Managed Funds

FOR

DUMMIES®

by Colin Davidson

WILEY

Wiley Publishing Australia Pty Ltd

Managed Funds For Dummies®

published by
Wiley Publishing Australia Pty Ltd
42 McDougall Street
Milton, Qld 4064
www.dummies.com

Copyright © 2011 Wiley Publishing Australia Pty Ltd

The moral rights of the author have been asserted.

National Library of Australia
Cataloguing-in-Publication data:

Author:	Davidson, Colin.
Title:	Managed Funds For Dummies / Colin Davidson.
Edition:	Australian ed.
ISBN:	978 1 74216 942 2 (pbk.)
Subjects:	Investments — Australia.
	Pension trusts — Australia — Management.
Dewey Number:	332.6780994

Cover image: © David Koscheck, 2010, Used under licence from Shutterstock.com

Typeset by diacriTech, Chennai, India

Printed in China by
Printplus Limited

10 9 8 7 6 5 4 3 2 1

About the Author

Colin Davidson has worked in financial services for more than 20 years, both in Australia and overseas, in London and Asia. A qualified chartered accountant, Colin worked in Hong Kong as a stockbroker selling equities to global and regional fund managers. In Australia, he has managed a major bank's online stockbroking business and Australia's largest direct managed funds broker. Currently working at one of Australia's largest full-service retail stockbrokers, Colin is RG146 accredited and a Responsible Executive managing the broker's financial planning business. He co-wrote the 2005 and 2006 editions of *Australia's Top 100 Managed Funds*.

Dedication

To the family, Louise, James, Ella, Alex, Claudia and Blossom, and to those gone but not forgotten, Jean and Marguerite, go well.

Author's Acknowledgements

Something I hadn't appreciated when writing this book was how much of a collaborative effort the whole process would be. Thanks to Bronwyn Duhigg who, before she left John Wiley, originally approached me to write the book and guided me through the commissioning process. Thanks to Rebecca Crisp for the subsequent direction and always kind words of encouragement, and to Hannah Bennett, the publishing equivalent of a footy coach, expertly guiding from the sidelines. Thanks to Kerry Davies, project editor extraordinaire, for the ever-wise suggestions, who somehow magically pulled everything together. Thanks also to Zoë Wykes in the United States for the fresh perspective with the final edits, and to Glenn Lumsden for the great cartoons!

Thanks also to Angus Robertson, financial adviser at Bell Potter Securities, for the technical review of the book. With many years' experience advising clients on superannuation and managed funds, Angus brings a tremendous amount of experience to the book. Thanks finally to Louise, who read chapters, offered advice and was given a good excuse to regularly lock me away in the study until I'd met my deadlines. I'm sure the family enjoyed the peace.

Publisher's Acknowledgements

We're proud of this book; please send us your comments through our online registration form located at www.dummies.com/register.

Some of the people who helped bring this book to market include the following:

Acquisitions, Editorial and Media Development

Project Editor: Kerry Davies

Acquisitions Editors: Bronwyn Duhigg, Rebecca Crisp

Technical Reviewer: Angus Robertson

Editorial Manager: Hannah Bennett

Production

Graphics: Wiley Art Studio

Cartoons: Glenn Lumsden

Proofreader: Catherine Spedding

Indexer: Michael Ramsden

The authors and publisher would like to thank the following copyright holders, organisations and individuals for their permission to reproduce copyright material in this book.

- Page 49: © Industry Super Network

- Page 70: © Standard & Poor's 'Index Versus Active Funds Scorecard: Australia Year-End 2009'. www.spiva.standardandpoors.com.au

- Pages 131 and 132: © Morningstar Australasia

- Page 150: © BT Financial Group

- Page 155: © Responsible Investment Association Australasia (RIAA)

Every effort has been made to trace the ownership of copyright material. Information that will enable the publisher to rectify any error or omission in subsequent editions will be welcome. In such cases, please contact the Permissions Section of John Wiley & Sons Australia, Ltd.

Contents at a Glance

Table of Contents

Introduction

· ·

When I started writing this book at the beginning of 2010, global stock markets were emerging from one of the worst periods since the 1929 Wall Street Crash in the United States. Investors' portfolios had been decimated by the global financial crisis (GFC) of 2007 and 2008. The performance of many fund managers had fallen off a cliff and the funds management industry had gone through a shakeout. The crisis highlighted the fund managers who deserved their fees and exposed the mediocre — those who had been carried along by the 2003 to 2007 bull market.

As a result of the crisis, investors who stayed in managed funds fled to safety and switched their investments into cash, earning a pittance from the lowest interest rates Australia had seen in years. Investors lost confidence in the markets and especially in the fund managers who were supposed to be growing their money. As markets recovered, investors returned slowly, not so much to managed funds but to owning shares directly and looking after their own money.

So, all-in-all, a great time to start writing a book about managed funds!

Although the GFC should make everyone more cautious, it shouldn't stop people investing. In fact, the GFC has highlighted the need for professional fund managers. In *Managed Funds For Dummies*, I look at how fund managers provide consistency of method and a disciplined approach to managing money.

About This Book

I wrote *Managed Funds For Dummies* as a plain-speaking and practical guide to managed funds. The book is aimed at anyone new to managed funds — or investing for that matter — and who might not know where to start. And just because you may use a financial planner to invest doesn't mean you won't find the book useful. This book helps you ask the right questions and, importantly, understand the answers.

Without wanting to sound like a politician, *Managed Funds For Dummies* especially targets the everyday Mum and Dad investor trying to save for a better future, for themselves and their children. Many investors want to manage their own investment decisions, and this book is a good starting point for the DIY investor — even more experienced investors who may want to brush up on their managed funds knowledge. It is certainly not meant to replace qualified professional advice!

Fund managers have a certain air of mystery about them. They're a naturally secretive bunch, but who can blame fund managers for wanting to protect the way they make money? I aim to peel away some of the mystery and show investors what they need to know about fund managers and their funds before they invest.

The book refers to a number of the major fund managers in Australia and around the world. Longevity in the marketplace and size usually dictate which managers I mention. Investors are bound to come across the names in advertising, when talking to a financial planner or even through a quick search of the internet.

The industry is changing, and none more so than in 2010. Fees and commissions are the big talking point, as is the desire to make everything simpler and easier to understand. Hooray to that! Legislation will change some of the things I've written about in this book over the next couple of years. I've foreshadowed those changes where possible and explained the likely impact for the investor.

Conventions Used in This Book

To help you get the information you need as fast as possible, this book uses several conventions:

- ✓ **Bold** words make the key terms and phrases in bulleted lists jump out and grab your attention. They also indicate the action part of numbered steps.

- ✓ *Italics* signal that a word is an important defined term.

- ✓ `Monofont` is used to signal a web address.

  When this book was printed, some web addresses may have needed to break across two lines of text. If that happened, rest assured that no extra characters (such as hyphens or spaces) are used to indicate the break. So, when using one of these web addresses, just type in exactly what you see in this book, pretending that the line break doesn't exist.

✔ Sidebars, text separated from the rest of the type in grey boxes, are interesting but slightly tangential to the subject at hand. Sidebars are generally fun and optional reading. You won't miss anything critical if you skip the sidebars. If you choose to read the sidebars, though, I think you'll be glad you did.

I use some terms interchangeably in the book. So a *fund manager* can refer to the actual company that has legal responsibility for a managed fund, but can also refer to the actual person who manages the fund. The context should make it obvious which is which. The term *financial adviser* is interchangeable with *financial planner*, and refers to anyone who is legally qualified to give financial advice. *Stocks* and *shares* also refer to the same thing.

Foolish Assumptions

When I sat down to write this book, I thought long and hard about who would pick it up and read it. Here are a few assumptions I made that may apply to you:

✔ If you're reading this book, you have an interest in investing and, in particular, in managed funds.

✔ You may have no knowledge whatsoever about managed funds other than seeing the occasional advertisement and wondering what they're all about.

✔ You may be an industry professional taking a quick flick through the pages, maybe even a fund manager, but perhaps that's assuming too much!

✔ You want a book that covers every aspect of managed fund investing but can also give you the practical detail you need to go about investing. At the same time, you don't want to wade through the finance industry double-speak that can leave investors perplexed. But you do need to understand some specific terms that go with managed funds, so I clearly explain each of these, with a handy glossary at the back of the book for quick reference.

✔ Last but not least, you want an independent view of managed funds, one that isn't trying to sell you anything or convince you that only managed funds will do. So I give you a guide and a way to answer questions you may have about managed funds and whether they're right for you. It may even help to answer questions you didn't know you should ask until reading this book!

How This Book Is Organised

Managed Funds For Dummies covers virtually every aspect of managed fund investing, and I start by giving you an understanding of what a managed fund is and why investing in managed funds is different from investing in shares and property. When you understand that, then you can figure out what type of investor you are, do the research and then fill in the forms. The book also gives the once-over to investment strategies such as margin lending and how these strategies may have a place in your portfolio.

The book is organised in six parts, covering everything you need to know about managed funds in Australia and how to invest in them.

Part I: Coming to Grips with the Basics of Managed Funds

Part I starts with a view from the top, looking at what you need to know, the pros and cons of investing in managed funds and how they are structured. It also examines the importance of asset class and investment style, and rounds off with how much investing in a managed fund is likely to cost you.

Part II: Doing the Research for Your Peace of Mind

This part is all about you, examining what type of investor you may be and how to work out what level of risk you're prepared to take when investing. I then look at how to set your investment goals, how you can research managed funds and what you need to look out for when judging if a fund is going to help you achieve your goals.

Part III: Choosing, Buying and Selling Managed Funds

Which comes first, choosing the fund or the fund manager? If you want to get to know the fund manager before choosing a fund, then this part explains the ins and outs. It also shows how you can invest either direct with a fund manager, via a financial planner or through a managed fund broker. I also give you practical hints on how to fill the forms in, as well as how to buy and sell funds.

Part IV: Determining How Funds Are Labelled

This part looks at the many ways managed funds are categorised by the industry. Increasingly, hedge funds are going mainstream and this part demystifies some of what they do. Administering your funds may not sound particularly exciting but knowing the services offered by fund managers and administrators is worthwhile, possibly saving you time and money.

Part V: Following Some Sensible Ideas for Happier Returns

So you've chosen your funds. This part examines what other strategies you may want to use to invest, such as borrowing to invest, regular savings plans and dollar-cost averaging. But what happens if it all goes wrong? This part explains who is keeping an eye on the fund managers and who to complain to if you're not happy.

Part VI: The Part of Tens

Managed funds investing doesn't need to be complicated and, in this part, I give a rundown of what to bear in mind before taking the plunge, including ten tips for getting you on the road to successful investing in managed funds, and ten traps and pitfalls — what the fund managers may not tell you and what you should look out for.

Glossary

The **glossary** of terms explains the key investing terminology around managed funds.

Icons Used in This Book

Everything in this book is worth reading, but some paragraphs may jump out at you as being an important piece of information to remember or a useful tip on managed funds. In the margins of the book, you can find the following icons marking certain paragraphs containing that special information. Here's what they mean:

Remember items are the yellow sticky notes of the book, the ones you should highlight with your own yellow marker. You'll find these notes useful when completing a task — such as filling in an application form, or what to remember when using a financial planner.

This is the stuff that is a little bit technical — usually related to tax, fees or legal information — you don't need to know this information but may find it interesting. If you want to know a bit more about how something works, then read this icon; if not, you can give it a miss and won't be any worse off.

A tip is a specific piece of advice on a particular topic. A tip may be a shortcut or some other helpful hint that may save you time, money or possibly heartache.

Warnings are just that — a heads-up that you need to be aware of something that could get you into trouble, cost you money or affect the fund you invest in.

Where to Go from Here

Put the book to work for you straightaway! Thumb through the book to see what catches your eye or head to the Table of Contents or the Index to find a section or topic that interests you. Or just turn the page and dive right into Chapter 1. The choice is yours but, whichever way you go, I hope you enjoy — and benefit from — *Managed Funds For Dummies*.

Part I

Coming to Grips with the Basics of Managed Funds

Glenn Lumsden

'Which part of the park has the least scary rides?'

In this part ...

Whether you know it or not, managed funds are very likely a part of your investing landscape. Contributing to a superannuation fund? Chances are you're investing in managed funds. So, if for no other reason, getting to know managed funds could help you achieve a better retirement. Part I introduces managed funds, what to look out for and how to choose them.

As much as I'm a big fan of managed funds, you get to look at the cons as well as the pros of using managed funds here, and a dose of the legal stuff of how funds are structured, with a pinch of technical guff on top. This part also introduces some of the investing techniques used by professional financial planners and gets down to what we all want to know — how much it costs.

Chapter 1

Getting Started with Managed Funds

I'm going to indulge the accountant in me and throw around a few statistics about the size of the managed funds industry. The Australian industry has $1.7 trillion-plus in funds under management, with 10,000 and more funds available from over 130 fund managers, making it the fourth-largest managed funds industry in the world.

All sounds pretty impressive but what does it really mean for the average investor? That lots of advisers and people in the finance industry are raking it in with all the fees being charged? Possibly, but what is important is that the numbers show Australia has a thriving and world-class fund management industry offering a wide choice for investors, despite the effects of the global financial crisis.

Australia's superannuation (often simply referred to as super) system drives much of the managed funds industry, and managing super drives much of people's investing decisions. Saving for retirement is big business and that's because it affects most of us in one way or another. Super should be front and centre of most people's investment strategies. Understanding that managed funds can make up a fair chunk of your super, the need to know about managed funds becomes important.

In this chapter, I cover how managed funds can play a part in your investment portfolio — whatever your investment plans, whether saving for retirement or for a deposit on a house. Understanding what managed funds are, how to choose one and what to look out for can help make your investment decisions a whole lot simpler.

Making a Start with Managed Funds

A *managed fund* is a way of pooling together money from many investors into one big pot, called a *trust*. Investors then buy units in that trust. The company or person looking after the money in the trust — the *fund manager* — invests the money across a host of different types of investments, from cash and property to bonds and shares. Most managed funds are *unlisted*, meaning that they're not traded on the stock exchange. However, a small number of funds are traded on the Australian Securities Exchange (ASX) as listed investment companies.

Considering managed funds beyond the GFC

The global financial crisis of 2008 to 2009 not only rocked the financial world; it also seemed to affect just about every aspect of our lives, including mine in setting out to write this book.

In investing terminology, writing a book on managed funds in early 2010 was the equivalent of buying at the bottom of the market. Things couldn't get much worse — for the industry or for investors. Many funds, especially those in the property and mortgage sectors, were badly hit, freezing investors' money. Many of these funds remain frozen while managers wait for the good times to return. So why would you even consider going back into the managed funds market after all that chaos?

The point is that markets go up and down, and the good times do return. Managed funds can and should have a place in people's investment portfolios regardless of the fallout from the GFC. The superannuation industry in Australia is worth around $1.3 trillion and relies completely on markets that work and fund managers that perform well. As long as people and their employers are contributing to superannuation, skilled money managers and their managed funds will always be needed.

If there is a good side to the GFC, it is the lessons that might be learned by fund managers and investors alike. Poorly managed funds didn't survive. Fund managers do make mistakes and do lose money, sometimes a lot. But occasionally you come across a manager who knocks your socks off performance-wise and who can deliver again and again. As an investor, these managers are the ones you want to seek out to manage your money, because these are the guys who genuinely add value to your investments over time.

Discovering that you're probably using managed funds already

Before thinking about investing with managed funds, take a step back and look at the investments you have already. 'Not a lot,' you may think. But hold on. For many people — and I include myself in this — aside from the family home, superannuation is probably the largest, single and most important investment they have.

If you're working for a company, you're probably contributing to a super fund set up by your employer or perhaps an industry super fund. Most employer and industry funds are set up to invest mainly in managed funds, with very few offering direct share ownership. Often though, super is the forgotten investment; you have it because it's the law. Thinking about your super probably only happens around tax time, when you get an annual statement telling you what your fund has been up to during the year.

Just because your managed funds are in an employer super fund doesn't mean you can't manage them. Your super is important and managed funds are probably a big part of it. Getting to grips with some of the basics of managed funds can give you a better understanding of how to get your super working for you. See Chapter 3 for more on superannuation.

Including managed funds in your portfolio

'Portfolio' sounds like a word only the very wealthy would use, those with a private banker to cater for their every investing whim. Don't be put off, as *portfolio* is just a way of identifying the money you set aside for investing. Managed funds are generally set up to cater for three distinct uses:

- **Superannuation:** Within your super account helping you save for retirement
- **Pension:** After you've retired, managed funds in your pension account that help to provide an income
- **Investment:** Anything that is not part of (outside) your superannuation and pension

The idea of investing *inside* or *outside* your superannuation and pension is important to understand. Using superannuation and pensions can be a way of minimising tax on your investments. If investing solely to fund retirement, superannuation is invariably the best way to go, and managed funds are set up to cater for super, pensions and investments.

Examining What's Managed in Managed Funds

In the United States, managed funds are called mutual funds and in the United Kingdom they're unit trusts. So why 'managed funds' in Australia? For once, the finance industry came up with a name that says exactly what the product does — it manages funds (money). Thankfully, no committee was involved in coming up with that name or who knows what we'd be calling them!

Lifting the lid on fund managers

Managing money involves both investment decisions and administration, regardless of whether a big company or an individual is looking after the money. *Investing* is about making your money grow or producing an income. *Administration* is keeping track of your money and having the right paperwork to complete your tax return. Fund management companies spend a lot of money trying to get right both the administration and the investing sides of the business.

Fund managers may have different styles of investing. Styles can include *growth* managers investing in stocks with long-term growth prospects, or *value* managers who look for investments believed to be relatively undervalued. Hedge funds are another style all together (see Chapter 16). All have different risk and return attributes so you need to know what you're getting yourself into before you invest. Chapter 4 tells you more on investment styles.

Choosing a fund manager is as much about performance as it is about a good reputation — that the manager won't run off with your money — and good client service. Consistently good performance over a long period is the difference between a good fund manager and a great fund manager.

Finding out how fund managers earn a crust

Fund managers earn money mainly in a couple of ways. The first is charging fees as a percentage of your money. Every month the fund manager shaves off a percentage equivalent to anywhere between 0.9 per cent and over

2 per cent per annum. The actual amount depends on the type of fund and how expensive it is to run. Funds investing overseas charge more than funds managing cash investments, for example.

The second way fund managers earn money is from performance fees, although these funds are in the minority. Performance fees are charged if the fund makes a return greater than a pre-set hurdle rate, such as 8 per cent per annum. The fund manager takes a percentage — usually 20 per cent — of that additional gain. Fair enough. Giving the manager an incentive has to be good for both investor and fund manager.

Expenses are taken from your investment monthly, taking a bite out of its performance. You won't see the effect, however, until you get your statement at the end of the year. Check out Chapter 5 for more on fees.

Plunging into Managed Funds without Taking a Bath

Before you invest, you need to do a little self-analysis to work out what type of investor you are. Imagine buying a set of golf clubs and then realising you don't like golf. This example might sound odd, because most people know whether or not they like golf. But getting to the point where you know what type of investor you are should be like knowing if golf is your thing or not.

Managing your risk and setting your goals

All investing is about managing risk, about planning for the worst but expecting the best. *Risk* is simply the chance of you losing money on your investment, and some investments can be riskier than others. For example, investing in developing countries can be akin to a white-knuckle roller-coaster ride. Investing in cash, however, is like a drive to the corner shops — not usually that eventful.

Different investment types are referred to as asset classes and, conveniently, each carries a different level of risk. Moving up the risk-and-return scale, cash is the least risky with lowest likely returns, followed by bonds and fixed interest, and then property, with Australian and international shares topping out the scale. Chapter 6 helps you work out your investor type.

Your attitude to risk — whether you're happy to bet the farm or would prefer something a little more sedate — determines the managed funds best suited to you. Add to that what you're trying to achieve — your goals — and a structure starts emerging to help select the most appropriate managed funds. For more on goal setting, see Chapter 7.

Thinking about what life stage you're at can also influence your decision-making. The closer you get to retirement, the more likely you are to want to preserve the money you have and to start producing an income. The opposite is also true — the further away from retirement you are, the longer you have to recover from hits to your portfolio.

The bigger your goals, the more risk you'll to need to take. At some point, though, taking on too much risk is no different from betting on the horses.

Picking managed funds from the myriad of options

With more than 10,000 managed funds to choose from, selecting managed funds can seem overwhelming at first. When you've matched your goals to your risk profile, you're able to whittle away a fair chunk of that 10,000. But managed funds come in many different colours and flavours (see Chapters 14 and 15 for some of the standard, and not-so-standard fund types). And you also need to consider the reputations and performance of the fund managers themselves (see Chapter 10). So, how do you get to a shortlist of, say, a dozen funds to choose from? A dartboard is one option but the more usual way is to do some research.

Fortunately, managed fund research companies such as Morningstar Australia and Standard & Poor's can help potential investors. Using an easy-to-understand five-star rating system, combined with a recommendation, the research companies allow investors to home in on the better-rated funds. The research companies also categorise managed funds as, for example, Australian equities large-growth funds, letting investors compare similar funds more readily.

Managed fund research companies are not all the same. Each has a slightly different way of measuring and rating managed funds. However, all use a mix of past performance measures and a subjective (qualitative) judgement of how a fund is being managed. Chapter 8 gives more on the ratings agencies.

Conquering the paperwork and working out the costs

Now I'm getting to the pointy end — cost! You'll discover most of the costs of investing in a managed fund in what's called the *product disclosure statement (PDS)*. Usually a fairly weighty document, sometimes in two parts, the PDS should tell you all you need to know about the funds you may want to invest in. From the legal stuff, like who's responsible for investing the money, through to an overview of what a fund invests in and what it all costs.

The PDS usually has the application form at the back, as well as the *financial services guide (FSG)*. The FSG is a short document setting out the fund manager's services, the costs of using those services and who to complain to if you have a problem. Yes, it's all exciting stuff! However, you must be given an FSG before you invest, as well as a PDS — it's the law. Signing the application form means you acknowledge you have read and understood the PDS. See Chapter 12 for more on forms and the PDS.

So, where do costs come into this? Very near the beginning of a PDS usually. The PDS sets out what costs may be charged and even some that aren't charged. The PDS should give an example of how the fees work and what you can expect to pay. The main costs are:

- ✔ **Contribution fees:** Paid when you set up a managed fund account and every time you contribute to it; usually up to 4 per cent of the amount you invest

- ✔ **Management fees:** An ongoing fee charged as a percentage of the value of your investment, typically around 1.5 per cent per annum

- ✔ **Transaction fees:** The difference between the price you buy a fund and the price you sell a fund, or the *spread*, typically around 0.4 per cent

You may be able to reduce or have rebated the entire contribution fee. You can ask the fund manager, negotiate with your financial planner or use a managed fund broker.

The other main cost of investing is tax. Managed funds don't pay tax on any income or gain made from selling investments. Paying tax is, instead, left to the investor. How you judge the success or otherwise of an investment is the return you get after tax. Chapter 5 gives you the drill on tax and other costs of investing.

Some fund managers also offer administration services through what are known as *master trusts* and *wrap accounts*. These services offer a menu of managed funds from different fund managers, enabling investors to track several investments in one document. These services also allow access to funds whose minimum entry-level investment is too high for the average investor. Reporting includes all buys and sells of units, distributions by the fund (income), valuations and a tax statement. Of course, you can expect to pay an administration fee of anywhere up to 0.9 per cent per annum on the value of your investment. See Chapter 17 for more on these administration services.

Dealing with and Keeping Track of Your Investments

Investors have several options when buying and selling managed funds — going direct to the fund manager, using a financial planner or using a managed fund broker. It all boils down to personal preference. After you've bought your investments, you need to keep track of what they're doing. Performance is why you're investing, so you need to know a little about how it's calculated. Chapter 13 tells you more about buying, selling and monitoring your investments.

Taking advice or going it alone

Investing can be complex and it's not only about selecting a managed fund. With superannuation, the rules can be a minefield for the uninitiated and this is where a financial planner can help. Financial planners may charge a fee for their service or get paid from the commission that fund managers pay planners for investing your money with them, or a combination of both.

Others prefer to make their own decisions, either through a broker or by giving instructions directly to the fund manager. Managed fund brokers offer access to most of the major funds and also offer a rebate on some fees, such as the 4 per cent contribution fee. The other option is to go direct to the fund manager. Again, investors may get some fees rebated but usually only if they ask the fund manager. Take a look at Chapter 11 before making a decision on which way to go.

Tracking your fund's performance

Managed funds have a reputation as set-and-forget investments, meaning you don't need to look after them much once you've invested. Up to a point that is true. You do need to keep track of how the fund is going, making sure the performance is meeting your expectations. If you don't, you run the risk of not meeting your goals when you need to. Chapter 9 helps you analyse performance figures.

Performance of a fund is made up of two parts — income and growth. *Income* is paid as dividends by the underlying investments, such as shares, to the fund. *Growth* is the increase in value of the underlying investments over a certain period. For example, XYZ fund shows a return of 10 per cent for the 12 months to 30 June 2010. Of that 10 per cent, 4 per cent is from dividends received and the rest is from the increase in value of the investments held.

You may be up for a tax bill on any part of the return — the income and the growth — from a managed fund, which must distribute all the income it receives to investors every year.

Adding some spice to your investing

Without too much fuss, you can take advantage of straightforward yet powerful investing techniques, potentially adding to your returns. Some of these are:

- **Borrowing to invest:** You can employ this strategy either through a margin loan or through a managed fund that is allowed to borrow to invest. This simple strategy can add a rocket to your investment's returns. Equally, if you're not careful, it can lose you a lot of money. Properly managed and with a full understanding of the consequences of it going wrong, borrowing to invest can be a way of growing your money faster.

- **Compounding:** A simple strategy for reinvesting any income you get back into the managed fund, this strategy is like earning interest on your interest.

- **Dollar-cost averaging:** Setting up a regular (fortnightly, monthly or quarterly) savings plan where you regularly contribute a set amount to the fund. This helps you save and, importantly, reduces the risk that you buy a managed fund when the market is high, only to see the price fall during the coming months.

Check out Chapters 18 and 19 for more on these investment strategies.

Knowing what to look out for and what to do if it all goes wrong

Nothing in investing is guaranteed, except taxes. The fund manager offering guaranteed returns needs to be approached cautiously. Somewhere behind the promise of a guaranteed return lies either a very long disclaimer with conditions attached, or someone who's either extremely naive or out to take you for a ride. Some funds, known as *capital-guaranteed funds*, use complex derivative products to guarantee to give you at least your money back if the market takes a dive. But expect to have some conditions attached to that guarantee (Chapter 16 also explains these structured products).

If you don't know or understand what you're investing in, then don't invest. Better to be safe than sorry. Some managed funds can be quite complex, especially capital-guaranteed products, with fees and structures that, although disclosed in the PDS, can be hard to fathom.

The Australian Securities and Investments Commission (ASIC) is the main watchdog for the managed funds industry in Australia. ASIC makes sure fund managers follow the rules. But, should your investment go horribly wrong through incompetence, then you can complain to the Financial Ombudsman Service (FOS). ASIC is likely to get involved if you lose money through fraud. When complaining, the first stop is the fund manager. If you can't get what you expect from the fund manager, you can then go to the FOS, which acts as a mediator between the investor and fund manager.

ASIC's consumer watchdog website, FIDO (www.fido.gov.au), provides some great information on what to look out for before you invest. You can also turn to Chapter 20 for more information.

Chapter 2

Understanding the Pros and Cons of Managed Funds

In This Chapter

▶ Appreciating what managed funds have to offer

▶ Understanding the meaning of diversification

▶ Finding a managed fund to suit you

▶ Noting four reasons why managed funds may not be suitable for you

▶ Comparing managed funds with other investments

Managed funds can be a great way for many people to invest. Accessing professional management, the ability to instantly spread your investments across a range of different investment types and not having to keep an eye on the investment every day are reasons enough to tempt a large number of Australians to use managed funds. A huge range of funds is available across different parts of the market and different types of funds appeal to different types of investors. Whether you're a slow and steady type or prefer a bit more zing to your investing, you can find a fund to cater to your needs.

Investors should be aware of some of the downsides to managed funds. Investing in managed funds isn't everyone's cup of tea. Having to step back from day-to-day investment decisions and not having a good idea of what a fund manager is doing can be too much of a leap of faith for some.

Even though *fund managers* are the experts in assessing companies' worth as an investment, loss of control can be a big factor and many people believe they can manage their investments better than fund managers. Tax considerations can also deter some investors from managed funds. This chapter helps you to weigh up the benefits of investing in managed funds against some potential drawbacks.

Accessing All Areas: The Everyday Investor's Backstage Pass

I get genuinely enthusiastic about the huge array of investing possibilities available with managed funds. That enthusiasm is not because of my sheltered early career as an accountant; more because managed funds can be used to invest in areas that may be out of bounds to everyday investors. Managed funds are the financial equivalent of lifting the velvet rope at the premiere of a Hollywood blockbuster movie. Admittance is to the inner circle where the big guns play.

Many of the barriers that stop potential investors from investing, such as lack of experience or large sums of money, by and large disappear with managed funds. Investors can immediately tap into many years of investing experience for a relatively modest initial investment of around $2,000.

For an example of how managed funds make investments accessible, you need look no further than commercial property investments. Some individuals can afford $100 million or more to buy a building in their own name, but not many. As nice as it would be, most investors can't afford their own office tower. A managed fund pools small amounts of money from potentially thousands of people so it can buy an office tower and the investors can each have a small slice. Investing this way can be tremendously liberating, especially for small investors.

With managed funds, you get to go beyond the velvet rope to bask in the glow of the professionals, and your investment activities are also easy to handle.

Opening up a world of investing opportunities

Managed funds offer an all-you-can-eat smorgasbord of investing possibilities. Looking to invest in Australia? No problem. Want to dabble in emerging economies such as China? Done. Whatever you want to invest in and wherever you want to invest, there's a good chance it's been packaged up as a managed fund and is available to the investing public.

The number of funds on the market is eye-popping. In Australia, more than 10,000 managed funds are available to investors, and, according to managed funds ratings agency Morningstar, more than 400 new managed funds were launched in 2009. Having loads of funds to choose from sounds like a great idea, but choice can be a curse. Investors can feel swamped by the number of funds available.

What is an even better idea is if someone else has done the hard work to whittle down the choices to a 'best of' or 'top ten' list. In fact, from the client surveys I've done on managed funds, investors don't like too much choice. Whether people are looking to book a hotel or invest in managed funds, they like to be able to narrow their options without too much fuss.

Experienced investors can very quickly take a list of more than 10,000 funds down to just a few dozen. Stepping through a well thought-out process to determine what funds suit you helps. It all sounds so easy! The process involves figuring out what type of investor you are — for example, conservative or aggressive, depending on how much risk you like (often called your *risk profile*) — and then setting out your investment goals. Quickly, you find the number of managed funds that fit your needs diminishes significantly. See Chapter 6 for more on figuring out your risk profile and Chapter 7 for more on setting goals.

Beware the 'exotic' managed funds — those, for example, that invest in vintage cars, artworks or premium wines. Investing history is littered with the wreckage of these types of funds, which are very much at the specialised end of the market. Exotic funds typically appear when the market is running hot, when rational thinking can evaporate and investors can get caught up in the moment. Be careful, unless you have some play money you don't mind losing if it all goes wrong or unless you have specialist knowledge of the underlying investment.

Investing with the professionals

Tapping into the knowledge bank and experience of the professional investor is a powerful incentive for investing in managed funds. Managed funds offer the opportunity to piggyback off the knowledge and experience of professionals who, in all likelihood, have been in the investment game for a number of years. Trusting your fund manager to look after and grow your money shouldn't be a leap of faith. Building trust comes from checking out the fund manager as much as possible before you invest.

Paying for experience

Investing can be a minefield for the uninitiated, a burden for the time-poor and just plain confusing for everyone else. But help is at hand. Behind every managed fund sit professional investors or fund managers whose job it is to look after the money entrusted to them.

Many fund managers — the people responsible for making the investment decisions — are backed by a team of researchers, otherwise known as *analysts*. Working with the fund managers, the analysts carry out a lot of the investment heavy lifting, raking through company information and balance sheets, interviewing company employees or visiting factories or mines in out of the way places. With oversight from the fund manager, the information is ultimately distilled into a recommendation as to whether or not a company is a good investment. All of this analysis takes time, money and experience.

Trusting the fund manager

The point comes when investors have to trust the fund manager to do its job. Doing the background checks, for some people, may be little more than throwing a dart at a list of fund managers and hoping for the best. For most people though, the process of selecting a fund manager is more scientific and involves some degree of research. Having researched the background of the manager and read the various pieces of marketing literature, perhaps spoken to a financial planner and emerged relatively unscathed from the process, the point comes when investors need to commit.

Don't succumb to commitment phobia! Commitment, especially financial, can be hard for some people and a piece of cake for others. Concerns range from losing control of your money to the financial stability of the fund manager, as well as being unsure about the choice of your investment.

Trusting the fund manager can present you with that leap of faith that can make some investors baulk at a managed fund, but doing your homework can relieve the angst. Researching a fund manager and the funds on offer beforehand can make investing less of a trip into the unknown and more of a long-term relationship based on trust.

Making investing convenient

Imagine yourself doing all the work the fund manager does. For example, when fund managers select a portfolio of shares, they buy and sell those shares, deal with all the paperwork and provide regular reporting to their investors. Each point in the process of selecting, buying and managing the investments involves some degree of skill or knowledge. This skill, knowledge and convenience are what you pay for in a managed fund.

Lacking knowledge or confidence about investing can be a big hurdle for many people. Managed funds can take a lot of the angst out of investing. Once you've decided to invest, the fund manager takes care of virtually everything else:

- ✔ **Administration:** As well as managing the investments, the fund manager looks after the paperwork, from the actual buying and selling of investments in the fund to making sure they collect all the income due to them on behalf of their investors.

- ✔ **Investing:** You decide what fund to put your money in. The fund manager then decides where to invest that money in the best way it sees fit but also bearing in mind what the fund is set up to do.

- ✔ **Reporting:** The fund manager provides periodic reporting on your investments. Reports include the value of your holding, money that you've put in or taken out and the income or distributions you may have received.

- ✔ **Tax:** You need to know how much income you've received for your annual tax return. At tax time the fund should give you all the information you need to complete your tax return in relation to your managed fund.

You can make life even easier for yourself by using one of the many administration platforms offered by the major fund managers. The platforms offer a comprehensive administration and reporting service, as well as a menu of different funds. The great thing is that the platforms offer managed funds from a wide range of fund managers. The *investment menus*, as the choices are known, offer enough types of funds to cater for most people's needs. I cover platforms in more detail in Chapter 17.

For a fund manager, selecting the investments is likely to involve researching potentially hundreds of listed companies, talking to company managers and then working out a value for the companies. Buying shares involves dealing with stockbrokers and share registries that keep a record of the fund's share holdings. Companies also provide income to the fund in the form of dividends. Companies occasionally make changes to the number of shares they have on issue, generally to raise more money for the business. Known as corporate actions, these dividends and money raisings all need administering by the fund.

People do invest directly in shares and do all their own administration, perhaps with the help of an accountant. Some people thrive on this level of involvement but, to others, it can take up a lot of time. For me, working full time, even at a stockbroking firm, I barely have time to manage my own investments.

Diversifying Your Portfolio

'Don't put all your eggs in one basket.' Investors hear that phrase often. Like a child being constantly told off by a parent, however, the advice can go in one ear and out the other. Diversifying a portfolio is about spreading risk. Investors need to make sure that, if the eggs in one basket get broken, other baskets still contain enough eggs — hopefully a few golden ones!

Many investment experts say the three rules of investing are to diversify, diversify and diversify! And with managed funds you get that instantly, although different types of funds diversify in different ways. Understanding how diversification works helps you to pick the fund that suits you.

Understanding why diversification can be an investor's friend

Diversification is all about hedging your bets and spreading your risk. In practical terms, diversifying your portfolio means investing money across:

- ✔ Different asset types, such as cash, shares and property, which all present different levels of risk
- ✔ Different areas of the economy, such as retailing, mining or finance — again, each of these areas holds a different level of risk
- ✔ Different countries or geographic areas, such as the United States or Asia, depending on the health of that economy

Figure 2-1 shows a simple example of diversification, using managed funds compared with direct shares. Jim invests $10,000 in the stock market and buys equal shares in five companies. On the other hand, Martha splits her $10,000 between two managed funds — one investing in Australian shares and the other in bonds and cash — instantly putting her $10,000 across a range of different assets. Intuitively you may be able to see that Jim's portfolio is more exposed to risk if one of his stockholdings falls in value. A 20 per cent fall in BHP is going to hit Jim's portfolio harder than Martha's because it makes up a bigger proportion of the portfolio — BHP is one of 40 stocks in her portfolio. The reverse is true, of course, if Jim's shares were to increase in value! Jim's portfolio is not necessarily a bad thing; he may want a higher level of risk in his portfolio.

Diversifying your investments takes discipline. Wanting to chase the best returns is a natural instinct but can hurt a portfolio's performance. The best performing investments last year are not necessarily the ones that perform well the next year. Get the spread of investments right and you can enhance the returns on your portfolio. For more on chasing returns, see Chapter 9.

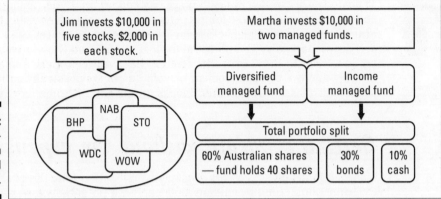

Figure 2-1:
Diversification from managed funds.

Of course, investors can get too much diversification. Sleeping better at night with diversified investments may mean lower returns. Like having a bath with a lifejacket on, investors can overdo the protection. As much as I try to not quote Warren Buffett, because he must be the most quoted investor on the planet, his one-liners are usually spot-on:

> *Wide diversification is only required when investors do not understand what they are doing.*
>
> —*Warren Buffett, much-quoted investment guru*

Buffett is not against diversification — just against too much. At some point an investor can spread his investments so thinly that all he ends up doing is matching the market's returns. Investors need to take on some level of risk, at the very least, to stay ahead of inflation.

Diversification gives you a free lunch?

Harry Markowitz, winner of the Nobel Prize for Economics, once said that diversification is 'the only free lunch in finance'. It's a catchy soundbite but what does it mean? Diversification is all about hedging your bets and spreading your risk.

When Markowitz wrote about diversification years ago, and linked investment risk with return, his ideas were nothing short of revolutionary. He explained that by divvying up your money across different investments you could lower your risk of loss without a big sacrifice in returns. Such a simple technique can make a big difference, so much so Markowitz figured it was like a 'free lunch'.

The two factors to diversification are *risk* and *return*. Underpinning both risk and return is *time*, or how long an investment is held. Over a short period of time, the values of higher risk investments such as shares can move up and down markedly. The potential for loss is high and therefore shares can be quite risky in the short term. Stretch the investment period to a number of years and the price movement or volatility becomes significantly less and so, in effect, less risky. Chapter 6 looks at risk and return in more detail.

Getting exposure without the expense

Managed funds give investors greater diversification than direct shares, for the same outlay (investment amount) and for a potentially lower cost than doing it themselves. Someone clever worked out that a portfolio should hold at least 12 investments to be considered diversified. The problem arises if investors have only a small amount to invest.

Here's an example. Throwing caution to the wind, Sarah decides to run her own investments and selects 12 stocks to invest in to ensure her portfolio has some diversification. The minimum amount of any share Sarah can buy on the stock exchange is $500 — this is an Australian Securities Exchange (ASX) rule — a total outlay of at least $6,000. Brokerage through an online stockbroker costs around $20 a trade, or $120 in total, 2 per cent of her investment. On the other hand, the $6,120 could go straight into buying units in a managed fund investing in 40 or more stocks. The ongoing management cost of the managed fund — assuming contribution fees are rebated (see Chapter 5) — is a typical 1.5 per cent per annum (or $90).

Costs of doing your own investing can quickly mount up. Paying brokerage every time you buy and sell shares could potentially increase your costs to a lot more than the annual cost of a managed fund. Brokerage costs can quickly erode any gains you make.

Managed funds are an ideal way for new investors with smaller sums of money to get exposure to the market. Set up a regular savings plan with the fund of around $100 a month and the minimum initial investment amount falls to $1,000 with most major funds. Without a savings plan, minimum investments in managed funds can range from $1,500 to $5,000.

Discovering how managed funds diversify

Most managed funds diversify their holdings; some more than others. Property funds investing directly in buildings diversify by looking for a mix of properties in different locations and paying different rents. Managed funds investing in shares generally invest in a minimum of 40 companies.

Managed funds also limit their exposure in any one holding by capping how much stock of any one company they may hold. For example, the maximum holding for a stock could be set at 10 per cent of the portfolio. Setting this maximum holding lessens the risk of the managed fund's returns being badly hit by the fall in value of a particular stock.

Funds adopt different levels of diversification depending on what the manager is trying to achieve. *Index funds*, which mirror the returns of a market index, are completely diversified and the risk is the same as the market as a whole. *Concentrated funds* are so called because they hold a smaller number of investments — perhaps 25 to 40 stocks — concentrating the risk and potentially magnifying returns and losses. Sitting in the middle are the bulk of managed funds with a *diversified* investment portfolio that still seek to beat the market. Figure 2-2 shows how the different funds stack up in terms of risk, reward and size of holdings.

When selecting a managed fund, look at the level of cash that the fund manager keeps in the fund. All funds need some cash to pay fees and other costs. A cash level of 5 per cent of the total value of the portfolio level is reasonable. For a share managed fund, having most of the money in shares for most of the time makes sense. If the manager regularly has more than 10 per cent of your money in cash, chances are you're not getting the diversification you're paying for.

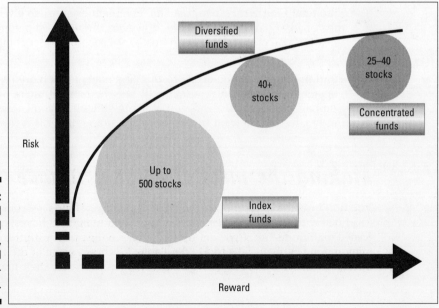

Figure 2-2:
Risk and reward for index, diversified and concentrated funds.

Funds for Every Investor

Whatever your needs, you're bound to find a fund to suit you. The bigger fund managers, such as Colonial First State, BT Investments and Perpetual, carry a range of different fund types, from cash funds to straightforward Australian equities funds and commercial property, to help you achieve your investment goals. These fund managers also run what are called *administration platforms*, grouping together an investment menu of funds from their own and other fund managers.

Finding the right fund for your money

Finding out what funds are available can be a daunting prospect. You have a number of options to help reduce the pain of sifting through hundreds of managed funds:

- **Direct fund brokers:** Brokers such as CommSec Direct Funds (www.commsec.com.au), InvestSMART (www.investsmart.com.au) and FundsFocus (www.fundsfocus.com.au) provide fund comparison tools, usually using information provided by Morningstar Australia (see the sidebar 'Morningstar Australia' for more information about Morningstar's services).

- **Financial planners:** A trip to a financial planner can also give you an idea of what funds are available. However, the financial planner should question you closely enough to be able to recommend a choice of just a few funds.

- **Fund managers:** Going direct to the fund manager is more time-consuming as you can generally only see the funds it offers. Comparison across the range of funds is difficult. If you know which fund manager you want to use, however, going direct is a good option.

Making the most of what you have

You don't need a lot of money to invest in managed funds — from as little as $1,000 with some fund managers. Other fund managers have $2,000 or $5,000 minimums but if you set up a regular savings plan with the fund, the minimum investment falls to $1,000. Table 2-1 shows some of the major fund managers and the minimum investment needed to access their funds.

Table 2-1	Some Major Fund Managers, Funds and Minimum Investments		
Fund Manager	**Minimum Investment**	**Regular Savings Plan Minimum**	**Number of Retail Funds**
Aberdeen Asset Management	$20,000	Not available	12
AMP	$1,500	$100 per month	78
AXA Investments	$2,000	$50 per fortnight or per month	57
BT Investments	$5,000	$2,000 initial; monthly contribution required but no minimum stated	195
BlackRock Investments	$5,000	No minimum	42
Colonial First State	$5,000	$1,000 initial and $100 per month	400+
MLC	$1,000	No minimum	400+
OnePath*	$1,000	$100 per month or per quarter	230
Perpetual Investments	$2,000	$1,000 initial; and $100 per fortnight, per month or per quarter	400+

__Note:__ OnePath is the new name for the former investment division of ING.

Many of the fund managers listed in Table 2-1 offer administrative services, or *platforms*. These services present a menu of managed funds from a range of different fund managers. In effect, platforms enable the big fund managers to broker for other fund managers. A big advantage in using a platform is the ability to access managed funds that usually ask for high minimum initial investments. For example, Perpetual's WealthFocus service allows investments in Platinum Asset Management funds for a minimum of $2,000. However, if investors go direct to Platinum, the minimum investment is $20,000. Chapter 17 sets out the administration services available and how they work.

Morningstar Australia

As one of the world's biggest managed fund research houses, Morningstar Australia is a good starting point. Morningstar's website at www.morningstar.com.au has some useful comparison tools for over 10,000 funds.

Register to get a login for the site and sort managed funds according to a number of different criteria. Research on funds can then be viewed along with a star rating. Morningstar only provides fund recommendations to users who pay for the privilege. The

Australian Financial Review's 'Portfolio' liftout and _The Australian_'s 'Wealth' liftout also publish the Morningstar fund tables every week. For more on Morningstar and other ratings agencies see Chapter 8.

You can also register with direct funds broker InvestSMART at www.investsmart.com.au to get free access to Morningstar recommendations. Or you can register with Morningstar Australia and pay for both the recommendations and research reports.

Four Reasons Why Managed Funds May Not Be for You

As much as it pains me to say, there are at least four reasons why managed funds may not be suited to everyone. Personal preferences play a major part. For some investors, using a managed fund is like buying a sports car and then getting a chauffeur to drive you around. Giving up control takes away the fun of doing it yourself.

Some investors also feel they can do better than the fund managers. And, for those who aren't experienced investors, the complexities surrounding managed funds, such as how the fund structures its tax responsibilities, can make this type of investment less than attractive. Other difficulties with managed funds can include making sure you're getting value for money and figuring out exactly _what_ you're buying into.

Losing control

Investors can expect to lose some control over certain elements of the investment process, as well as over the underlying investments. Losing control can either be a good thing or a bad thing, depending on your circumstances and how you like to manage your money.

Many people want to get rid of some of the anxiety of managing and monitoring their money. For others, knowing exactly what's happening to their money and being accountable for their own decisions may be a vital part of the investing process. Some investors also get a kick out of making their investment decisions and enjoy the buzz of getting it right. Investors can't do this with managed funds because they don't own the underlying shares and don't make the day-to-day investment decisions.

Stepping back from the investment decisions

After selecting your managed fund and having invested your money, the only decision you need to make is whether or not to keep the investment. At the point your money's invested, you're placed in the hands of the fund manager. You no longer have a direct say in what is done with your money. Like having surgery under general anaesthetic, you have no idea of what's going on and trust the surgeon to do the right thing!

Fund managers fiercely protect the way they make their investment decisions. Marketing brochures and product disclosure statements tell you only so much. Sometimes these methods are known as a *black box* — not a lot is known about what goes on inside but it's where all the secrets are stored. These processes are a fund manager's reason for being; it's what makes one manager different from all other fund managers. The last thing a fund manager is going to do is tell the world how it makes money!

Giving up legal ownership

On a practical level, owning units in a managed fund or trust is one step removed from owning the shares directly. For more on managed fund structures, see Chapter 3.

The trust for the managed fund, not the investor, has legal and beneficial ownership of the investments (usually shares), whether directly or through the help of another third party called a *custodian*. *Legal ownership* simply means that the name on the share certificate is that of the trust. *Beneficial ownership* means that the trust is entitled to the benefits that arise from owning shares, such as receiving any dividend income paid. That being said, by law, trusts must give that income to investors who own units in the trust.

Watching out for tax

The current tax position of a managed fund may not be the first thing, or even the last thing, you think of when you're about to invest. Tax and managed funds can be hazardous for the unwary. Understanding how managed funds are taxed can avoid a rude shock when investors get their statement from the fund manager. For more on tax see Chapter 5.

Finding out what tax is paid

Most managed funds don't pay tax because any income earned during the year must be paid to investors. As a consequence, tax is then paid by the investors at their *marginal rate*, or the highest rate at which the investor's income is taxed. Tax on managed fund income is paid once, at the end of the financial year. The exceptions are investment bonds or family bonds, which do pay tax — see Chapter 5.

Investors receive an annual statement from the fund manager showing how much money they received during the year from the fund. The distributions are split between income and capital gains, and investors have to pay tax on some of both types of distribution. Even if you opt to have all your income from the fund reinvested in the fund (by buying more units), you still may have to pay tax on the income.

Buying into a managed fund's tax position

The way a managed fund invests money affects the tax that investors pay. Managed funds make money for investors in two ways — from income received from investments and from gains made by either holding or selling those investments as values increase.

Funds that buy and sell investments on a regular basis make gains or losses from those trades. Buying and selling is known as *turnover* and refers to the percentage value of the portfolio that is bought and sold each year. Low turnover funds may buy and sell about 40 per cent of the value of the portfolio. High turnover funds can trade 150 per cent or more of the portfolio value. The more a fund turns over the portfolio, the greater the chances of the investor having to pay capital gains tax (CGT) on those transactions at the end of the year. *Capital gains* are the difference in price between what the fund paid for the investment and the price the fund sold the investment.

Watch what time of the year you buy into a managed fund and watch for any tax liabilities in the fund you may 'inherit' when you buy into it. Buy at the wrong time — just before the end of the tax year on 30 June — and it's like turning up late to a dinner party only to find you've missed the food and it's your turn to do the dishes. From personal experience, a CGT bill from a managed fund can be a shock. I bought into a fund in June after a particularly good year for investments on the stock market. Receiving the fund manager's statement two months later, I found I was liable to pay CGT on gains the fund had made over the year. The tax bill was about 4 per cent of the value of the investment. And I'd held the investment for only a couple of months!

You have to pay tax on gains eventually, such as when you sell units in a fund. However, if you don't want to pay a large amount of tax on income from your managed fund every year, preferring to defer it, look for a managed fund with a low turnover.

Hugging an index might not leave you feeling warm and fuzzy

'Hugging an index' isn't as touchy-feely as it may sound. *Index hugging* is the practice where a fund manager runs an investment portfolio that, by and large, matches the performance of a benchmark index. Some of the terms you hear associated with this practice are:

- ✔ **Benchmark:** This is a gauge or reference point against which fund managers measure their own funds' performance. Fund managers typically select an index, such as the S&P/ASX 200 (read on), as the performance benchmark for their fund. Using a well-known index has the advantage of providing an independent yardstick for investors to compare a range of similar funds.

- ✔ **Index:** This is a measure of a portfolio or group of share prices and is used to show the change in value of those share prices over a period of time. One well-known financial index, the *S&P/ASX 200*, measures the performance of the top 200 shares by size on the Australian Securities Exchange (ASX).

- ✔ **Tracking error:** Another way of saying how much the performance of the fund differs from the performance of the benchmark index. With zero being the benchmark index, the tracking error of the fund is shown as a positive or negative 1, 2 or 3.

Hugging the index can be an intentional or an unintentional consequence of the way the manager runs the investment portfolio. Funds with low tracking errors, say less than one, are almost mirroring the performance of the index. Unless invested in an index fund, investors would have to question why they're paying a fund manager to mirror the index. Paying for a fund manager's expertise means paying for the fund to outperform the index.

Trading for a living

Investors who want to take advantage of short-term movements in share prices can't do this with managed funds. These types of investors are more commonly known as *traders*. Traders take a short-term view of the market from as little as a few seconds to several months. As shares move up and down in value, so traders try to take advantage of those movements.

Traders may make or lose only small amounts each time they trade. By making several trades, sometimes in a day or in a week, they amplify gains and losses. Being able to buy and sell shares quickly is vital for the average

trader as seconds can mean the difference between a successful trade and a loss. You can't trade like this with managed funds that are priced daily, or sometimes only monthly, and require signed documentation for any purchases and sales.

Trading shares regularly can see costs mount up. Even if you're a confirmed trader, consider putting aside a portion of your investments in managed funds. Doing this helps to spread the risks should you have a bad month trading and averages out your investment costs.

Lacking transparency

Managed funds can seem like staring into a murky pool of water cloaked in a veil of legal structure, government regulations and marketing hype. Add a dash of periodic reporting by the fund manager and investors may have good reason to question what they're buying into.

Fund managers don't want to share all their information with investors and the market for good commercial reasons. If you've found a winning investing formula, then you're very unlikely to want to broadcast your secrets. Investors are left judging a fund by what's available in the marketing brochures and the fund's performance. Research from ratings agencies can help with an independent view, but even these ratings aren't foolproof. Some or all ratings may rely on what the fund manager tells the agency.

Stacking Up Managed Funds against Other Investments

How do managed funds stack up against other investments? I'm not talking about performance here, as I tackle that in Chapter 9. I mean how managed funds compare on things like costs and how easy it is to get in and out of different types of investments. Direct shares and property are the most popular types of investments that managed funds may be compared against.

Accessing your money

Buying and selling most managed funds is straightforward. Some paperwork is involved and investors need to be organised to complete the forms.

For the purposes of this book I decided to raid the kids' piggy banks and open up some managed funds on their behalf. 'But Dad, I really wanted a smart phone!' cried my son. 'But you're only nine and your mother doesn't even have a smart phone — the fact she can't use one is a different matter. Besides, you'll thank me later when you get your bill for uni fees,' I said, knowing I may as well have been talking to a tree for all the acknowledgement I got.

I'm pleased to say that, apart from my son's withering disapproval, the process of buying a managed fund from scratch was relatively painless. In fact, it was much less painful than opening an everyday bank account.

Always have an exit strategy before you invest. Ask yourself, 'If I put my money in, how and when can I take my money out?' If you don't have an answer to this question that you can live with, then seriously consider why you're making the investment.

Be careful you understand exactly what type of fund you're buying into. Some funds make it difficult to take your money out and may have a set timeframe that you need to stay invested in the fund. To my mind, buying into a fund that has frozen its redemptions, for whatever reason, makes little sense. This means you can put your money in but can't take it out. Many property and mortgage funds during the GFC froze investors' funds and many remain frozen.

Comparing funds against share ownership is fairly straightforward. Investing in shares has many similarities to investing in a managed fund (see Chapter 13 for more on buying and selling managed funds). After all, managed funds themselves tend to invest in shares.

Property investing covers a range of options as vast as Australia itself, from buying residential rental properties to property development and agricultural holdings. For the purposes of this section, I have residential rental properties in mind when making the comparisons. These investments are perhaps the most popular form of property investment in Australia.

Shares

The nature of shares and the way they trade means a certain amount of paperwork is needed, especially when getting started. All stockbrokers have standard account-opening procedures. However, if you choose to get advice from a broker, you'll need to fill in more forms and answer more questions.

Dealing with different types of stockbrokers

Everyday investors, as opposed to traders, can choose between two different types of stockbroking services — advice or non-advice. Advice tends to be offered by what are known as *full-service brokers* such as Patersons Securities, Bell Potter Securities and RBS Morgans. Non-advice is generally offered by the *online* or *direct brokers* such as CommSec, E*Trade Australia and Bell Direct. The differences between the two services are outlined in Table 2-2.

Table 2-2	Costs and Service Provided by Different Types of Stockbrokers	
	Full-Service Brokers	**Online or Direct Brokers**
Advice	Yes	No
Cost per trade	From a minimum $70 or 1% of value per trade up to 3% of total value	From a minimum of $10 or 0.11% of value per trade
Research on stocks	Yes, usually produced by the broker for exclusive use by its clients	Yes, some research may be produced in-house and some by independent research agencies
Invest in managed funds	Yes, but shares are what these brokers know and love	Yes and no; some online brokers provide access to managed funds
Ongoing contact	Yes, if the broker is doing the job right	General email updates on the market or stocks in your portfolio

Setting up an account to trade shares

Typically an investor needs to set up the following to buy and sell shares:

- **Stockbroking account:** Investors need to set up an account with a stockbroker if they want to trade shares, involving identification checks and possibly credit checks. I was surprised to learn not all brokers do credit checks! Identification checks include checks to prevent money laundering of the proceeds of crime, such as from drug dealing, through legitimate financial services and products.

- **Cash account:** A bank account is linked to every new stockbroking account when it's opened. Money is taken out to buy shares and deposited when shares are sold. Dividends and other income from shares are also put into the bank account.

> ✔ **CHESS sponsorship account:** This stands for Clearing House Electronic Subregister System and, despite the mouthful of a name, is just a way of managing the legal ownership of shares. Each time shares are traded, CHESS makes a note of the change in ownership based on the CHESS account details submitted to it by stockbrokers. Every share investor needs one of these accounts.

If you decide to take advantage of advice from a stockbroker you need to complete what is known as a 'know your client' questionnaire. Gone are the days of stockbroking when a client would sign up over a long lunch and a handshake. Nowadays, stockbrokers offering advice need to make sure they ask prospective clients about their financial circumstances. The resultant questionnaire is then part of the account-opening process.

Bricks and mortar

Compared with managed funds and shares, property is a whole different kettle of fish when it comes to investing. With shares and managed funds, investors are essentially dealing with pieces of paper that give them ownership of shares in a company or a trust.

Property investors, on the other hand, have a physical asset along with a piece of paper to say they own it or, more likely, the bank owns it until they've paid the mortgage. And property comes with a whole heap of different expenses, both when bought and when sold, as well as a raft of ongoing costs.

The ongoing debate in the media and from investment commentators is whether property or shares (and shares in managed funds) are better investments. Performance is the obvious way to compare the two asset classes. Chapter 4 takes a closer look at the performance of different asset classes. Many other factors need to be taken into consideration, though, when deciding if direct property or investing in the sharemarket is right for you. You may, of course, decide — and many people do — that both offer exciting investment possibilities.

Summarising the differences

Managed funds, shares and property are all similar in that they are affected by factors beyond most investors' control, such as what's happening in the overall market. And any transaction requires a willing buyer and a willing seller, with prices affected by the simple laws of demand and supply. The similarities end there though. I summarise the main differences between each type of investment in Table 2-3.

Table 2-3	Aspects of Managed Funds Compared with Shares and Property		
	Managed Funds	*Shares*	*Property*
Transaction fee, buying	Entry fee, from nil to 4%	Yes, brokerage from 0.11% to 3.3% (incl. GST on brokerage)	Yes, estate agent's fees, generally 2%
Transaction fee, selling	Exit fees may be charged, nil to 4%	Yes, brokerage from 0.11% to 3% (incl. GST on brokerage)	Yes, estate agent's fees
Stamp duty	No	No	Yes, varies between states
Ongoing costs	Yes, annual management fees 0.4% to 2.5%	Generally nil; brokers may charge an annual fee on international shares	Council rates, strata fees, insurance, land tax, maintenance costs, agent's fees
Liquidity (how easy it is to offload the investment)	Most can be bought and sold daily; check with fund manager	Depends on the stock; large companies tend to be very liquid and can be bought or sold easily during market open	Relatively long selling process from around six to eight weeks; can be much longer, depending on the property
Settlement (when you get your hands on the cash)	Usually within a few business days of sale but can be longer	Three days after the sale, known as T + 3 for Australian stocks	On settlement, usually a few weeks after sale, agreed by exchange of contracts

Chapter 3

Examining the Structures of Managed Funds

In This Chapter

▶ Understanding all the legal stuff

▶ Getting to grips with superannuation

▶ Finding out what your options are in retirement

▶ Exploring other managed fund structures

*H*aving a general understanding of how managed funds are set up helps you protect yourself and your money. In this chapter, I lift the veil on the way managed funds are set up in the eyes of the law. Although I can't promise a lot of laughs here, I do explain why the legal stuff is relevant. Important legal differences between funds also prevent certain types of investors from using certain funds. Retail and wholesale funds are the two most common funds you'll come across. Knowing the difference between the two and how to access wholesale funds could save you money in the long run.

Here I also go into why superannuation and pensions are a great way to legally reduce tax on retirement investments. Slight differences exist between everyday retail managed funds and those used for super and retirement. I take a look at what those differences are and how managed funds can be used as a part of a superannuation and retirement portfolio.

The source of much of the legal information in this chapter is the corporate regulator, the Australian Securities and Investments Commission (ASIC) and the relevant legislation. The summaries I provide give investors some useful checkpoints before taking the plunge into managed funds.

Easing through the Legalese

Legally speaking, managed funds in Australia fall under the gaze of the *Corporations Act 2001*. Here I summarise the important stuff from the relevant sections of the Act.

In the legislation, just to confuse things, a managed fund is defined as a *managed investment scheme (MIS)*, covering a multitude of different types of funds. The law also sets out how managed funds need to operate and how they should be run. ASIC is the industry watchdog, set up to keep a close eye on how fund managers operate.

Defining a managed investment scheme

Investors are unlikely to come across anything calling itself a managed fund that isn't an MIS. However, finding out what defines an MIS is worthwhile because the law ensures a minimum set of standards and protection for investors in an MIS.

What is a managed investment scheme?

The law has an exhaustive list of what is and is not an MIS. The following investments are what you'll most likely encounter:

- Australian equity (share) trusts
- Cash management trusts
- International equity trusts
- Mortgage funds, including unlisted mortgage funds
- Property trusts and unlisted property trusts

Anything classed as unlisted can't be bought or sold on a stock exchange. The bulk of the managed funds offered in Australia are unlisted and available directly through fund managers. However, some companies listed on the Australian Securities Exchange (ASX), known perhaps unsurprisingly as listed investment companies, look and feel like managed funds but can be bought and sold on the market. I talk about listed investment companies in the section 'Understanding the Differences between Various Funds' later in this chapter and in more detail in Chapter 15.

Other types of managed investment schemes you may come across are:

- Agricultural schemes (such as in horticulture, forestry or aquaculture; even racehorse syndications fit into this category)
- Schemes that provide film financing

    ✔ Strata title schemes that are actively managed

    ✔ Timeshare schemes

Investor appeal for agricultural schemes is waning, as many went belly-up during the global financial crisis. However, most of the types of schemes listed here are tax-driven investments supported by exceptionally generous government tax incentives to encourage investment. Investing in any of these types of schemes comes with some serious caveats, which are covered in more detail in Chapter 15.

The definition of an MIS *does not* include the likes of regulated superannuation funds, approved deposit funds, franchises and direct investment in shares. Importantly, schemes operated by an Australian bank in the ordinary course of banking business, such as a term deposit, are also not considered managed investment schemes.

A four-point managed investment scheme checklist

Having read mountains of product disclosure statements over the years, I could easily get complacent about all the legal stuff. Most of the time you deal with major fund managers who you'd think could be trusted to set things up correctly, and most of the time you'd be right. But, with just five minutes of basic checking, you can avoid the 'if only I'd checked …' moment if things do go wrong. Here's my checklist of questions to ask:

    ✔ **Is the fund an MIS as defined by the legislation?** Occasionally a product that looks like a managed fund may be something completely different. Check what you're investing in, because it can affect your rights as a consumer.

    ✔ **Is the fund registered with ASIC?** ASIC's website `www.asic.gov.au` and its consumer website `www.fido.gov.au` let you search for registered managed investment schemes.

    ✔ **Does it have a product disclosure statement (PDS)?** If the fund is registered with ASIC it should have a PDS. Use this information as the basis for making your investment decision.

    ✔ **Am I a wholesale or retail investor?** In most instances if the fund isn't registered and doesn't have a PDS, it's generally only available to wholesale investors. Do you meet the definition of a wholesale investor? (I cover this in the section 'Understanding the Differences between Various Funds' later in this chapter.) If you don't meet the definition, be careful investing.

Having problems understanding any aspects of the investment process such as reading the PDS? Never be afraid to ask and seek advice from a qualified professional; just understand you'll be charged for the service.

If an MIS isn't registered with ASIC, it can be offered only to wholesale investors, with some exceptions, which I outline in the section 'Understanding the Differences between Various Funds' later in this chapter.

Making sense of managed fund structures

The law says managed investment schemes must all have one thing in common, regardless of what they invest in. Whether investments are in Australian shares or sandalwood forests in Western Australia, to qualify as an MIS, the scheme must:

✔ Bring together people looking to invest in something in common

✔ Combine investors' money in the same investing pot

This idea of an investing pot, typically in order to invest in shares, gives managed funds the title *pooled investments*. Investors' money is combined, The legal entity that holds the pooled money is a trust. Figure 3-1 shows that, when you invest in a managed fund, you're buying units in that trust, which then invests in different investments on behalf of unit holders.

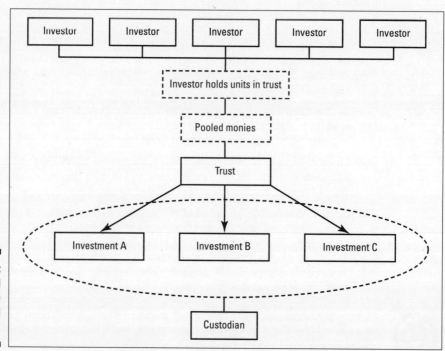

Figure 3-1: Managed funds are pooled investments.

The trust, in all likelihood, will have been in existence for some time before you buy the units and will continue to exist long after you've sold your units. Like a balloon, the size of the managed fund expands as investors put money into the trust by buying units and contracts as investors take money out by selling units.

Figuring out what fund operators need to do

The law makes sure fund operators are correctly set up to run a managed fund. The main requirement is that most funds must be registered with ASIC if they have more than 20 investors or are being promoted by 'someone who is in the business of promoting investment schemes'. This last statement is a catch-all clause intended to cover most schemes in the market.

ASIC also wants operators to jump through a number of hoops before a scheme can be registered. These regulations include:

- **Detailing a complaints resolution system:** An MIS must have a procedure in place to handle complaints and be a member of the industry's external complaints body, the Financial Ombudsman Service (FOS).

- **Keeping investors' money separate:** Investors' money must be kept separate from the property of the operator and other schemes. If the operator goes bust, at least investors should get their money back.

- **Putting in place a compliance committee:** The fund must have a board of directors with at least three external directors, or a compliance committee with at least three members, the majority external.

- **Setting up a responsible entity:** Each MIS must have what is known as a *responsible entity* to look after the operation of the scheme. The responsible entity is subject to its own licensing arrangements and must be a public company.

- **Submitting a product disclosure statement (PDS):** A PDS must be issued by any scheme wanting to raise money from the public. The PDS is designed to disclose all the relevant scheme details, fees and the like so investors can make an informed decision.

- **Writing a constitution and compliance plan:** Respectively, these documents outline the rules of the scheme and how the scheme intends to comply with the law.

A PDS must be lodged with ASIC if it's for a listed financial product; that's to say, a product that can be traded on a financial market. However, even if a PDS is lodged, ASIC gives no undertaking that the scheme is a good investment, so investors beware!

Finding out who's involved in running a managed fund

A managed fund's PDS can list a mind-boggling number of different companies and entities involved in running a fund. In my experience though, the average PDS falls short of explaining the role of each participant involved in running a managed fund. Four main players are involved in running a managed fund; here's who they are and what they do:

- ✔ **The fund manager:** Has responsibility for all the day-to-day investment decisions of the fund.

- ✔ **The responsible entity:** Looks after the operations of the managed fund, such as making sure the bills get paid and that the admin is done. Just to confuse things, the responsible entity and the fund management company are usually one and the same.

- ✔ **The trustee:** Most managed funds are set up as unit trusts. Each trust has a trustee to look after the interests of the managed fund and the investors. In reality, the trustee and the responsible entity are, again, usually one and the same. You can see a pattern developing here ...

- ✔ **The custodian:** Usually a specialist third-party company or a bank responsible for actually holding (having legal title over) the investments in the fund. Best practice is for managed funds to appoint a custodian, regardless of size, to provide an extra degree of comfort for investors. But, again, if the fund manager is big enough, it can also be the custodian. The custodian collects income on behalf of the fund and reports on asset values.

Managed funds are set up to protect investors' money should the actual operator go broke. Custodians are put in place to make sure that the investments are held separately from the assets of the fund management company. If the operator of the fund does go broke, the investments should be protected and returned to investors.

Visit the government's consumer watchdog website at www.fido.gov.au to find out more about the law governing managed funds. The website is run by ASIC with a brief that includes watching over managed fund providers. Refreshingly for a quasi-government agency, the website provides a plain-English guide to the law.

Superannuation and Managed Funds

Superannuation is an administrative and tax structure designed to help people save for retirement, and only for retirement. The government incentives and tax structure make superannuation a must for any investor's armoury. This section looks at the three main superannuation investment vehicles available to investors — employer super funds, where an employer makes superannuation contributions on your behalf, self-managed superannuation funds, which you run, and industry superannuation funds, where you or your employer contribute to a not-for-profit superannuation fund.

For most people contributing to a superannuation fund, their investments tend to end up in managed funds, especially for employer super funds and industry super funds. Self-managed super funds do use managed funds for their investments but to a lesser extent than direct equities.

Knowing about employer super funds

An employer super fund is offered by a company to its employees and generally only for use by its employees. A specialist superannuation company may run the fund or it could be set up by the company and run by external trustees on behalf of the employees. Certainly, many larger companies run their own funds.

Most employer superannuation schemes offer a menu of managed funds for investors that are set up specifically for superannuation investors. Each time an employer contributes to your super, the fund pays 15 per cent of that contribution in tax. This is different from non-superannuation managed funds that generally don't pay tax and where the investor is left to pay tax once a year on any income received from the fund.

Finding out about the superannuation guarantee

Generally, all employers must pay money into a super fund on behalf of employees. These payments are called *super guarantee (SG)* payments or *employer contributions*. At the time of writing, to be eligible for these payments employees must usually be over 18 years of age and under 75. Employees also need to be paid more than $450 before tax in a calendar month. Eligibility rules affect people under the age of 18, who generally have to work more than 30 hours a week to qualify for super contributions. For more information, visit the Australian Taxation Office (ATO) website (www.ato.gov.au).

Currently, employers are obliged to pay a minimum 9 per cent of base earnings into your super account. Your base earnings do not include overtime but do include bonuses and commissions. Employers must pay contributions at least every quarter. Currently, contributions must be paid on a maximum of $42,220 of earnings per quarter.

You should receive a contribution statement from your super fund at least annually. Check the statement to make sure you've been paid what your employer owes you. Employers are faced with a super guarantee charge for late payment or non-payment, which compensates employees.

Contributing to your super in other ways

Super fund members can also contribute by making voluntary contributions over and above the contributions made by their employers. Those contributions can be:

- **Concessional:** Additional contributions can be made from a person's salary or wages before tax is deducted. This method is highly tax-effective for super fund members. The government knows this is a great tax break so limits the contributions. Check the ATO website at www.ato.gov.au for the latest limits. The limits include the employer's superannuation guarantee payment.

- **Non-concessional:** Personal contributions are made after tax so generally no tax is payable by the super fund on the contributions, unless you contribute too much. Currently the limits are $150,000 per annum or $450,000 in any three-year period, depending on your age.

- **Government co-contributions:** Designed to help boost the super balances of low-income earners, the government matches contributions on behalf of employees up to $1,000 per annum, subject to maximum earnings, currently at just under $62,000.

Understanding your choices

You have a choice as to what fund you use, be it your employer's super fund, an external fund or even an industry super fund. Regardless, you will be confronted with an investment menu of fund choices, which are all, almost invariably, managed funds. Some funds do offer facilities to invest directly in shares but, for most, it's managed funds or nothing.

Spend time selecting funds from the investment menu; after all, this is your retirement that you're planning for. Most employer super funds also offer access to a financial planner to help employees with their selection. Use this service if you're in any way unsure; chances are you're already paying a small annual fee from your super for this financial planning service, so it makes sense to get your money's worth.

Doing it yourself: Self-managed super funds

Self-managed super funds (SMSFs) are a tremendously popular way for people to manage their own superannuation money. ATO figures show that at the end of December 2009 more than 415,000 SMSFs were in operation, with more than $385 billion in assets. Over 30,000 new funds were opened in 2009. Listed and unlisted managed funds made up around 17 per cent of assets held, or around $65 billion. A huge $103 billion, or 27 per cent, of assets were held in cash and $116 billion, or 30 per cent, were held in listed equities.

Many investors choose to set up SMSFs because they offer autonomy over investment decisions; however, with freedom comes responsibility and, often, increased expense.

Liberating your superannuation

The idea of managing your own super can be hugely attractive. The many advantages of SMSFs include controlling what you invest in, and when and how you invest. SMSFs can hold a wide range of investments, including shares, managed funds, cash, and even art, antiques and other collectibles.

Any assets held by an SMSF must pass what's called a *sole-purpose test*. Assets can be used only for the sole purpose of superannuation investments. Investing in a vintage sports car and driving it for pleasure is a no-no. The car needs to be insured and locked up in a storage facility until sold and the same goes for artworks; these all need to be stored away and not used for personal enjoyment. The restrictions also mean that you can't take cash out of the fund to pay your electricity bills, for example. The ATO, responsible for regulating SMSFs, takes a particularly dim view of the misuse of funds.

Taking on the responsibilities

Setting up a self-managed super fund is a big step from managing your investments through your employer super fund. Significant responsibilities are involved and the ATO is particularly eagle-eyed when it comes to SMSFs. Apart from the day-to-day accounting and administration of the fund, you need to ensure that the fund meets its tax and reporting obligations. Put the investment decision-making on top of all the administration work and an SMSF is not something for the faint-hearted!

An SMSF is a legal entity governed by a trust deed and administered by trustees for and on behalf of the members of the fund. SMSFs are open to a maximum of four people — you and three others (the members), who can't be your employees and who are usually but not limited to your spouse or relatives. The fund members are the individuals who ultimately benefit from the fund on retirement. The trustees of the fund, usually the members, bear all the responsibility for ensuring the fund manages the investments correctly on behalf of the members, as well as all the reporting and administration.

Setting up an SMSF can be relatively expensive. The general rule is you need at least $200,000 in an SMSF to make it cost-effective. You can expect to pay anywhere between $2,000 and $5,000 a year in administration fees, or more, depending on the size of the fund.

Look to pay no more than around 2 per cent of the total value of your superannuation account in annual fees. Anything less than $200,000 in your account and the fees start to look expensive. Most trustees use accountants or specialist administrators to manage the administration, legal, compliance and tax reporting. With so many professionals involved, the costs can quickly mount up.

Understanding industry super funds

Industry super funds are open to people who work in a particular industry, such as healthcare or construction. These funds operate, by and large, in a similar way to the employer super funds, offering an investment menu of managed funds.

Finding out why industry funds are different

A key difference between employer and industry funds is that industry funds are not-for-profit, most of which are *public offer super funds*. For these funds, an employer can generally make contributions on your behalf or you can make the contributions on your own behalf if self-employed.

The other big difference and selling point of industry super funds is that they don't pay commissions to financial advisers. As a result, industry funds typically cost less than employer super funds. Figure 3-2 shows the potential difference between using an industry fund and a retail superannuation fund, assuming a 30-year-old with an annual income of $60,000 and $20,000 in superannuation. The chart shows the difference that paying lower fees can make to your super balance until retirement at 65 years old.

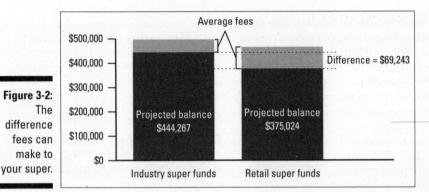

Source: Industry SuperFunds and Super Ratings.

Figure 3-2: The difference fees can make to your super.

Figure 3-2 is taken from the Industry SuperFunds fee comparator tool, found on its website at www.industrysuper.com. Figure 3-2, with modelling data current at 30 June 2010, assumes payment of the annual 9 per cent superannuation guarantee, annual salary increase of 3.5 per cent, investment returns of 7.225 per cent per annum and retirement at 65 years. No insurance deductions have been made.

Super changes for superannuation

The federal government is on a mission to improve superannuation in Australia. Regardless of which party is in power, the general consensus is that, the way super-annuation stands, most people will find they won't have enough savings in retirement to live off. In early 2009, the government commissioned a review of superannuation in Australia and a raft of recommendations were released in 2010. Not all of these recommendations will be taken up but the ones most likely to come into being are:

✔ **Lower fees:** For the 80 per cent of workers who use their employer's default fund, the proposal is to launch a new product that will cut fees by 40 per cent. The maximum fee will be 0.66 per cent per annum, almost half of what many superannuation fund members currently pay. Retirement savings will be significantly boosted if this fee cut is introduced.

✔ **Efficiency:** More than $13.6 billion is lying unclaimed in superannuation accounts in Australia. Frequent job changes and failure to notify changes of address have left many people with several super accounts that they have lost track of. The plan is to use a person's tax file number (TFN) — it escapes me why this isn't the case now — to keep track of super-annuation accounts.

✔ **Better benefits in retirement:** Super is one of the cheapest ways to take out life insurance. However, an average of 30 per cent in insurance premiums is paid to financial advisers. These commissions will be banned.

Discovering what funds are available

Most industries, from construction through to healthcare, rural services and hospitality, are covered by 16 industry super funds. And, if you can't find a fund specifically for your industry, the Labour Union Co-operative Retirement Fund (LUCRF) covers all industries. You can find out more about industry super funds at the industry governing body, Industry SuperFunds, at www.industrysuper.com.

Industry super funds are not geared to cater for financial planners. The funds don't pay commissions to planners, the assets behind each option are often opaque and their administrative systems aren't easily accessible by financial planners. Financial planners need to know the product and have a reasonable basis for recommending it. If funds don't adequately disclose the assets, financial planners can't recommed them. For these reasons, you're highly unlikely to be recommended an industry super fund by a financial planner.

Working Out Your Retirement Options

When retiring, investors move from what is known as the *accumulation phase* to the *pension phase*. People stop saving for retirement and start taking an income from their savings. People moving into retirement have the option of setting up either a pension or an annuity. The main difference between the two is that pensions can be bought only from superannuation fund providers and only with money from a superannuation account. Annuities can be bought only from life insurance companies but can be bought with funds from either a superannuation account or other money, in some cases.

Two main types of pensions and annuities are available:

- ✔ **Market-linked pensions and annuities:** A minimum amount of income is drawn every year but investment returns fluctuate according to the underlying investments.

- ✔ **Fixed-income pensions and annuities:** The income received is agreed in year one and then increases at a fixed rate every year, usually at the rate of inflation. How long an income is paid depends on the type of product purchased.

Income and lump-sum payments from pensions and annuities are generally tax-free when you reach 60 years of age. Some types of pensions and annuities don't allow lump sum withdrawals and pay only a regular income.

Learning about market-linked pension accounts and annuities

Market-linked pension accounts (previously known as allocated pensions) and annuities are sometimes known as *account-based pensions* and *account-based annuities*. An investment account is set up and retirees can choose how they want to manage their money. Commonly, money from a retiree's existing superannuation fund is used to buy into managed funds specifically set up to cater for pensions. The larger fund managers offer a pension version of many of their managed funds.

Market-linked pension accounts can be bought only with money from a retiree's existing superannuation account. However, annuities can be bought, in some cases, with other money, in addition to money from a superannuation account. The level of income from market-linked pensions and annuities is not guaranteed as it's subject to the returns generated from the underlying investments, as well as fees.

Market-linked pension accounts and annuities invest money in shares, managed funds or similar investments that are held in a special pension account. Each year a minimum amount of income must be withdrawn from the account, depending on how old you are. From the age of 60 onwards, as long as the rules on income are met, tax is zero. Should you need to take out a lump sum, say, to buy a car, these withdrawals are also tax-free after the age of 60.

Managing your income with fixed-income pensions and annuities

Many retirees like the certainty of a regular income every year and one that increases with the rate of inflation. Three types of fixed-income pensions and annuities exist and all of them offer income increases every year in line with inflation:

- ✔ **Fixed term:** A regular income is paid for a fixed term. The risk is that the beneficiary outlives the term of the investment. Any remaining money upon death is distributed to the estate. The fixed term is set by the person taking out the pension or annuity.

✔ **Life expectancy:** You choose a period to receive income based either on your life expectancy at the time you buy the pension or annuity, or your life expectancy plus five years, which has the effect of extending the payment term. On death, payments may be made to what is known as a *reversionary beneficiary*, usually the partner or spouse, or the remaining money is distributed to the estate. The insurance companies set the life expectancy periods. If you outlive the life expectancy period you won't receive any further payments.

✔ **Lifetime:** These pay an income over the life of the holder or beneficiary. When the holder dies, payments can still be made to a reversionary beneficiary until that person dies.

The companies selling these products use complex life expectancy tables to work out how long they may have to pay out income on a pension or annuity. If you live too long, it can cost the company a lot of money! Investors also need a reasonable sum of money in the first place to be able to generate enough income to live off.

Understanding the Differences between Various Funds

Investors are likely to come across a menagerie of managed fund types, such as retail and wholesale funds, closed-end and open-ended funds, and unlisted and listed managed funds. Bear in mind, each of these is a distinct type of managed fund and is designed for different types of investors.

Retail and wholesale funds

The terms *retail* and *wholesale* for me conjure up images of either a fancy shopping mall with pricey goods open to everyone with a credit card, or a dark warehouse stacked full of boxes being sold off cheap for cash and in bulk, where you need to be a member to get in the door. In truth, this distinction is not that far off what actually happens in practice with retail and wholesale funds, although perhaps not the bit about payment in cash!

Defining retail and wholesale investors

The main difference between retail and wholesale funds is based on what type of investor the fund can be offered to. Whether you're a retail investor or a wholesale investor depends on how much money and investment experience you have. The law says that if you have more than a certain amount of money you're deemed to be an experienced investor. Whether you are or not is a different matter!

Table 3-1 summarises the differences between retail and wholesale investors and the nature of the investments they can purchase. Within the definition of a wholesale investor sits also a distinction between *sophisticated* investors and *professional* investors.

Table 3-1	Retail versus Wholesale Investors	
	Retail Investor	*Wholesale Investor*
Offer document	A PDS must be provided to all potential investors in the product	No requirement for a PDS; an investment memorandum may be issued that outlines the details of the offer
Wealth test	No wealth test	Yes; sophisticated investors must meet one of the following conditions: Have net investable assets of more than $2.5 million (must be certified by a qualified accountant) Have income greater than $250,000 for each of the last two years (must be certified by a qualified accountant) Be investing more than $500,000 Be classed as a professional investor under the Corporations Act; mainly bodies licensed as such or individuals who control more than $10 million for investing in securities
Types of investments	Retail products offered only through a PDS or a prospectus	Wholesale or excluded offers that are not available to retail investors
Complaints procedure	Yes; investors should be protected to some extent; fund manager must be a member of the Financial Ombudsman Service (FOS)	No external complaints procedure or ombudsman for investors to fall back on

Retail managed funds are generally more expensive than wholesale funds. You can access wholesale funds through administration platforms without having to meet the definition of a wholesale investor. See Chapter 17 for more on administration platforms.

Advantages and disadvantages of retail managed funds

Retail funds are an attractive way of investing for a number of reasons. A big plus is that funds are required to provide detailed disclosure of what they do via a PDS and give greater protection or means of redress for investors.

The flipside of the protection retail funds offer is that they're generally more expensive than wholesale managed funds. Retail managed funds are more costly to run because of their much greater disclosure and reporting obligations, and, with more investors, administration costs mount up. Whereas an investor may pay an ongoing annual cost of around 0.9 per cent on the value of the investment for a wholesale fund, a retail fund might charge 1.5 per cent annual fee — almost double.

Accessing wholesale managed funds

Investing in wholesale managed funds isn't out of the question for inexperienced investors. Fortunately, the big platform providers like Westpac BT, Colonial First State and Perpetual Investments, among others, provide an opportunity for retail investors to invest via their platforms. Platforms are, in effect, an administration and reporting service for a range of investments covering managed funds, shares and cash. For more on platforms see Chapter 17.

The platforms can be aimed at retail investors directly but usually via financial planners. Size means platforms can invest large slabs of money into wholesale funds on behalf of retail investors. Platforms can take advantage of the lower costs charged by wholesale funds and pass these on to investors. Importantly, the retail investor can get access for between $1,000 and $5,000 and not the $50,000 to $500,000 they would need if going direct to the fund manager.

Open-ended and closed-end funds

Open-ended funds are definitely in the majority in the world of managed funds and these are the ones you're most likely to come across. Open-ended funds don't generally have an end date, whereas closed-end funds will have a date when the fund will be wound up.

Opening up on open-ended managed funds

Open-ended managed funds are those that can issue and redeem units in the trust at any time. For example, an investor wanting to buy or sell units in an unlisted managed fund can do so by either the fund manager issuing (creating) new units or redeeming (cancelling) the units from the investor. Investors don't generally buy or sell units to or from other unit holders. The fund manager looks after all the transactions.

Investors pay cash to the fund manager for the issue of new units in the managed fund. Equally, the investor receives cash from the fund manager when selling units. The price at which units are issued or cashed in largely reflects the value of the underlying investments of the fund divided by the number of units on issue, plus some tweaking for fees and other items. For more on how managed fund units are priced, see Chapter 13.

Learning about closed-end managed funds

Closed-end funds generally issue all the units they're going to issue at the outset of the investment. If investors wish to buy more units, they have to find another investor willing to sell shares to them. Investors can do this by using a broker, or the fund manager may introduce willing buyers and sellers.

Closed-end funds generally, but not always, say when and how the fund manager allows investors to sell their units or shares back to the fund manager. Most funds have a limited life, of say ten years, after which time assets are distributed back to the unit holders in the form of cash. Closed-end funds tend to invest in longer term assets, such as property or toll roads, where money is needed upfront to buy the asset. The attraction is that the investment generally provides a regular and growing income over the life of the investment.

Getting your money out of a closed-end fund before the end date may be tricky. An active market for the units means you could find a buyer for your units quite easily. However, if demand for the units is low, you could wait a long time to find a buyer.

Unlisted and listed funds

The obvious difference between listed investment companies and unlisted managed funds is that listed funds are traded on the ASX. Other key differences are shown in Table 3-2.

Table 3-2	Listed Investment Companies versus Managed Funds	
	Listed Investment Company	*Managed Fund*
Structure	A company with a board of directors and shareholders	A trust with a trustee and custodian to make sure investments are held separately from the running of the fund and unit holders
Holdings	Investors hold shares	Investors hold units
Access	Listed on the ASX; buying and selling of shares through a stockbroker	Purchase of units direct with the fund manager through an application form; redemption by letter or form
Liquidity	Depends on the company and how actively it is traded on the market; may take a while to buy or sell a large holding if demand is low	Depends on the fund; most large Australian equity funds offer to sell or buy units to or from investors on a daily basis but some funds, such as some infrastructure and property funds, may trade only once a month
Income	The listed company receives income and dividends from the investments it holds	The managed fund receives income and dividends on the investments it holds
Income to investors	Pays a dividend to investors; may or may not be 100% of income received	Legally required to distribute all income and capital gains it receives to investors every year
Tax	Company pays tax on the income it receives; investors may receive franking credits on some of or the entire dividend	Managed funds pay no tax; the investor may pay tax on the distributions paid

Watch out for the price of listed investment companies on the stock market. Sometimes the price doesn't reflect the true value, or *net tangible assets (NTA)*, as it's known, of the underlying investments held by the company. For example, the price per share of the company may be 95 cents but the value of the underlying investments is actually $1 a share. In this example, the company is trading at 5 per cent discount to its NTA value. Discounts to NTA value can be as high as 15 to 20 per cent.

A listed investment company trading at a discount is great if you're looking to buy, because you get a good price. But the discount is not so good if you're a holder of the shares. As an investor, you want your holdings to trade closer to the true value of the company. At 30 June 2010, of the 25 listed investment companies on the ASX, 21 were trading at a discount to NTA.

Chapter 4

Identifying Asset Classes and Investment Styles

In This Chapter

▶ Exploring the meaning of asset classes

▶ Understanding how different asset classes can affect returns

▶ Finding out about the investment styles of fund managers

Class and style — not descriptions that immediately leap to mind when thinking of fund managers! Snappy dressers aside, most fund managers do have their own particular sort of style. Like chefs cooking a particular type of food, such as Italian or Chinese, so fund managers have their own ways of managing money.

Style reflects a fund manager's view of the world and how that manager looks for and judges investment opportunities. Diners know what dishes to expect when they go to a favourite Italian restaurant. Similarly, investors can get to know what potential returns to expect with certain styles of fund manager. In this chapter, I run through the various styles so you can almost visualise the menus each of them offers.

This chapter also explores the meaning of asset class — essentially shares, bonds, cash and property. Asset class is a simple way of grouping similar types of investments with similar attributes. Understanding how each asset class works can be a big help when it comes to deciding the best place to put your money.

For fund managers (and investors), style and asset class go hand in hand. How different managers view the world is likely to determine what asset classes they use. Simply put, asset classes are about the returns investors can expect for a certain level of risk. Investors can mix asset classes to potentially reduce risk and this chapter shows you how to do it.

Learning about Asset Class

Asset class is a way of lumping together similar types of underlying investments that have similar characteristics, such as potential returns and likely risks. Assets in a particular class are also generally subject to the same laws and regulations. The four main types of asset class are cash, shares, fixed-interest securities (bonds) and property. Each of these classes can be broken down further and I set this out in the section 'Setting Out the Types of Asset Class' later in this chapter.

Highlighting the importance of class

Sorting assets into different classes is more than a just a convenient way to group investments. Understanding how risk and reward work together is the key to understanding asset class. Each asset class combines similar assets with similar risks. What results is known as a *risk profile* — basically, how likely you are to lose money if you invest in that asset.

Using asset class to build a portfolio

Fund managers use an asset class or a mix of asset classes to manage their risks and returns. However, creating a fund is not just a case of 'build it and he will come'. Fund managers need to have an eye on what investors want. Some investors want a low level of risk and are prepared to accept lower returns. A cash fund may be appropriate in this case. On the flipside, some investors want high returns and take on higher risk to achieve them. An international share fund may meet this demand.

Knowing that funds have different levels of risk, with potentially different returns, does make it easier for investors when it comes to choosing a fund. As fund managers look to mix asset classes to achieve certain returns, so should investors think about doing the same with managed funds.

Figuring out risk and reward is crucial to any investment decision. The riskier the investment, the greater the reward you want in return. Each asset class generally offers a certain type of risk and reward.

Understanding the risks and rewards of asset classes

All investing involves some risk, but not all risk is bad. In fact, investors need to take some risk if they want to beat the effects of inflation — how much the cost of living goes up each year. With, for example, an average annual inflation rate of 3 per cent, $100 today will be worth only $56 in 20 years' time.

You *can* manage risk. Used sensibly, risk can enhance returns to a portfolio without scaring yourself silly. As with any investing, the level of risk is up to you and what you feel comfortable with. Your own circumstances, what your investing goals are and, importantly, how much you're prepared to lose help you determine the right investments for you. See Chapter 6 to see how you can decide what level of risk suits you.

The return on an investment, in its simplest form, is how much money you make over the time you hold the investment, less any costs you incur. Risk is a little trickier to measure but can be summed up by how much an investment moves up and down in value over a period of time. This movement in values is known as *volatility*. Investments that rollercoaster up and down are said to have high volatility and investors definitely need a strong stomach to ride out the highs and lows!

Risk and return profiles across the asset classes generally follow a pattern. Table 4-1 outlines the basic risk and return profiles of each asset class.

Table 4-1	**Asset Types: Risks and Potential Rewards**		
Asset Type	*Description*	*Risk and Potential Reward*	*Timeframe*
Defensive assets — lower risk, focused on income and capital preservation			
Cash	Bank bills or similar securities that provide regular income that can generally be accessed quite quickly	Low	No minimum
Fixed-interest securities	Government bonds, corporate bonds, hybrid securities (bonds with shares attached)	Low to medium	1 to 3 years
Growth assets — higher risk, a mix of income and capital growth			
Property securities	Listed property trusts	Medium to high	3 to 5 years
Australian shares	Direct investment or through managed funds	High	5 to 7 years
International shares	Shares in overseas markets, which offer numerous opportunities, although currencies can move against you	High	5 to 7 years

Table 4-1 provides a guide only — within each asset class are investments that can be riskier than others. For example, the shares of smaller mining companies are generally riskier than those of large companies or the big banks. Equally, fixed-interest assets such as US treasury bonds are seen as less risky than bonds that may be issued by companies. The risk of the US government not meeting its obligations is seen to be a lot lower than that for most companies that sell their own bonds.

Figure 4-1 shows how the value of $100,000 has increased using the different asset classes from January 1989 to December 2009. Over the longer term, Australian shares have been the top-performing investment.

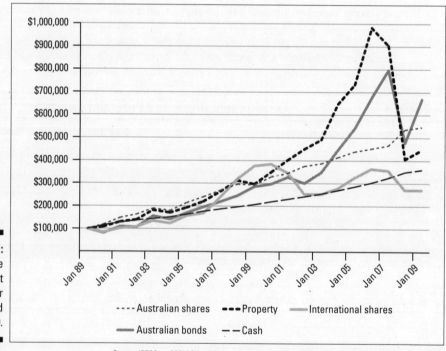

Figure 4-1:
Performance of asset classes over the period 1989 to 2009.

Source: IRESS — S&P/ASX 200 Accumulation Index; MSCI World ex-Australia (net dividends) Index in A$; S&P/ASX 300 Property Index; UBS Bank Bill 0+ years; UBS Composite 0+ years index.

Making the right choice

It's not whether you're right or wrong that's important, but how much money you make when you're right and how much you lose when you're wrong.

—*George Soros, hedge fund guru*

Making the right choice about asset class boils down to each investor's own attitude to risk. Combine risk with the returns you need and your time horizon to help you determine what asset classes to invest in. To find out more about risk and to work out your investor type, see Chapter 6.

Dividing up your investments by using different asset classes is called *asset allocation*. Asset allocation comes in two types, strategic and tactical. *Strategic* allocation is working out *what* asset classes to use and *tactical* allocation is working out *when* to invest. As Peter Haggstrom of Independent Strategies and Bill Raffle of Bennelong Private Wealth put it:

> *In military terms, strategic asset allocation is the equivalent of 'invade Russia' while tactical asset allocation is: 'Do it in summer'. Reality is: 'You will be sitting around a fire in winter toasting a rat on a stick.'*

Asset allocation needn't be complicated. Fund managers and professional investors may spend an inordinate amount of time trying to get this right, but the science behind asset allocation is inexact at best. Don't fret over whether you should have 50 per cent or 53 per cent in Australian shares. As long as you're getting the approximate split across asset classes, fiddling at the edges isn't going to make a heap of difference.

Setting Out the Types of Asset Class

Asset classes come in four main flavours — cash, fixed-interest securities (bonds), property and shares. This section takes a closer look at what assets are generally lumped under each asset class, how managed funds invest in them, the risks associated with each class and the likely returns.

Being conservative in cash

Cash covers a whole range of different types of investment that are called cash. Putting your money in a savings account is perhaps most people's idea of a cash investment. By placing your money in a bank account or with a credit union, you're effectively lending your money to the bank, which then pays you interest. Investing in cash through a fund is a little different.

Finding out about investing in cash

A host of products act much as if you've put your money in the bank but they can pay slightly different returns and usually for a set period. You can 'lend' your money out by either buying these cash products directly, such as term deposits or bank bills with a bank. Or you can invest indirectly by buying into managed funds that specialise in cash products.

Cash investments take various forms:

- ✔ **Cash:** Straightforward cash in the bank. Most investors and all fund managers keep a portion of their investments in hard cash, readily accessible to meet expenses or for emergencies.

- ✔ **Cash managed funds:** These funds invest in a range of different cash assets, notably government and semi-government securities, bills of exchange, negotiable certificates of deposit, promissory notes and call deposits, to name a few. *Cash managed funds* sound complicated but essentially operate like cash, with a low risk of loss.

- ✔ **Cash management trusts:** In the good old days before the global financial crisis, cash management trusts were all the rage. Not so now. A *cash management trust* is set up like a managed fund but works like a bank account, except they're not a bank account. Confused? The trust invests in, usually, fixed-interest products, such as company bonds, that pay a regular income. The trust uses that income to pay a return to investors that is usually better than a standard high-interest bank account.

Technically, cash management trusts and cash managed funds could be classed as fixed-income products, given the underlying investments may be bonds. However, I include them in cash because investors tend to treat them as a cash product.

Understanding the risks of cash

Any investment carries risk — even cash. Cash in a bank is at risk from the bank going into default. Although not impossible, the odds of this happening in Australia are low. Cash management trusts and cash funds carry some risk of the value of the underlying investments declining. Again, the risk of that happening in these funds is generally low.

Fixing your interest with fixed interest

Fixed interest is a general term for investments that pay a set level of income over a certain period. At the end of that period, the original amount is returned to the investor. Income is the main reason for investing in fixed-interest products but some may provide the opportunity to grow the value of the investment.

Finding out about investing in fixed-interest securities

Investing in fixed-interest products is effectively lending your money to a borrower who pays you interest for the pleasure. The general rule is that the higher the rate of return, the higher the risk. Fixed-interest funds cover a wide range of products, such as:

- ✔ **Bond trusts:** *Bond trusts* invest in bonds issued by governments or companies, both in Australia and overseas. A *bond* is a form of debt that pays an income. The income divided by the value of the bond is what's known as the *yield*. For example, a ten-year Australian government bond may be issued by the government for $100 per bond, paying an income of $6 per annum, or 6 per cent yield. Corporations look to raise money by also issuing bonds but, because the risk may be greater with a corporate bond, the rate of interest is higher, at maybe 7 per cent.

- ✔ **Debenture notes:** These products are a way for companies to borrow money in return for paying a set interest rate. Companies use monies raised via *debenture notes*, basically a loan similar to a bond, to finance a wide range of activities. Notes can be either listed on a stock exchange or unlisted and offered through a prospectus. Managed funds invest in debentures for the income that is generated by the notes in the form of interest. The underlying value of the debenture may also change over time but this is not the primary reason for investing in debentures.

- ✔ **Mortgage trusts:** A *mortgage trust* invests in a wide range of mortgages, both residential and commercial, that pay an income over the life of the loans. By investing in a large number of loans across a range of properties, the trust spreads its risk.

Understanding how bonds and other fixed-interest products stack up as investments can be tricky. Ratings agencies can be a help here. You may be familiar with specialist agencies such as Standard & Poor's, Fitch, and Moody's. Using an easy-to-understand system, such as stars, ratings give a good guide of the creditworthiness of the underlying issuer of the bond. The level of credit rating given to a company affects the cost of borrowing for a company or government. The worse the credit rating, the higher the interest rate paid to investors.

Understanding the risks

The risk of losing money in fixed-interest products is generally low to medium. However, be wary of any product paying an interest rate that seems too good to be true. Some of the most recent and biggest corporate failures have involved fixed-interest products of some sort. In these failures, investors lost most of their original capital.

The consumer website of the Australian Securities and Investments Commission (ASIC), www.fido.gov.au, gives extensive guidance on what to look out for when investing in fixed-interest securities.

Building your wealth in property funds

When I refer to property here I mean investing in property through managed funds, not direct investment in property, where an investor takes physical ownership. This section looks at the various property funds available and what to look out for.

Finding out about investing in property

Some large funds offer exposure to different areas of the property market, from commercial office buildings and warehouses, retail shopping centres, pubs and hospitality through to property development. The advantage of investing in a *property managed fund* is the ability to access a professionally managed portfolio of properties, across a diverse range of property sectors, with different tenants and leases, without the complexities of direct property ownership. With property trusts, investors get exposure to both income from rent and potential growth in value of the underlying properties.

Investments generally take the form of listed and unlisted property trusts:

✔ **Listed trusts:** Some property trusts are listed on the Australian Securities Exchange (ASX). *Listed trusts* are also known as *A-REITs* or *Australian real estate investment trusts*. Listed trusts are generally *stapled* securities, which means they have two parts — a management company that acts as trustee for the other part, the trust. The management company pays a dividend to investors and the trust pays a distribution. Shares in A-REITs can be bought or sold via a stockbroker. A-REITs invest in property directly and are responsible for all aspects of management, maintenance, leasing and rental collection. Income is generally paid quarterly or half-yearly to shareholders.

✔ **Unlisted trusts:** Some investors buy or sell units in an *unlisted property trust* directly with the fund manager. Unlisted funds can invest directly in property and manage properties in the same way as listed property trusts.

✔ **Property securities trusts:** Investments in the shares of property companies are known as *property securities trusts* and can be unlisted or listed on the ASX. Property securities trusts do not invest in or manage properties directly.

Property trusts can offer what is known as *concessionally taxed income*, or *tax-deferred income*. This income is taxed at a lower rate than normal and that has to be a good thing! The level of the tax-deferred income is between 50 and 100 per cent of the fund's distributions. The tax-deferred income recognises that fixtures and fittings reduce in value over time, and that fall in value can be claimed against the investment. While no income tax is payable, the income is deducted from the original *capital base* (the amount you've invested), potentially increasing the capital gains tax (CGT) payable when you sell the investment.

Understanding the risks of property

Property investment, even via a managed fund, is considered a higher risk asset class than cash or fixed interest, along with shares. Fluctuating property prices and rental incomes driven by what's happening in the wider economy are the key risks. Also bear in mind that property security trusts investing in listed property companies are also potentially affected by general movements in the stock market.

Property funds can seem complicated to the uninitiated but need not be so. You do need to put some work into assessing whether a property fund is a reasonable investment. Some things you should be looking out for include:

- ✔ **Borrowings:** Some trusts borrow money (or *gear*) to buy properties. As with a residential mortgage, gearing is fine as long as the income more than offsets the repayments (negative gearing doesn't apply to trusts, as it implies having another source of income to service the debt — if the income can't cover the repayments, the trust has to sell off the investment). How much debt the trust has is the key to its survival.

- ✔ **Income:** The quality of the tenants, the average length of the tenancies and how much of a building is occupied at any one time (*occupancy rate*) all affect the rental income stream flowing back to the trust.

- ✔ **Property type:** Whether the trust invests in residential, commercial, industrial or retail property or a mix of property types, each type has different risks attached to it, moving up or down at different times during the course of the economic cycle. So, while residential house prices may be in the doldrums, the market in warehouses could be on the up. You need to get a feel for where each sector is in the cycle before investing.

- ✔ **Quality:** The location and condition of the property impacts on the value of the trust. The product disclosure statement (PDS) should provide a description of each property, along with a commercial grading for the property.

- ✔ **Timeframe:** Property trust investing is not short term and investors should have a five- to seven-year investment timeframe in mind.

The mix of property in a trust either concentrates the risk or reduces it. Trusts that invest in one property type, such as retail shopping centres, are exposed to very specific risks peculiar to that sector, such as changes in consumer spending habits. Property trusts that have a lot of exposure to property development take on a higher level of risk altogether. Trusts that have a good mix of property types, also known as *diversified* funds (refer to Chapter 2), spread the risk across different segments and so should be able to manage their risk better.

Watch out for high debt levels in property funds. Too much debt was the undoing of many property trusts during the global financial crisis. Some funds caught up in the mess are still trying to sort themselves out. These funds allow new investors to buy units but don't let them sell those units. Make sure any fund you invest in isn't closed for withdrawals!

Raising the stakes with shares

Over the longer term, Australian shares as an asset class have generated higher returns than most other asset classes. However, investing in shares isn't all fun and games, so you need to understand some of the definite risks.

Finding out about investing in shares

A tremendous number of managed funds invest in both Australian and international shares. A diversified fund invests in a spread of different companies to reduce the overall risk of the fund. Others are concentrated funds focused on a small number of stocks, concentrating the risk if some of the stocks don't perform. Others are high-yield or high-income funds investing in stocks that produce consistently high dividends or income. Refer to Chapter 2 for a general overview of managed funds and see Chapter 14 for more on the standard fund types.

Understanding the risks of shares

Shares can move around a lot more in value and carry more risk than most other asset classes. Most product disclosure statements carry a list of the types of risk that investors could be exposed to by investing in a managed fund. Because funds invest in such a wide range of shares, they also potentially carry a number of different risks. The three main risks are

✔ **Liquidity risk:** Fund managers, for whatever reason, may not be able to readily sell out of a particular investment, which means investors won't be able to get their money out of the fund when they want. For example, some small company shares do not trade large amounts of stock, so selling a sizeable chunk of shares may take some time.

> ✔ **Market risk:** All companies listed on a stock exchange face the risk that the market falls beyond their control, affecting all listed companies. Most companies can do little to manage this risk so the task generally falls to the investors. Investors can manage the risk by simply deciding how much money to have in or out of the market.

> ✔ **Specific company risk:** Companies are exposed to the general risks of doing business in whatever industry they operate. For example, the risks faced by a mineral explorer are different from those faced by a bank, or you'd hope so. A company's management looks to offset this risk by operating in an environment where it can control its operating risks as much as possible.

The skill of fund managers is their ability to pick the stocks that are best at managing their risks for the returns they're likely to generate. When the market falls, some stocks fall further than others. By selecting a range of different stocks across different industries, the manager can, to some extent, reduce the impact of falls in the market on the total value of the portfolio.

How Stylish Is Your Fund Manager?

I doubt you'll see any fund managers showing off their style on the fashion runways of Paris or Milan. Yet managers do like to parade their style in front of potential investors. The big difference between fund managers and the world of fashion is that fund managers tend not to change their style every year, thank goodness. Being consistent with style can ultimately affect the overall performance that a fund manager delivers.

A fund manager's style is more than skin deep. Style, sometimes known as *bias*, goes to the core of how a fund manager works. *Style* is a real methodology adopted by many fund managers to describe how they manage money. The first assessment is whether the fund manager is an active investor or passive. Active management is then further categorised according to the types of investment the fund manager focuses on. Classing fund managers this way helps investors as well. Investors know what they're potentially getting when investing with a growth manager or a value manager, for example.

Other managers shun style and won't be labelled. They tend to have a foot in both the value and growth camps, and are referred to as being style-neutral, or core, investors. Still others are described as going for growth at a reasonable price. Then there are the high-risk hedge funds versus traditional fund managers. I talk more about hedge funds in Chapter 16.

Some fund managers run a number of different funds, each with a different style. Table 4-2 shows the generally accepted style of the major Australian fund managers.

Table 4-2		Styles of Different Fund Managers			
Active Investors					*Passive Investors*
Value	*Growth*	*Style-Neutral (Core)*	*Growth at a Reasonable Price*	*Hedge Funds*	
Investors Mutual	Colonial First State	BT Investments	AMP OnePath	Hedge Funds Australia	BlackRock iShares/State Street
Maple-Brown Abbott	Merrill Lynch	Goldman Sachs JBWere		PM Capital	Vanguard Investments
Perpetual Investments					
Tyndall					

Passive or active management

Broadly speaking, style can be divided into passive or active management. As the names suggest, *passive* fund managers deliberately don't do very much and attempt to follow the performance of an index such as the S&P/ASX 200. On the other hand, *active* managers put more effort into trying to beat the performance of an index using their skill and expertise. Passive and active investing are quite different styles that cost investors quite different amounts. See Chapter 5 for information on fees and costs.

Learning about passive investing

Passive funds are designed to mirror the performance of a selected index and no more. The type of funds that follow indices are better known as *index funds* and can be either unlisted, like a traditional managed fund, or listed on a stock exchange.

Listed index funds are generally known as *exchange-traded funds (ETFs)* and can cover a range of market indices both in Australia and internationally. Separately, another type of listed index fund, known as *exchange-traded commodities (ETCs)*, works exactly the same as a fund except it replicates the movement on commodity markets such as gold, wheat or oil.

Why would investors choose to use index managed funds or exchange-traded funds, if these instruments aren't going to beat the market? Index funds are attractive to investors for a number of reasons:

- ✔ **Asset class exposure:** Investors can get instant exposure to shares across a whole market should they choose, both in Australia and overseas, and they're readily traded on the ASX.

- ✔ **Costs:** The cost of managing an index fund is relatively low compared with the cost of active managers. Passive managers don't pay fancy fund manager salaries to manage the investments but instead have a piece of software (albeit a quite sophisticated one) to build and manage the portfolios. Annual management costs can vary from 0.1 per cent up to 1 per cent depending on the index, compared with actively managed funds costing on average 1.6 per cent per annum or higher.

- ✔ **Returns:** Passive investment managers believe that their funds can produce returns as good as and sometimes better than active managers.

Index funds don't track an index exactly. In fact, index funds most likely underperform the index very slightly because costs and management fees are deducted from the performance. This underperformance is called *tracking error* and is something investors should check out. A tracking error of more than 1 per cent per annum and you'd have to question the ability of the fund to match the index.

Morningstar's style box

Managed fund research house Morningstar Australia (www.morningstar.com.au) provides what it calls a *style box* with each piece of managed fund research. The style box is a quick reference guide that describes a fund's style profile according to growth and value (or a blend of the two) and then according to whether the fund generally invests in big, medium or small companies.

Active or passive funds: How the results stack up

The argument rages between active and passive managers as to which style is better value for investors. Ratings agency Standard & Poor's (S&P) in Australia regularly produces a fascinating comparison of how these two types of funds stack up against each other.

The research produced is known as the Standard & Poor's Index versus Active (SPIVA) funds scorecard. The SPIVA for the 2009 year end shows how well, or should I say how badly, actively managed Australian equity share funds performed compared with various market indices, such as the S&P/ASX 300 Accumulation Index and others.

And what was the conclusion? The performance of active funds doesn't stack up too well over the five-year period to the end of 2009. The following table shows the percentage of managed funds in each asset class segment beaten by the index. Some sectors did better than others. For example, over five years, 63 per cent of Australian Equity General funds were beaten by the index. That is an astonishing number. Almost two-thirds of funds didn't outperform the index. The opposite is true for Australian Equity Small Cap funds, with almost two-thirds beating the index over five years.

Comparing Active and Passive Fund Performance to December 2009

Active Fund	Comparison Index	Percentage of Funds Beaten by Index			
		Last Quarter	One year	Three years	Five years
Australian Equity General	S&P/ASX 200 Accumulation Index	57.81	50.77	49.41	62.87
Australian Equity Small Cap	S&P/ASX Small Ordinaries Index	30.30	38.81	26.98	39.62
International Equity	General MSCI World Ex Australia Index	49.03	24.05	62.58	68.89
Australian Bonds	UBS Composite Bond Index 0 + Y	25.00	16.67	87.10	89.66
Australian Equity A-REIT	S&P/ASX 200 A-REIT Index	31.43	21.13	52.17	62.69

Source: S&P Indices/Morningstar. There has been no deduction of expenses from index returns.
Data to 31 December 2009

The Nobel-winning professor, William F Sharpe, is quoted by S&P in its SPIVA report as summing up S&P's view on indexing:

> Should everyone index everything? The answer is resoundingly no. In fact, if everyone indexed, capital markets would cease to provide the relatively efficient security prices that make indexing an attractive strategy for some investors. All the research undertaken by active managers keeps prices closer to values, enabling indexed investors to catch a free ride without paying the costs. Thus there is a fragile equilibrium in which some investors choose to index some or all of their money, while the rest continue to search for mispriced securities.
>
> Should you index at least some of your portfolio? This is up to you. I only suggest that you consider the option. In the long run this boring approach can give you more time for more interesting activities such as music, art, literature, sports, and so on. And it very well may leave you with more money as well.
>
> —*William F Sharpe, 2002*

Getting active with your manager

Active investing is where the fund manager builds a portfolio that is designed to beat a particular index. Using skill and expertise, the fund manager then takes a view, or an opinion, on which shares will perform better than the market. Active managers produce a range of different funds that give investors a choice of risk-and-return profiles:

- ✔ **Concentrated funds:** These funds are also known as *high-conviction funds*. The manager has a strong view on a small number of stocks. If the manager gets it right, the fund can make great returns. Get it wrong and the results can be horrible.

- ✔ **Diversified funds:** Investment here is in a range of different areas of the stock market across different sectors, such as property and banks. Risk is spread across a range of different investments.

- ✔ **Sector funds:** These are specialist funds investing in stocks in one particular sector, such as property, resources, small companies, large companies or ethical companies, to name but a few.

- ✔ **Yield funds:** These funds invest in stocks that provide good income in the form of dividends. Unlike an index fund that invests in all stocks regardless of the quality of income, yield funds select stocks specifically for their income.

The common theme with active funds is that investors pay managers for the skill they bring to the table. When selecting a fund, investors should pay serious attention to how consistently an active fund manager beats the market. If the manager doesn't beat the market, investors have to question why they'd invest in that fund. Investing in an index fund gives you the market return without the expense of an active fund.

Index managers do no more than capture market returns, and there's nothing wrong with that! Market returns are referred to as *beta*. In a year, for example, beta could be 10 per cent. Active managers look for returns above beta, or better than market. These returns are known as *alpha* and may be 15 per cent in a year, for example. So, for an active fund manager with returns of 15 per cent in a year, 10 per cent is beta, or purely down to the market, and 5 per cent is down to the skill of the manager.

Finding out about growth and value

The whole concept of dividing it up into 'value' and 'growth' strikes me as twaddle. It's convenient for a bunch of pension fund consultants to get fees prattling about and a way for one advisor to distinguish himself from another. But, to me, all intelligent investing is value investing.

—Charlie Munger, Berkshire Hathaway,
and business partner of Warren Buffett

Among active fund managers, styles can generally be divided into growth, value and core (style-neutral) managers, as well as funds reflecting growth at a reasonable price, or GARP (read on). Most core and GARP managers have some growth and/or some value style attributes to the way they invest. These styles are all discussed in this section.

Getting to grips with growth managers

Growth managers look to buy shares that are expected to grow at a higher rate than the market or index. The type of companies that growth managers look for have strong earnings growth potential due to a highly competitive market position. Typically, these types of companies don't pay out high dividends but instead reinvest earnings to build the company.

The growth style of investing is generally seen as more aggressive than that of value investors and can potentially deliver better returns. Growth funds tend to do well during healthy economic times and less well when there's a downturn in the economy. The underlying investments of growth managed funds can be more volatile and so riskier than other types of funds. A growth stock stops being a growth stock when it stops reacting to good news.

Learning about value investing

Value investors look to purchase shares at less than their intrinsic value and shares that might be out of favour with the market. Fund managers spend a lot of time working out how much they think a particular company is worth. This value is based on a range of different criteria, including the value of the underlying assets of the company and how much money or earnings the company is likely to make in the future.

The basis for value investing is that the market has undervalued a particular company. The other assumption is that the fund manager knows how to value a company and that, over time, the market will also come to appreciate the company's real value and will re-rate the stock upwards. A value stock stops being a value stock when returning to what the fund manager or investor believes to be the fair value.

Figure 4-2 shows the differing performance of value funds versus growth funds from 2000 to 2010. Importantly, the chart shows that growth and value funds can both perform well or badly at the same time.

Figure 4-2:
Performance of Morningstar's retail value funds index, versus its retail growth funds index over ten years to 30 June 2010.

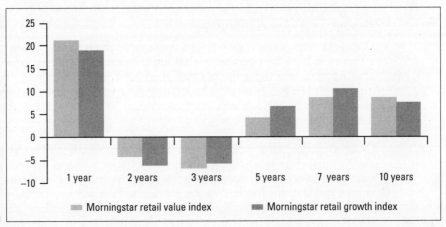

Beware of falling into the trap of chasing returns when one style of fund is outperforming another. The classic situation is when an *investment bubble* begins to build, a bubble being where the price an investor has to pay for shares far outstrips the underlying value of those shares. The price growth in the shares becomes self-perpetuating as the fund managers pour more money into the shares until the bubble bursts. The tech boom of 2000 is a prime example of a market getting ahead of itself, when investors poured money into the growth funds to chase the returns, with disastrous results when the dotcom companies collapsed.

Getting to the core of investing

Some fund managers refuse to be boxed in by a label or management style. However, not to be outdone on the name front, the industry refers to these types of fund managers as *style-neutral* or *core* investors. The objective of style-neutral funds is to produce consistent returns over a period of time without a particular growth or value bias.

Instead, these fund managers keep their options open! Core fund managers select stocks that they believe are undervalued compared with the market or offer good long-term growth prospects over and above the general market, reflecting characteristics of both growth and value managers.

Growth at a reasonable price

Managers who adopt a *growth at a reasonable price (GARP)* style of investment look for companies that are generating good earnings but are also, as the name suggests, reasonably priced. Typically, these companies may have seen a downward blip in their share price because of some bad news. However, the bad news is expected to be short-lived because the underlying business is strong.

GARP managers also look for companies that are undervalued by the market. Investors don't know much about the stocks and haven't given them much attention. GARP managers seek to uncover the hidden value of these stocks and wait for the rest of the market to find out!

GARP managers are sensitive to price relative to the earnings that the company is making. This measure is known as the *price-to-earnings ratio (PER)*. PER is essentially the price per share divided by the earnings per share. The ratio is a relative measure and doesn't mean a great deal on its own. The general rule is that the bigger the PER — compared with the market or a similar stock — the more expensive the share.

PER is commonly used by investors to measure how a company's share price stacks up relative to other similar companies. Because of this practice, GARP managed funds tend to be slightly less risky than ordinary growth fund managers. GARP funds also tend to have lower turnover rates than ordinary growth funds and can generally be more tax-efficient than more aggressive growth funds.

According to the ASX, the average PER of the Australian market, the S&P/ASX All Ordinaries Index, from 2000 to 2010, has been around 15.5. Stocks with PERs significantly above or below that level could be seen to be either expensive or cheap compared with the market.

Hedged or unhedged

The hedging of investment portfolios adds a whole new dimension to managed fund investing. Most people know hedging, outside of the world of gardening, in the context of 'hedging your bets', or reducing the risk of something happening. Fund managers classify themselves as either traditional fund managers or hedge fund managers. The two types of fund manager are quite different.

Hedge funds were originally set up, as the name suggests, to protect against unexpected downward movements in the stock market by smoothing out returns. Hedge fund managers today have morphed into a vast array of different investment styles, methodologies and sophisticated investment products. Hedge funds have, rightly or wrongly, become known for excessive risk, making huge bets on the direction of, for example, currencies or commodities. Smoothing out returns is sometimes far from the main objective of some hedge funds — making as much money as possible!

Traditional fund managers tend to shy away from using hedging methods precisely because of the perception of the higher risk involved. The average equities fund manager is also known as a *long-only* manager, meaning that the fund manager buys shares only to make money. Well, that seems logical, I hear you say. However, a typical hedging technique is for a manager to sell shares that it doesn't own, also known as *going short*, or *shorting* stock. Managers go short by borrowing stock, selling it and then buying it back at a lower price to give back to the person they borrowed it from. I get a headache just thinking about it, let alone figuring out how it's done in practice!

Check the terms of the trust deed of any traditional fund manager you plan on investing in. Most traditional fund managers aren't allowed to short stocks, which should be disclosed in the fund's product disclosure statement. If a fund is allowed to borrow stock, you're potentially investing in a hedge fund with a different risk profile from a traditional long-only fund.

A traditional hedge fund manager investing in overseas equities is exposed to the movements in the Australian dollar against whatever currency it's buying the shares in, be it US dollars or Thai baht. Some fund managers try to minimise the impact of currencies by using hedging instruments that remove the effect of currency.

For example, say a fund manager buys US$1,000 worth of shares in the United States when the exchange rate has one Australian dollar equal to 80 US cents. So the investment costs the manager A$1,250. If the exchange rate moves to 90 US cents to one Australian dollar, and assuming the value of the shares remains the same, then the shares are worth A$1,111 or a loss of A$139. Equally, currency movements can be in favour of managers and enhance their returns. Chapter 16 looks in more depth at how hedge funds work.

Chapter 5

Revealing the Cost of Investing: Fees and Commissions

. . . .

In This Chapter

▶ Examining what costs you can expect to pay for different funds

▶ Working out management and administration costs

▶ Finding out what tax does to your investment

▶ Getting to grips with upfront fees

▶ Looking at ongoing commissions

▶ Checking out performance and exit fees

. . . .

*O*ver time, costs can eat into the potential returns of a managed fund. Finding out what fees you can expect to pay, and when and how they're paid, is an important part of investing in managed funds. Ignoring fees is like swimming with sharks and can be bad for the health of your fund. This chapter runs the ruler over the costs you can expect to stump up when investing in managed funds.

Costs can vary between funds and range from the annual management fee, entry and exit fees, and commissions paid to financial planners, to performance fees, to name but a few. With such a scope of potential fees, the likelihood of creating confusion for investors is strong. Reducing investor confusion and increasing transparency are the reasons the law is very specific about exactly how costs and fees should be shown to investors.

Tax is perhaps not the first thing that comes to mind when thinking of costs. However, tax is perhaps the biggest cost an investor has to pay, and it does impact on returns. This chapter also dips its toes into the dark and unforgiving pool that is tax and seeks to bring to the surface the main points as they affect managed funds.

Examining the Costs of Investing

As with most things in life, in investing you get what you pay for. Generally, the more a fund manager plays with the underlying investments, or how active the fund manager is, the more expensive the fund can be. Costs are relative though. Some funds charge like a wounded bull but give poor performance. Investors are left questioning what value a fund manager adds when performance is poor. Other funds are expensive but show fantastic returns and so, relatively speaking, the costs are quite reasonable.

Understanding what you can expect to pay

A fund manager is likely to charge you fees when your money moves in or out of a fund. Fund managers also charge ongoing service fees. In the application forms, fund managers give investors the option to pay financial planners out of their initial investment, as well as pay ongoing fees to planners.

The product disclosure statement (PDS) for the fund should show at least some of the following fees:

- **Establishment fees:** These fees are charged when you first set up your investment. Most funds don't charge this fee, instead charging a contribution fee.

- **Contribution fees:** Also known as *upfront* fees or *entry* fees because they're paid as soon as the investment is made, typically contribution fees are up to 4 per cent of the value of the investment. Contribution fees are paid every time you contribute money to your investment, such as through a regular savings plan.

- **Management expenses:** The operational costs to run the fund make up the bulk of the ongoing fees in the fund. (See the section 'Uncovering Management Costs through the Indirect Cost Ratio' later in this chapter for more information.)

- **Transaction costs:** These costs apply when you buy or sell units in a fund. You usually see this expressed as the *buy–sell spread*, which is the difference between what price the fund will sell you units and what price it will buy units for. This price difference can be anywhere between 0 per cent and 0.75 per cent of the value of the investment. (For more information on the buy–sell spread, see Chapter 13.)

- **Performance fees:** These fees typically sit in the realm of hedge funds (see Chapter 16) and can be as much as 20 per cent of profits the fund manager makes over and above a set performance hurdle.

- **Switching fees:** If you switch your money from one fund to another within the same fund manager, these fees may apply. Most fund managers don't charge for this.

- **Withdrawal fees:** These fees are applicable when some or all monies are withdrawn from the fund. Most fund managers don't charge this fee.

- **Termination fees:** Like withdrawal fees, you may be charged when the account is closed.

- **Ongoing or trailing commissions:** Fund managers pay these commissions to financial planners for ongoing service to clients. Typically around 0.25 per cent to 0.4 per cent of the value of the fund is paid annually to the financial planner. These commissions are included in the management expenses charged by the fund.

Different funds attract different fees

Funds that have a lot of work done on them by the fund manager generally attract higher fees than those funds that have low manager involvement. The following four structures of managed funds attract different levels of fees:

- **Index funds:** At one end of the scale sit index funds, with low management involvement and low costs. Index funds mirror the performance of a particular index, such as the S&P/ASX 200, and have a low cost base because the manager has virtually no involvement. A typical index fund cost can be as low as 0.5 per cent per annum.

- **Actively managed funds:** In the middle of the scale are active funds, where investments are closely managed. Fees here depend on the underlying assets — you can expect to pay less to invest in a managed fund investing in cash products than one investing in international equities, for example.

- **Structured products:** At the other end of the scale are the potentially heavily fee-loaded structured products using complex strategies to protect investors' money and to grow it. Sounds like the perfect investment! If you stick with the structured product investment for its life, usually five to ten years, you will, at the very least, get your money back. As you can imagine, the costs involved can be high, at around 7 per cent. For more on structured products see Chapter 16.

✔ **Hedge funds:** These high-risk funds have different fee structures again. Hedge funds usually follow what's known as the '2 and 20' rule — 2 per cent annual management fee with a 20 per cent performance fee. For hedge funds, performance is everything, which explains how, if successful, they make eye-popping amounts of money. (See the section 'Working out performance fees' later in this chapter for more.)

Uncovering Management Costs through the Indirect Cost Ratio

Management and administration make up the bulk of the costs that a managed fund charges. The *indirect cost ratio (ICR)* is the standard method of showing the annual expenses attributable to managing a fund.

The indirect cost ratio (ICR) is, perhaps not surprisingly, a measure of the indirect costs that a fund charges investors. The ICR is shown as a percentage of the total value of a fund's assets, such as 1.8 per cent, and excludes separately disclosed fees. The ICR should not be confused with the management fee or expenses that make up part of the ICR.

The indirect costs included in the ICR are generally investment management and performance fees, and legal, accounting, auditing and other operational and compliance costs. The ICR is the same for all investors in a particular managed fund. The costs excluded from the ICR are specifically contribution fees, transaction costs, additional service fees and establishment fees, switching fees, termination fees and withdrawal fees. All of these fees should be disclosed separately to investors in their annual statement. See the section 'Paying tax: Who pays what?' later in this chapter for more on annual statements.

Fees and costs, including the ICR, must be shown as *gross of tax*; that's to say, without any tax having been deducted. However, the costs and fees must include any GST (goods and services tax) paid and applicable stamp duty. For more on the tax cost of investing see the section 'Managing Tax in Managed Funds' later in this chapter.

The ICR replaced the management expense ratio (MER) and, in 2006, became the industry standard fee comparison measure enshrined in the Corporations Act. The ICR is designed to provide a consistent way for indirect costs to be calculated and, therefore, make cost comparison between funds a lot easier than with the MER. Surprisingly, some of the larger fund managers still don't quote the ICR or even the old MER. Instead, these managers just show a management expense.

How does the MER rate against the ICR?

Up until 2004, management expenses were shown as the management expense ratio (MER). This ratio was the industry standard measure of costs for a fund and was phased out in favour of the indirect cost ratio (ICR). The MER is still used by some fund managers and you're bound to come across it. In practice, there isn't a huge difference between the ICR and the MER. The biggest difference is that fund managers are left to decide what expenses go into the MER, making it harder to easily compare funds.

Managing Tax in Managed Funds

Talking about tax is rarely exciting unless it involves a refund. However, tax has to be a major consideration in any investment and managed funds are no exception. Tax affects a fund's performance and ultimately the amount of money investors end up with in their pockets.

Generally, tax can arise in a managed fund on three occasions:

- ✓ **Tax within the fund:** The underlying investments held by the fund, such as shares, may produce income from dividends, or capital gains or losses when bought and sold. This usually applies only to investment bonds.

- ✓ **Distributions to unit holders:** Managed funds are obliged to distribute to unit holders all income received and all realised net gains made during the financial year (after expenses). Capital losses made by the fund must be held in the fund and can't be distributed, though they may be used to offset gains, so affecting income distribution. The unit holder may be liable for tax on the income portion of the distribution.

- ✓ **Tax on the sale of units:** The investor may be liable for tax on capital gains or be able to offset capital losses on the sale of units in the fund. These gains or losses are separate from the net gains that may make up part of the distribution to unit holders.

Tax considerations can drive many investment decisions. However, tax shouldn't be your sole purpose for investing, which should be about generating an acceptable return. Ensuring you pay as little tax as legally possible can make a significant difference to the overall performance of your investments. After all, what you have in your hands after tax is the most important measure of the success of an investment.

See a tax adviser if you have any questions in relation to tax on managed funds. This section gives general information about tax but a tax adviser can tell you how your particular circumstances are taxed.

Existing tax in managed funds

Managed funds set up as trusts don't pay tax on investment income. Instead, all income earned and gains on investments in a financial year are distributed to the unit holders. Investors then pay tax at their marginal, or highest, rate on both the income and the gains.

Invest in a managed fund and you potentially buy the tax history of that fund. The tax history includes dividends a fund may have received from investments during the year, as well as realised gains and losses made on selling investments. Investors are liable to pay the tax on the income made by the fund as well as capital gains.

Even though you may have only just bought into a fund, you may be obliged to pay tax on income or capital gains that took place months before you bought the managed fund units.

Paying tax: Who pays what?

The basic rule is that the investor is liable to pay tax earned on income and capital gains in the fund. At the end of the financial year, as an investor you receive a statement from the fund manager listing, among other items, the distributions you have received from the fund. Distributions comprise income from dividends and any money made from the sale of investments, known as capital gains.

A year-end statement is likely to be similar to that shown in Table 5-1. The main elements of an end-of-year statement are as follows:

- **Distributions:** A detailed breakdown of distributions, including income from investments held by the fund. On the statement, you may see this as 'non-primary production income' (see the next point).

- **Non-primary production income:** This includes income received from Australian dividends (franked and unfranked), interest and other income.

- ✔ **Franking credits:** These are the tax credits received from the distribution of franked dividends, on which tax has already been paid at the company rate of 30 per cent. Investors can generally claim a tax offset for the tax already paid.

- ✔ **Australian franking credits from New Zealand companies:** Australian franking credits are attached to dividends or distributions paid by a New Zealand company, which are also claimable against tax.

- ✔ **Capital gains:** Two types of capital gains exist. The first is paid on realised capital gains, or on how much money a fund made on the sale of any investments during the year. The second is a capital gain payable on units sold or transferred by the investor during the year. Normal capital gains tax rules apply, which means that if you've held the fund units for more than 12 months you pay only 50 per cent of the capital gains tax due (often expressed as a 50 per cent CGT discount).

- ✔ **Total year capital gains:** The investor's share of capital gains realised from the sale of investments is the sum of discounted capital gains (gross) plus other capital gains. Investors may not necessarily have to pay tax on the full amount, as it does not include any losses made by the fund from selling investments.

- ✔ **Net capital gains:** These are the capital gains (less capital losses) realised when the fund sells investments and distributes the net gains to investors. This is the sum investors are most likely to have to pay tax on.

- ✔ **Foreign source income:** This is income derived from investments that have some or all of their income generated overseas. Foreign income tax offset rules allow Australian resident taxpayers to receive a non-refundable tax offset for foreign income tax paid on an amount that is included in their assessable income.

- ✔ **Deferred tax:** Although not included on the statement shown in Table 5-1, a property fund may also have *tax-deferred income* arising out of a revaluation of a property asset or from various other tax allowances. The tax on the distribution is deferred and is usually only taxable on sale of the asset.

- ✔ **Other fund expenses:** Investors may also see other fund expenses listed on the statement, which may be tax deductible.

Table 5-1	A Typical End-of-Year Statement			
Fund Name	**Account No: 1234567A**	**Unit Price**	**Units**	**Value at 30 June**
XYZ Australian Share Fund		1.5408	10,000	$15,408.00
BCD Income Fund		2.3056	10,000	$23,056.00
EFG International Fund		0.5678	10,000	$5,678.00
TOTAL				$44,142.00
Tax Return Components				
Non-primary production income				$2,032.68
Franking credits				$221.56
Franking credits from New Zealand companies				Nil
Total current year capital gains				$945.00
Net capital gains				$1,430.00
Assessable foreign source income				$76.54
Other net foreign source income				$76.54

Franking credits, also known as *dividend imputation credits,* are designed so investors aren't taxed twice on the same investment income. For example, a company earns $100 profit and is taxed at 30 per cent, leaving $70 distributed to investors as a dividend. Without franking credits, investors may potentially have to pay tax at the top marginal rate of 46.5 per cent (including the Medicare levy of 1.5 per cent) on the dividends. The Australian Taxation Office (ATO) gives investors a 30 per cent credit to offset against the tax they have to pay.

Watch out for managed funds that buy and sell investments regularly. Buying and selling is known as *turnover* and refers to the percentage value of the portfolio that is bought and sold each year. Low turnover funds may buy and sell about 40 per cent of the value of the portfolio. High turnover funds can trade 150 per cent or more of the portfolio value. The more a fund turns over the portfolio, the greater the chances of the investor having to pay capital gains tax on those transactions at the end of the year.

You have to pay tax on gains eventually, such as when you sell units in a fund. However, if you don't want to pay a large amount of tax on income from your managed fund every year, preferring to defer it, look for a managed fund with a low turnover.

Handling Upfront Fees

From my days working with a direct fund broker, I struggle with how the industry justifies upfront or contribution fees charged by managed funds. Whichever way you look at them, upfront fee payments to financial planners can be a huge impost on your investment. Typically, these fees are about 4 per cent and are paid immediately your money hits the fund manager. Upfront fees come straight out of your money and you pay upfront fees every time you put new money into the managed fund.

Understanding upfront fees

By law, fund managers can pay commissions, including upfront, contribution or entry fees, only to licensed financial advisers. Such fees are an efficient way for financial advisers to be paid for their services. No messy invoices or late payments; the fund manager pays the upfront fee direct to the financial planner.

Table 5-2 shows the difference upfront fees can make to your investment returns. The example in the table shows the impact of fees when investing $2,000 every year with an average 10 per cent per annum return until the age of 65. Over a period of time the difference in return does add up to a not insubstantial amount!

Table 5-2	The Effect of Upfront Fees on Returns		
	Value of $2,000 p.a. Invested until Age 65 with 10% p.a. Average Returns		
Start Date	*4% Entry Fee; 1.5% Ongoing Fee*	*No Entry Fee; 1.5% Ongoing Fee*	*Difference*
Aged 30 years	$547,655	$570,474	$22,819
Aged 40 years	$201,004	$209,379	$8,375
Aged 50 years	$65,519	$68,248	$2,729

Investors shouldn't begrudge any financial adviser getting paid, as along as the adviser can demonstrate the value added to the investment process, especially for a typical upfront fee of 4 per cent! Make sure you know what advice you're paying for. If you use a financial planner, you may be able to negotiate a rebate of the upfront fees so it's paid by the fund manager to you in the form of additional units in the managed fund.

Check the product disclosure statement (PDS) carefully to understand if upfront fees are charged and, if so, how much. Even if you don't have a financial adviser helping you with the investment and you go direct to the fund manager, you're very likely to be charged the fees. The fund manager picks up the 4 per cent and you're left with 96 per cent of your investment on day one.

Reducing upfront fees

Fund managers may be prepared to negotiate reductions in upfront fees, so you should always ask the question. However, fund managers can't, by law, pay the 4 per cent upfront fee to an individual who doesn't have a financial services licence. You can reduce the upfront fees you pay by doing one of the following:

- **Negotiate with your financial adviser to reduce or rebate some or all of the upfront fee.** Consider asking the financial adviser to adopt a fee-for-service arrangement whereby you agree to a flat fee for the advice that the financial adviser gives you.

- **Ask the fund manager to reduce or rebate the full upfront fee.** If you don't use a financial adviser and apply directly to the fund manager, you may be able to get a rebate in the form of additional units, so that 100 per cent of your money is invested in the fund. This rebate is very much at the fund manager's discretion and subject to the law.

- **Use a direct funds broker.** A number of direct brokers are around who can provide all the information and product disclosure statements that you need. Typically, direct brokers rebate up to 100 per cent of the upfront fee they receive from the fund manager in the form of additional units. Direct brokers live off the much more modest ongoing commission the fund manager pays, which is around 0.25 per cent per annum of the total value of your investment.

Filling in the forms correctly can make all the difference to the level of fees you pay upfront. Usually, a section in the application form states what fees you pay. If your financial planner is filling this in for you, make sure you agree beforehand what that fee is going to be. (Chapter 12 is devoted to forms.)

Paying Ongoing Commissions

Ongoing commissions, also known as *trailing commissions*, are paid by managed funds, in theory, for the ongoing management and service provided by a financial adviser. Trailing commissions are typically between 0.25 per cent and 0.5 per cent per annum of the total value of the investment but can be much higher. Unlike upfront or contribution fees that are paid immediately you make the investment, ongoing commissions are paid either quarterly or half-yearly to financial planners.

Understanding why ongoing commissions are paid

The system for paying ongoing commissions is quirky and unusual, to say the least, but it's not illegal — yet! Fund managers, in good faith, pay a commission to financial advisers so that the advisers continue to provide an ongoing service to clients. Nothing wrong with that, except that fund managers have no way of knowing if the financial planner is providing that service. And if you're not using a financial planner or fund broker, the fund manager keeps the commission.

Some fund managers make a standard provision to rebate ongoing fees to investors who have a large portfolio with the manager. I've seen fund managers offering to rebate around 0.2 per cent to 0.4 per cent of the value of a portfolio that's larger than $400,000. This rebate certainly won't apply to a lot of investors but it's worth remembering!

Some financial planners may charge clients a fee to review their portfolio of managed funds, usually once a year. Closely question the financial planner charging a review fee; often he is already being paid a fee by the fund manager — out of ongoing trail commissions — to do so.

Avoiding ongoing commissions

Trying to avoid ongoing commissions is like trying to avoid going to the dentist when you need a tooth pulled. You may be able to reduce the pain a little but eventually you have to get there. You're unlikely to avoid paying ongoing commissions altogether, but you may find ways to reduce them:

✔ **Negotiate with your financial adviser to reduce or rebate some or all of the ongoing commission.** Agree to a fee-for-service schedule setting out the ongoing service the adviser will give and how much you'll pay.

✔ **Ask the fund manager to rebate the ongoing fee in the form of additional units in the fund.** If you don't use a financial adviser and apply directly to the fund manager, asking for a full rebate may be justified; otherwise, the commission stays with the fund manager. By law the fund manager can't pay you the commission unless you have a financial services licence, but may be able to give you additional fund units instead.

✔ **Use a direct funds broker to reduce your fees.** You're unlikely to get a full rebate of ongoing fees, as this is how most funds brokers make their money. However, some brokers, such as InvestSMART (www.investsmart.com.au) cap the amount of trail commission investors pay each year.

Commissions to be decommissioned?

The whole area of commission payments by financial services product providers, such as fund managers, to financial advisers is in a complete state of flux. In April 2010, the federal government stated it plans to ban commissions paid to financial advisers on financial products by 2012. The intention is to remove the potential for conflict of interest.

The advice given by financial planners must be in the client's best interest and not influenced by payments from fund managers. In addition to commissions, financial planners may also get extra payments when their clients have a certain amount of money with a fund manager. These are known as volume-based payments

and something the government wants to phase out.

The financial planning industry has been forced to sit up and take notice. The industry's ruling body, the Financial Planning Association (FPA), has already started to encourage its members to look at changes to their businesses to meet the government proposals.

Financial planners will eventually have to look at charging a fee for the service they give, rather than rely on commissions. Planners and their clients will have to agree on the fees every year, which is very different from the current situation, where fees can be paid for years after the first investment by a client.

Considering Other Fees

Other fees you're likely to come across include performance fees and exit fees. Such fees are generally not common among most funds and typically apply to specialist funds using a particular investment method, such as hedge funds. Exit fees are more typically found in managed funds investing in long-term assets such as infrastructure projects, or in funds that don't charge an initial entry fee (called nil entry fee — NEF — funds).

Working out performance fees

Some funds charge a performance fee on money they make over and above an agreed annual return. Such fees are common among hedge fund managers but less so in everyday managed funds.

A performance fee is usually charged on the fund's performance above a set benchmark. For example, a fund may set itself a benchmark return of 15 per cent per annum or it may decide that the benchmark is an index such as the S&P/ASX 200. For any amount of money that the fund makes above the benchmark, the fund manager charges a performance fee of anything up to 20 per cent.

The important thing to understand is that the fund manager sets the benchmark and leaves the investors to decide if it's reasonable. Performance fees can be a massive incentive for hedge fund managers but they can also come at a high cost for risky investments.

Some hedge funds also adopt what is called a *high-water mark hurdle*, based on the value of the pool of money it manages. High-water marks are an investor-friendly way of charging fees and preventing a fund manager paying itself fees more than once on the same performance. The fund manager can take the fee only if it beats the previous highest value of the fund. In some ways, fund managers have created a rod for their own backs. Failure to beat the previous high-water mark value means no fee! To find out more on hedge funds see Chapter 16.

Watching out for exit fees

Exit fees aren't commonly used by managed funds but you may come across them, so it's worth understanding them. Exit fees can be charged as a percentage of the value of the money being withdrawn or as a flat fee. Managers charge exit fees to discourage investors from pulling their money early from a fund. A fund manager may charge exit fees for one of three reasons:

- ✔ **Because they can:** And exit fees are another way to make money.

- ✔ **The nature of the underlying investment is long term:** When money is invested in projects such as commercial property or infrastructure, raising cash quickly to pay out an existing investor is inordinately difficult for a manager. Imagine trying to buy and sell office blocks every time a large number of investors want to cash out — it's not a quick process!

- ✔ **To keep costs down:** Fund managers spend a lot of money on sales and marketing to bring money into a fund. Minimising those sales costs by discouraging investors from taking their money out makes sense for a fund manager.

Nil entry fee funds don't charge an initial entry fee but charge an exit fee instead.

Some fees are also charged on a sliding scale, reducing each year for a number of years until the fees are nil. For example, if funds are withdrawn in the first 12 months, the exit fee may be 2 per cent of the total value, reducing by 0.5 per cent in the second year to 1.5 per cent. Withdrawal after five years may attract no exit fee.

Part II
Doing the Research for Your Peace of Mind

Glenn Lumsden

*'Our investors have had a fabulous year.
I feel a correspondingly fabulous growth in
fees is called for.'*

In this part . . .

Figuring out what type of investor you are and how much risk you're prepared to take might not put you on the path to enlightenment but it can help you choose funds that suit you. So, here you get to indulge in some navel gazing and self-analysis. Don't be put off, because it's all for a good cause.

At the risk of stating the obvious, I show in this part how investors should set out their investing goals. Making as much money as possible is a great goal to have but setting achievable targets helps to avoid disappointment.

When you start to choose funds, you need to do the research, sifting the fund manager marketing spin from what really lies behind the fund. Help is at hand in the form of ratings agencies that set out easy-to-follow five-star rating systems. Everything in investing, regardless of what you invest in, boils down to performance. In this part, I also take a scalpel to the numbers and show you how to interpret performance.

Chapter 6

Assessing Your Appetite for Risk and Avoiding Indigestion

The policy of being too cautious is the greatest risk of all.

—*Jawaharlal Nehru, India's first prime minister*

When Jawaharlal Nehru said this, I doubt he was referring to his investment portfolio! But the point is clear — there are two sides to risk. Minimising risk is all very well but shouldn't be at the expense of making decent money. As much as investors need to be careful of risk, they also need to embrace risk, understand it and learn how to exploit it.

This chapter sets out to explain the risk-and-reward trade-off that is such a fundamental part of investing. Reward is what investors get for putting hard-earned money to work for them. How much reward the investor gets depends, by and large, on how much risk they take. Putting your money into a high-interest bank account carries less risk than investing in shares in emerging economies.

Risk is the chance of something bad happening to an investment that wasn't expected. That something bad could be losing some or all of your money, not getting the income you were expecting or even not being able to get the money out when you need it. Although investors don't expect anything bad to happen, managing risk means planning for the worst and expecting the best.

Understanding the Risk-and-Reward Trade-Off

Risk and reward go hand in hand. I don't think anyone intentionally sets out to lose money with an investment. Investing is done in an environment of uncertainty — and, where there's uncertainty, risk is lurking in the background. Risk never goes away but it's easy to forget about it when things are going well. The dangers of risk have a habit of creeping up behind and taking investors by surprise when least expected.

Heaps of academic papers attempt to quantify and measure risk. The two basic ideas about risk are:

- **The higher the returns, the greater the risk.** This general rule is true up to a point. As risk gets too high, the relationship snaps and investors potentially lose all their money before they've even had a chance to generate a return!

- **Risk gets less over time.** The longer you hold riskier assets, the more the risk depletes.

One thing is for sure, investors have different tolerances towards risk. Being too cautious can stop investors from taking on enough risk, resulting in potentially lower returns. Investors can also take on more risk than they realise but only become aware of the risks when everything goes wrong.

The risk-and-reward trade-off boils down to how much is enough. How much risk are you, as an investor, prepared to take on for the reward you want? The trade-off is a balancing act and is as much a science as an art. Financial advisers have their clients poring over questionnaires to help them figure out how much risk they can take. Questionnaires are the science and, although far from perfect, can point investors in the right direction. Putting a measure on gut instinct when investing — now, that's an art!

Working out how much you can afford to lose

Working out how much you can afford to lose may seem extreme. This idea is really about how much risk you can stomach. Setting out in black and white what loss you could bear draws a line in the sand when it comes to your risk tolerance. Working out how you'd manage with a 20 per cent fall or a 50 per cent permanent fall in the value of your investments makes risk very real.

Weighing up the risks with managed funds

As with all investment types, managed funds have their own sets of risks that investors should be aware of. All of the risks can be offset to some extent by setting up a diversified portfolio but risk can never be totally removed. In Chapter 4, I set out the three main risks of investing in shares (company, liquidity and market risks). The risks for managed funds, which can include other asset classes, are similar but with some extras:

✔ **Currency risk:** Managed funds investing in international markets can be exposed to currency risk. Even if all other things remain the same, the movements in a currency add or detract from a fund's performance. Some international managed funds try to iron out the effects of currency by what is called *hedging*, which, perhaps confusingly, doesn't make it a hedge fund — see Chapter 16 for more on hedge funds. Most funds don't hedge against currency risk because, as much as this method protects a fund from currency losses, hedging also irons out any potential gains from a favourable currency movement.

✔ **Economic and political risk:** Changes to the strength of the economy, interest rate moves and legal or political changes can all hit market values. Interest rate changes, in particular, affect bond and other fixed-rate instrument values. As rates fall, so the *yield* a bond is paying (the bond's interest rate or coupon rate divided by the value of the bond) becomes more attractive. More investors then want the bond and the price of the bond increases, and vice versa.

✔ **Investment risk:** Certain investments carry associated risks. For example, investing in cash carries a different risk than investing in the shares of gold-mining companies.

✔ **Liquidity risk:** The underlying investments in a managed fund may not be readily bought or sold. This liquidity risk is particularly the case with funds that invest directly in property. Unlike share managed funds that issue and redeem (buy and sell) units daily, investors may find they can sell their property fund units only at certain times of the year. Other funds may require the seller to find a willing buyer for his units.

✔ **Manager risk:** Another risk when investing in shares through a fund is that the fund manager doesn't perform as expected. Investors have to weigh this against the risk of investing directly in shares and ask the question: Can I do it better than a fund manager?

✔ **Market risk:** This is the risk that the underlying markets in shares, bonds and property fall for whatever reason. The fall in value of the markets could be due to any number of factors, such as changes in company earnings or nervous investors.

✔ **Portfolio risk:** Some funds have a relatively small number of holdings in their portfolio. These are called *concentrated* funds. Not spreading the risk across a larger number of holdings increases risk but also means potentially greater returns.

✔ **Other risks:** You may come across some other risks, such as credit risk that a provider of a bond or other fixed-interest product defaults on its obligations; gearing risk that comes with borrowing to invest; derivative risk of using complex financial instruments; and emerging market risk that comes with investing in developing economies.

Having no risk at all can be almost as bad as having too much risk. Low or no risk usually means sacrificing returns. Over time, inflation can gnaw away at the real value or purchasing power of money — that $100 today may be worth only $90 in five years' time. Returns need to at least beat inflation.

Allocating your assets

Money can be invested many different ways in many different asset classes, from cash and fixed-interest securities such as bonds, to property and shares both in Australia and internationally. (Refer to Chapter 4 for more on asset classes.) Risk varies across the asset classes, with cash and fixed interest having the lowest risk, property and Australian equities seen as being high risk and international equities the riskiest of all asset types.

The risk of having funds frozen

The risk of not being able to take your money out of a fund once you've invested — liquidity risk — became a reality for many Australian investors during the global financial crisis. The property and mortgage funds sector was deeply affected by the sharp fall in value of the underlying property investments and were forced to suspend withdrawals.

Investors woke one morning in 2008 to find that their monies were locked down in these funds. Even now, several thousand investors are still affected, with about $25 billion in funds they can't access. Even more galling for these investors is the fact that property and mortgage funds had not been deemed high risk but medium to high risk.

Property funds suddenly found that the value of their investments had plummeted, that income was starting to dry up as tenants shut up shop, and the banks were calling in their debts. The funds were forced to stop investors from withdrawing their money so they could manage the situation without the added concern of having to sell assets to give money back to investors. Understandably, fund managers had to freeze the funds to prevent sell-offs of property at fire-sale values. For more on frozen funds, see Chapter 20.

Understanding asset allocation

Spreading investments across different asset classes, through *asset allocation*, changes the level of risk and reward. Careful mixing of asset classes allows investors to tailor a portfolio to meet their needs. How much is invested in each class boils down to the answers to two questions:

- ✔ **What sort of investor am I or, simply, how much risk can I tolerate for the reward I want?** Finding out what type of investor you are works out how much risk you're prepared to take on and then matches your resulting risk profile with the right asset mix. The end result of this process may be a risk profile you're happy with, but prospective returns may not be enough. Asset mixes can be tweaked to add risk and therefore potential returns. The next two sections of this chapter, 'Discovering What Type of Investor You Are' and 'Understanding Your Investor Type', help you answer this question.

- ✔ **Where will I get the best returns without taking on risk outside my comfort zone?** Work out what return you need and work backwards to find out what asset class or mix is likely to pay you the return you want. Obviously you have to be a realist when deciding returns. A return of 50 per cent per annum is unlikely unless you adopt a high-risk strategy investing in complex option and derivative instruments. The long-term average return on Australian shares is around 10 per cent. With that sort of return in mind, it should be easy enough to put together a mix of asset classes that gives the return and minimises the risks. The last section of this chapter, 'Matching the Results to Your Goals', helps you out with this question.

The Australian Securities and Investments Commission (ASIC) has a consumer watchdog website called FIDO, at www.fido.gov.au, which has a spreadsheet that can help calculate risk and return. To use the calculator effectively, you do need to have an understanding of how much risk you're prepared to take on. Play around with the different risk profiles to explore expected returns across different asset classes.

Changing asset allocations over time

Over time, an investor's attitude to risk and asset allocation can change for two main reasons:

- ✔ **Life stage:** Your investment needs change as you get older (see Chapter 7). Someone who is 30 years old has a much longer time horizon to retirement than someone who is 50. The 30-year-old investor has more time to recover from bad markets or rash investing mistakes and can afford to take more risk. On the other hand, the 50-year-old probably has more money, is not that far off retirement and doesn't want to bet the farm on highly speculative investments. The 50-year-old's asset allocation is likely to have lower risk assets than the 30-year-old.

✔ **Market risk:** Asset allocation also depends on the state of the market. Asset classes move in and out of favour. For example, during the global financial crisis of 2008–09, shares were definitely the riskiest asset class. Investors shifted much of their holdings into cash. Managed funds held unprecedented levels of cash in their portfolios — up to 35 per cent of their holdings, when usual levels are less than 10 per cent.

You can use managed funds to access all asset classes. Investing via managed funds is a convenient way to allocate assets and keep control over your investments. Some investors are happy to construct a portfolio just using managed funds across the various asset types. Others prefer to use managed funds for a certain percentage of their portfolio and mix this with direct holdings in shares, cash or property, for example.

Be careful about double-dipping when allocating your assets. If you invest in shares directly and then invest in a managed fund that invests in shares, make sure that both share investments are counted towards the percentage of your investments you allocate to shares. The same goes for all other asset classes, such as cash.

Discovering What Type of Investor You Are

Working out your financial goals first means figuring out what type of investor you are. Some investors like to hang on to their cash, short of stuffing it under the mattress. Other investors adopt an investment approach that may be one step removed from the casino. Whatever your style, knowing what that style is can help put together your investment plan.

Most people probably have a sense of how they like to invest without the need for detailed psychoanalysis. However, a number of different questionnaires are available to investors to help identify their investing style. Most of the better questionnaires have been touched by a behavioural psychologist.

Questionnaires don't provide financial advice about any particular financial product or asset class. Rather, they give you an insight about how people with certain risk profiles may choose to allocate their funds among the major asset classes.

Taking the test

Investors can figure out what type of investor they are in various ways. Several websites offer online assessment tools, some of which you pay for and others that are free. Needless to say, you get what you pay for. The free tools offer useful insights but are designed to get you to pick up the phone to a financial planner. The ones you pay for go into a lot more depth, although they still suggest you speak to a planner. Some of the better online assessment tools are:

- ✔ **AMP:** The risk profile at `www.amp.com.au` (click on Advice and Calculators at the bottom of the page, then click on Calculators in the left-hand menu and look for the question 'What investor style am I?') is a simple dashboard-type chart that adjusts according to where you place the risk parameters, and it's free. Regardless of what investor type you are, this website recommends you speak to one of AMP's financial planners. I tried it out and was ranked as an 'aggressive' investor, which I wasn't expecting!

- ✔ **Colonial First State:** The risk-profiling tool at one of Australia's largest fund managers is found at `www.colonialfirststate.com.au` under Forms and Tools — click on the Calculators tab and scroll down to the question 'What investments suit your risk profile?'. The site suggests taking two profiling tests, one for superannuation ('How much super is enough?') and one for your investments outside of super. Both calculators are free. The site asks eight questions and then produces two easy-to-read charts of your risk profile and suggested asset class mix. Here I was high growth.

- ✔ **FinaMetrica:** For the purposes of research, I stumped up my $39 to find out how I rated at `www.myrisktolerance.com`. The patented survey is in two parts — 25 questions that ask about your attitude to risk and another about your personal circumstances, such as age.

  I was surprised by the results — my score was 81 out of 100, with zero being no tolerance to risk and 100 being the riskiest. I thought I might be around 70. If nothing else, this questionnaire goes into a lot of detail around the good and bad of using such questionnaires.

- ✔ **MSN's MoneyCentral:** This 20-question risk profile is another free profiler and is available at `www.moneycentral.msn.com`. The results are not as comprehensive as other sites but the commentary is useful. My risk tolerance score was 38 out of 50, so not quite as high risk as other quizzes say I am!

I've also pulled together my own basic risk profile, included in the online cheat sheet for *Managed Funds For Dummies*, which you can find at `www.dummies.com/cheatsheet/managedfundsau` (this web address is also on the inside front cover), along with another useful tool — a managed fund checklist — and some interesting fast facts about managed funds in Australia.

The problem with all these types of test is that they're only as good as the questions they ask and how honestly they're answered. To really understand how investors feel about losing a lot of money, I've heard the suggestion that they need to be kicked in the stomach at the same time as being asked the question. A bit extreme, but the point is that the questions aren't real-life situations and people can react differently when faced with the loss of money.

Interpreting the results

Fortunately, interpreting the results can be done quite easily. Questions are multiple choice and each choice is ranked with a score linked to how risky the answer may be. So, for example, for the question 'How much of a loss on your portfolio are you prepared to take?' the choice 'none at all' carries one mark and the choice '50 per cent or more' might carry five marks. At the end of the test, the scores are added up. The final score falls within a range of total scores that match a particular risk profile; for example, 50 points may equate to a conservative risk profile.

Don't take the results as gospel but use them as a guide only. The results are a starting point in the process of helping to set a plan and achieve your investing goals. See Chapter 7 for more about setting goals.

Understanding Your Investor Type

If you sign up with a financial adviser or a stockbroker, you'll be asked to complete a risk-profile questionnaire. Table 6-1 takes a quick glance at how investors may be categorised. Each investor type is examined in more detail later in this section. The typical characteristics give a broad-brush description of the investment aims and outcomes, along with a risk profile. The asset allocation guide gives a very general feel for what a typical portfolio may look like. The timeframe is the suggested minimum length of time that an investor should take when investing.

Under the asset allocation column, Table 6-1 also distinguishes between defensive and growth assets, which is another way of broadly grouping the asset classes. Not to be confused with the growth versus value investing I mention in Chapter 4, which are investment styles adopted by fund managers, defensive and growth assets are characterised as follows:

   ✔ *Defensive* assets, as the name suggests, are designed to protect your initial investment, provide some potential for growth, but not much, and to give income.

✔ *Growth* assets are designed to increase your initial investment and, depending on how risky these assets are, produce a little income. A longer term outlook is needed, five years or more, when investing in growth assets because of the amount those growth assets can move up and down in value in a short period.

Table 6-1   Summary of Investor Types and Asset Allocation

Investor Type	Typical Characteristics	Asset Allocation	Timeframe
Defensive	Concerned with protecting investments or capital ahead of earning potentially higher returns by investing in riskier investments. Risk is that the investments may not grow sufficiently to counter the effects of inflation and tax.	Defensive assets 75% to 100% Growth assets 0% to 25%	Short term (a few months) or medium term (1 to 3 years)
Conservative	Objectives are primarily income but prepared to take some risk to generate additional returns. Some risk that inflation could reduce the value of the investment over time.	Defensive assets 65% to 80% Growth assets 20% to 35%	1 to 3 years
Balanced	Returns from a mix of capital growth and some income to smooth out returns. Prepared to take some short-term risk with fluctuations in the value of the assets.	Defensive assets 25% to 45% Growth assets 55% to 75%	3 to 5 years
Growth	Looking for long-term growth and willing to accept a higher level of risk to achieve goals. Income is not a priority, with growth in the value of the investments more important.	Defensive assets 10% to 30% Growth assets 70% to 90%	5 years plus
Aggressive growth	Willing to accept higher levels of short-term risk and volatility to achieve higher longer term returns. Investors should have a much longer timeframe for achieving desired outcomes.	Defensive assets 0% to 15% Growth assets 85% to 100%	5 to 7 years plus

Financial planners, fund managers and investment research houses produce much more detailed asset allocation plans to help investors get the right mix. Within each asset class, such as Australian shares, is a number of subclasses, such as large company shares or shares that are known for producing good dividends (income). Each of these subclasses has its own risk and reward profile. More detailed asset allocation models are provided later in this section.

Table 6-1 is a guide only and is no substitute for a full financial plan. The table should be used only in conjunction with a complete assessment of your investment needs, your current financial situation and what you're trying to achieve.

With each investor style described in the following sections, I include a chart showing a typical investment portfolio. Table 6-2 sets out the different suggested asset allocations for each portfolio so you can see how they differ overall. Alternative assets here refers to those asset classes outside the mainstream and include commodities, infrastructure and hedge funds. These suggested allocations do change over time and should be used as a rough guide only. As an investor's risk profile moves from defensive to being more aggressive, so the level of riskier assets in a suggested portfolio increases.

Table 6-2	Typical Asset Allocations for Each Investor Type				
	Defensive	**Conservative**	**Balanced**	**Growth**	**Aggressive Growth**
Australian equities	12%	21%	27%	34%	42%
International equities	7%	12%	16%	20%	25%
Listed property and infrastructure	5%	8%	10%	14%	17%
Alternative assets	8%	11%	20%	20%	16%
Fixed interest	45%	33%	21%	20%	0%
Cash	23%	15%	6%	2%	0%

Source: Van Eyk Research.

Leaving nothing to chance: Defensive

The defensive investor leaves little to chance. The main objective is to keep the initial investment intact. This objective could be achieved by investing in managed funds that invest in fixed-income securities from governments or companies that have been rated highly by the credit ratings agencies, such as Moody's. Investment in these types of securities usually comes with a reliable, ongoing income stream. The risk is generally relatively low.

If investors want to include managed funds that invest in equities, the funds should be investing in large and established companies that pay a regular income. With equities, however, investors also have to accept a higher, albeit still relatively low, degree of risk.

With any investment, after-tax returns are the best way to measure success or otherwise. Defensive investing may produce very low after-tax returns that may not keep pace with inflation, meaning, in real terms, that the value of your investment goes down over time.

Figure 6-1 shows a typical asset allocation for a defensive investor, with mainly fixed-interest and cash investments.

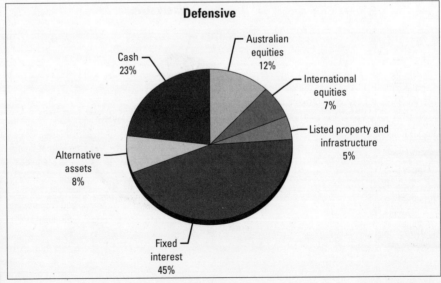

Figure 6-1:
Typical defensive investor portfolio.

Source: Van Eyk Research.

Adopting a measured approach: Conservative

The conservative investor looks for better than a basic return but with low risk. The approach is to keep the initial investment intact, generate income and produce an overall return a little bit better than the rate of inflation. Over the medium to long term, a conservative approach should provide relatively smooth investment returns, while aiming to preserve that initial investment.

Different fixed-interest managed funds have different risk profiles according to what underlying investments are in the funds. Fixed-interest funds can invest in hybrid securities, income securities and convertible notes, each of which can lead to higher risk and increase the fluctuations in the value of the fund. Adding funds that invest in shares and/or property securities can enhance returns.

Figure 6-2 shows a typical portfolio of assets for a conservative investor, slightly increasing investments in equities and decreasing those in fixed interest and cash, for example.

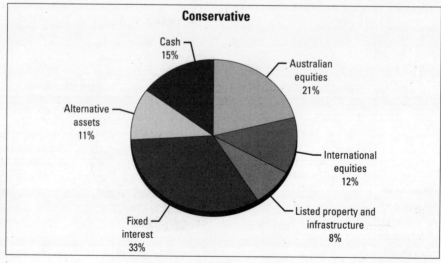

Figure 6-2: Typical conservative investor portfolio.

Conservative

Cash 15%
Australian equities 21%
Alternative assets 11%
International equities 12%
Listed property and infrastructure 8%
Fixed interest 33%

Source: Van Eyk Research.

Keeping an even keel: Balanced

The balanced investor likes an each-way bet — the thrill of the win but with some security of a second-place payout in case it doesn't quite work out. The balanced investor is looking for a balanced portfolio of diversified investments, providing some protection against both taxation and inflation.

To achieve this objective, the balanced investor adds more growth assets to the portfolio and includes more share managed funds. These share funds could make up to 75 per cent of the value of the portfolio. The higher risk of these funds is offset to some extent by a mix of fixed-interest and property security funds. The asset mix looks to produce a combination of both income and growth.

The long-term average exposure to growth and income assets is expected to be approximately 65 per cent and 35 per cent respectively of the total portfolio, although this ratio could vary in the short term. Investment returns undoubtedly fluctuate over the short term, including the possibility of a loss of value in some periods. The investment needs to be viewed over at least a three- to five-year period.

Figure 6-3 shows a classic balanced portfolio, with 73 per cent of investments in equity and property funds, as well as alternative assets, and 27 per cent in fixed interest and cash.

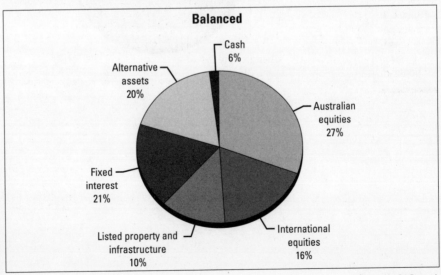

Figure 6-3:
Typical balanced investor portfolio.

Source: Van Eyk Research.

Growing your wealth: Growth

The growth investor uses a more aggressive investment strategy than the balanced investor, with more exposure to growth assets over a slightly longer timeframe of, say, five years or more. The portfolio is likely to have above-average risk and values may fluctuate a lot in the short term, but performance is expected to be higher in the medium to long term.

In Figure 6-4, the chart shows the portfolio has again boosted equity and property investments, and decreased those in fixed interest and cash.

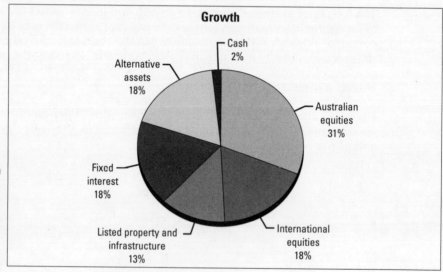

Figure 6-4: Typical growth investor portfolio.

Source: Van Eyk Research.

Betting the farm on red: Aggressive growth

The aggressive growth investor is prepared to take on a high level of risk and to ride out the likely high fluctuations in value for longer term gains. Managed funds are higher risk and may include *small-cap stocks* (companies that have a relatively small value on the stock market, usually less than $1 billion), *cyclical stocks* (those companies whose earnings move up and down with changes in the economy) and stocks that fluctuate more than the market does. Aggressive growth investors want to maximise investment performance. Preserving their initial investments takes second place to making money.

The aggressive growth portfolio shown in Figure 6-5 has dropped investment in fixed-interest securities and cash completely.

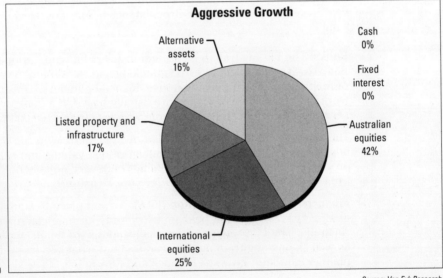

Aggressive Growth

- Alternative assets 16%
- Cash 0%
- Fixed interest 0%
- Australian equities 42%
- International equities 25%
- Listed property and infrastructure 17%

Figure 6-5: Typical aggressive growth investor portfolio.

Source: Van Eyk Research.

Matching the Results to Your Goals

Now for the fun part! The tests for understanding your investor type aren't fail-safe. You should use these test results as a means to an end, rather than an end in itself. What type of investor you are is a good way of figuring out which investments match your goals. See Chapter 7 for more on goal setting.

Seeking advice

Leaving a visit to the doctor or the dentist until it's too late can end in tears. The same can be said for a visit to a financial planner. Investors who don't feel comfortable going through the whole self-analysis process to figure out what type of investor they are and then try to spread their risk across asset types need to see a financial planner.

Finding a financial planner is fairly straightforward. As with any service, you want to get the best for your circumstances. Here are a few places to check out:

- **Banks:** The big Australian banks and insurers like the National Australia Bank (NAB), ANZ Bank, Westpac Banking and the Commonwealth Bank of Australia (CBA) all have in-house financial planners. These planners work directly for the bank and are usually based at a bank branch. The service is generally aimed at people with less than $100,000 to invest.

  The banks also have what are called *tied* planners, who run their own businesses but use the banks' administration systems and sell bank products. Speak to your bank branch. You'll very quickly be put in front of the right level of planner for your situation.

- **Financial Planning Association (FPA):** A good place to start is the FPA at www.fpa.asn.au, the peak industry body for financial planners in Australia. The FPA regulates the qualifications for financial planners as well as ongoing training. You can find out what services a financial planner can offer, how she charges and how much.

  The FPA has another website for consumers at www.goodadvice.com. au, which also has a directory of financial planners who are members of the FPA. You can also find easy-to-read educational pieces on investing, financial planning and the like.

✔ **Independent planners:** These planners aren't part of a bank or insurance company. The FPA has a list of such planners. Count Financial, iPAC and PIS are some of the larger independent financial planning groups

✔ **Insurance companies:** The big insurers like AMP and MLC also have in-house and tied planners operating in the same way as those in the banks.

Ask friends or relatives who've used a financial planner to recommend one. First-hand experience of a financial planner and his service is a valuable reference check. Shop around and have conversations with at least a couple of planners to understand the process and to see if you like each other.

Planners linked to banks or insurance companies are more likely to recommend the financial products of the company they work for or are tied to. On average, planners linked to the major banks and insurance companies sell their company's product 75 per cent or more of the time, according to the Roy Morgan research company in its *Superannuation and Wealth Management* report. The danger is that investors may not be getting the best outcome if the financial planner just sells her own bank products.

Keeping things simple

Whether you've taken the advice of a financial planner or are going it alone, you need to find the managed funds that match your investor profile and your goals. For more on how to set your goals, see Chapter 7.

Using the managed fund research houses such as Morningstar and Standard & Poor's can guide your investment choices. Ratings houses organise funds according to their style and the sectors of the market they invest in. Finding a good-quality fund that matches your risk profile then becomes a relatively straightforward process.

Making sure you're investing in the best possible tax environment is as important as the type of investments you choose. Using a superannuation account to save tax-efficiently for retirement makes sense. Saving for short-term goals, such as a deposit for a house, can only be done outside of super. Once your money is in super, you can't easily get it out.

Most of all, when it comes to investing, keep things simple. Matching your investor type with your goals and eventually with the right funds may seem overwhelming. This shouldn't be. For investors with small amounts of money, splitting investments to the nth degree or by exact percentages isn't going to make a heap of difference.

For example, someone who is a conservative investor and has only $10,000 to invest shouldn't try to match the asset allocation profile in Figure 6-2, even though that shows a typical conservative portfolio. Figure 6-6 shows how a conservative investor can match short- and long-term goals with managed funds.

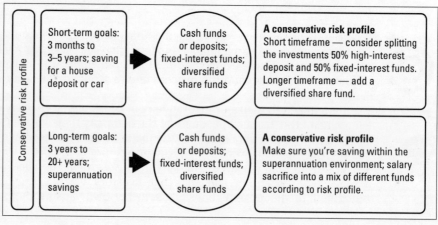

Figure 6-6: An investment strategy for a conservative investor can cater for both short- and long-term goals.

Conservative risk profile

Short-term goals: 3 months to 3–5 years; saving for a house deposit or car

Cash funds or deposits; fixed-interest funds; diversified share funds

A conservative risk profile
Short timeframe — consider splitting the investments 50% high-interest deposit and 50% fixed-interest funds. Longer timeframe — add a diversified share fund.

Long-term goals: 3 years to 20+ years; superannuation savings

Cash funds or deposits; fixed-interest funds; diversified share funds

A conservative risk profile
Make sure you're saving within the superannuation environment; salary sacrifice into a mix of different funds according to risk profile.

Chapter 7

Setting Your Goals and Making a Plan

. . . .

In This Chapter

▶ Understanding how making a plan can help

▶ Working out your investment goals

▶ Finding out how timing affects your investments

▶ Matching goals with timeframes

. . . .

If you don't know where you are going, you'll end up someplace else.

—*Yogi Berra, sportsman*

*B*uilding a house without a set of plans is either for the foolhardy or for the extremely experienced. Similarly, you need to have a plan before you dive headlong into investing in managed funds. Setting out what you want to achieve financially lays the foundation for the success or otherwise of your investing career.

Setting your financial goals can be as wide-ranging as wanting to make as much money as possible, through to paying for an education for your children or grandchildren, saving for retirement or even just preserving the wealth that you have. However, you need to set realistic expectations about what can be achieved. Making as much money as possible is a goal but it's not one that can be easily measured. We'd all love to make as much as possible, I'm sure!

You also need to consider other factors when setting goals. Understanding what's happening in the markets, what level of risk you want to take and the limitations of certain investments are all important. Of all the factors to consider, time has the biggest effect on your investments. The sooner you start investing regularly, the longer you have to meet your goals and the more likely you'll get to where you want to go. This chapter looks at the importance of setting financial goals, how to set those goals and then putting those plans in motion.

Making a Plan

Where do you start when making a plan? A blank piece of paper is usually a good place to begin but it can be intimidating. You can very quickly fill up a sheet of paper with information that enables you or a financial professional to start building a plan. Separating out your short-term goals from your long-term aims also helps when it comes to putting your plan into action.

Whether you work in conjunction with a financial planner or you feel you can take on the task yourself, you should end up with a plan that looks something like this:

- **Current financial position:** A summary of your current situation sets out what money and assets you have to work with. You can also work out what the gap is between what you have and what you want.

- **Goals:** The plan sets out what your future needs are likely to be, whether that's saving for a house or planning for retirement.

- **Investment strategy:** A strategy can range from simply identifying opportunities to save more money to working out what type of investments or managed funds you can use to meet both your short- and long-term goals. You need to be realistic, though. Having a goal to increase your wealth 10 per cent per annum if you only want to invest in cash products has no point, because it isn't going to happen.

- **Measuring success:** Regularly reviewing a plan makes sense. If things aren't going to plan and you're not meeting your goals, you may have to tweak your strategy. Doing this sooner rather than later helps to avoid disappointment.

Setting your course to financial freedom

Financial freedom can mean many different things to different people. A previous boss of mine, at the time a young hotshot stockbroker, said that financial freedom to him was being able to live 'off the interest off the interest' on his money in the bank. Knowing my boss's jetset lifestyle and the fact he was supporting a fleet of expensive sports cars, I figured he would need at least $100 million in the bank to achieve his financial freedom. At 5 per cent interest he would earn $5 million a year on which he would earn another $250,000 a year. Come to think of it, $100 million doesn't seem enough!

Here I set out a few goals and steps to achieving them that are just a little more realistic.

Common investing goals

For most investors, financial goals are perhaps more modest than having $100 million in the bank, and cover a range of different options. Some common goals include:

- ✔ Buying a home, whether you're saving up for a deposit or making sure you have enough income to help pay off a mortgage

- ✔ Saving and investing for the future, either for a rainy day or as part of a strategy for retirement

- ✔ Planning for retirement and working out the minimum amount needed to retire on the income you'd like to become accustomed to

- ✔ Protecting or enhancing lifestyle, such as regular overseas holidays, buying a new car or a second home, or paying for an education for a dependant or yourself

- ✔ Transferring wealth to future generations and making sure that the money is protected when it's transferred

List all your goals, no matter how crazy or unrealistic they may seem. As you work through your plan, prioritise those goals that you're most likely to achieve. Move down the list as the goals get harder and scrap the ones that really are out of this world. Relying on a major win on the lotteries shouldn't be part of your life plan!

Your own investing goals

Figuring out your goals can be made easy by following a few basic steps. If you don't feel comfortable doing this yourself, then seek professional financial help. Here are six basic suggested steps for you, as an investor, to follow when setting out your financial goals:

1. **Set your short-term goals.**

   These include saving up for a deposit on a house, paying off credit cards and other personal debt such as car loans, or setting up regular contributions to a savings account. Short-term goals can range from a few months to three years or more.

2. **Set your long-term goals.**

   Decide what you'd like to achieve in 10 or 20 years or more, such as paying off a mortgage or buying that beach house you've dreamed of. Your short-term goals may help you achieve your long-term goals.

3. **Refine your lists to some specific goals.**

   Make your goals concrete and measurable. For example, 'I want to make as much money as possible so I can retire' could become 'I want to have an income of $80,000 from my investments so I can retire'.

4. Convert those goals into achievements.

This can be tricky. Perhaps contributing more to your superannuation may help, or building up a portfolio of managed funds through a regular savings plan. You may need professional help to work out your options.

5. Take hold of the present — inertia kills.

Act now before the moment and the enthusiasm disappears. Start researching your options or look up a financial planner. Making a start gets you on the road to building a successful investment plan.

6. Constantly review your goals.

As you put your plan together, regularly go over your list of goals, as much to remember what they are as anything. As you find out more about how to achieve what you want, you may have to tweak your goals.

Goals are affected by your stage in life. People leaving full-time education to start work have time on their side but are unlikely to have access to the same amount of money as someone who's been working for 20 years. However, when you're young, you can afford to take on more risk. Younger investors have time to recover from sharp falls in the value of investments. Closer to retirement, investors are likely to be focused on preserving their wealth rather than risking it. Achieving your goals depends on your timeframe as much as the investments you choose.

Considering other factors when setting goals

You need to bear in mind several other factors when setting your goals. These factors are to do with matching your goals with available investments or managed funds. So how do you match funds and goals?

Five aspects determine what investments you use to reach your goals:

- ✔ **Inflation:** A dollar today won't be worth a dollar in five years' time, so inflation is a serious consideration. Returns from investments need to keep ahead of inflation or your wealth goes backwards in real terms.

- ✔ **Returns:** The returns on your investments are linked to your timeframe. Different asset classes produce different levels of return over different time periods. Again, the returns you need to meet your goals need to be matched with what is realistically available from each asset class. Returns can mean an income, an increase in the value of the investment or both.

✔ **Risk:** The likelihood of loss on an investment is closely tied to both the timeframe and returns. The greater the returns, the riskier the investment is likely to be. However, over time, that risk can reduce. You need a longer time horizon for riskier investments. Refer to Chapter 4 to see how risk reduces over time for each asset class.

✔ **Tax:** Finding the right structure to invest through is important. Superannuation is one of the most tax-efficient ways for most people to invest for their retirement. However, when your money is in super, the government doesn't like you taking it out! If you think you'll need your money before you retire, be careful about using super.

✔ **Time:** Some asset classes, such as share managed funds, have a much longer timeframe to generate a reasonable return (five to seven years usually) than, say, a cash managed fund (one to three years). You need to match your timeframe for your short- and long-term goals with each asset class. For more on asset classes, refer to Chapter 4.

You need to know what type of investor you are. Easier said than done, perhaps? Fortunately, a number of questionnaires are available that can help answer this for you. Questionnaires are mainly used by financial planners but some are available online for free (refer to Chapter 6).

Being flexible as circumstances change

People's circumstances change — as sure as eggs are eggs. Some changes are planned, such as retirement, buying a house or changing jobs. Other changes people may have little or no control over, such as redundancy, illness or even the arrival of children.

Short-term goals can change dramatically if you suddenly lose your income or ability to earn money, or find that your expenses ratchet up with the birth of a child. Out the window goes the regular savings plan and investments are cashed in to help replace the lost income.

Knowing where you are in life — financially, that is (spiritually or emotionally, you may need to look at another *For Dummies* book!) — is a good starting point when planning for change. Knowing where you want to end up is also a good starting point but that end point is never easy to set in stone. Unless you are very fortunate, your financial situation most likely won't move up in a straight line. You'll find bumps along the way and you need to plan for change, especially for the unexpected. Later in this chapter, in the section 'Understanding life's investing stages', I examine the three main investment life stages.

Working Out What You Want from Your Investments

The goals you set yourself may include extra income to supplement your earnings. Other longer term goals may include saving money over a long period to help fund education fees or buy a house. Your goals, along with a timeframe for each goal, determine what types of funds you invest in.

Spreading your assets

Putting your money into the right mix of investments helps you manage your risk and gives you the returns you need to meet your goals. Spreading your money across cash, shares, property and fixed-interest investments is called *asset allocation*. Generally, the greater the return you want or need, the greater the risk you need to take on. Moving up the risk scale, cash is the least risky, followed by bonds and other fixed-interest investments, through to property and shares. International shares are seen as having the greatest risk. For more on asset classes and asset allocation refer to Chapters 4 and 6 respectively.

Investors need to sort their goals into those that are about making an income and those that are about increasing the value of investments, or growth. Growth investments are better suited to goals that require a lump sum, such as saving for a house deposit, an education or even retirement. Given growth investments or funds are inherently more risky than income funds, an investor's timeframe for growth assets should be at least five years. Moving into retirement, income assets may be more appropriate, as investing becomes more about preserving wealth and generating an income.

Working out how much income is enough

For retirees who intend to fund their own retirement rather than rely on the government, having enough income is crucial. Russell Investments has come up with a useful guideline when it comes to figuring out how much savings you need in retirement. As a general rule, for every dollar of retirement income (indexed for inflation) payable for a 30-year period, $20 of retirement savings is needed. Figure 7-1 shows the level of savings retirees need for certain levels of income.

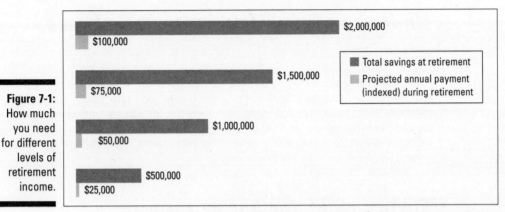

Figure 7-1:
How much
you need
for different
levels of
retirement
income.

Source: Russell Investments. Assumes inflation of 3 per cent, payments for 30 years, portfolio of 35 per cent shares and 65 per cent fixed interest, 0.7 per cent alpha in addition to assumed asset class returns, management fee of 1.8 per cent. Return assumptions are shares 9 per cent, fixed income 6 per cent.

The $20 of savings for $1 of income is a guide only, as investment returns vary from year to year. Selecting annuity-style investments can provide a guaranteed income over a period of time. These types of investments pay an income that is agreed beforehand with the product issuer and, as such, the income the retiree receives is not dependent on the returns of the market. Refer to Chapter 3 for more on annuities.

Setting Your Investment Timeframe

When you've worked out your investment goals, setting a timeframe helps to decide how realistic those goals are. Sooner or later, investors need to face facts and understand that age affects what can be achieved. Younger investors, according to my teenage children, have all the time in the world and, of course, know everything. When investors draw closer to retirement and the wisdom that comes with age, they know they don't know everything. However, they do know that priorities inevitably change and that income-producing investments are now more important than rapidly growing and risky ones.

Different goals have different timeframes. Saving for a house may take three to five years; saving for an education may take longer than ten years, while saving for retirement should be an ongoing plan.

Understanding life's investing phases

Generally, three main life stages count when it comes to investing — accumulation, pre-retirement and retirement. Table 7-1 shows the typical priorities and financial goals of investors at each of the three stages, and what investment strategies may be used to achieve them. Some overlap exists in both goals and strategies between the life stages but each also has its own distinct needs. The table is also a generalisation; for example, an increasingly large number of people over retirement age don't want to retire or perhaps still need to keep working.

Sitting tight for better returns

For longer term goals, investors need to be prepared to ride out the ups and downs of the market over the short to medium term. What matters in the longer term is being in the market. If you want your investments to grow, you need to be positioned in the market when it moves. Later in this chapter, in the section 'Timing the market', I talk about how this is as much about luck as good judgement.

Chapter 9 shows what can happen to your investments if you miss the best performing days in the market. If you had missed the top 70 performing days from 2000 to 2009, your money would have lost 10 per cent rather than made 10 per cent.

 Using managed funds is no reason to *set and forget*, meaning you still have to manage your investments just as if you were managing your own selection of shares. Managed funds have bad runs of performance, as do other investments. If a fund you select is performing poorly, consider switching to another.

Deciding When to Invest

The sooner investment plans are started the more likely they are to be successful. Committing money to the market can be a nerve-wracking experience, especially when hard-earned cash is at stake and the markets look jittery. But you can take some practical steps to put a plan in motion, and this section takes a closer look at how.

Table 7-1	The Three Main Investment Life Stages		
Investor Life Stage	*Priorities*	*Goals*	*Strategies*
Accumulators (up to 50 years old) — singles, couples, families with younger children	Paying off debt Accumulating wealth	Paying off mortgage Investing for retirement Buying investments to grow wealth Minimising tax Saving for dependants' education	Building wealth and achieving lifestyle goals by investing in higher risk assets such as share managed funds Increasing superannuation balance by salary sacrificing Taking on some higher risk by borrowing to invest in managed funds or shares (gearing) Setting up regular savings plans Offsetting any spare cash against the mortgage
Pre-retirees (45 to 55 years old) — singles, couples, families with older children either in full-time education or about to leave home	Protecting investments Planning for retirement	Tax planning and optimisation Working out how much is needed for retirement	Retirement planning Salary sacrificing Some borrowing or gearing to enhance returns Boosting savings, especially those in the superannuation environment, which is the most tax-effective way to invest
Retirees (55 years plus) — singles, couples, no dependants and generally no debts	Receiving income Preserving investment values	Generating a regular income Minimising income tax Protecting investments	Moving into what is called pension phase Reducing exposure to higher risk assets to protect capital and produce income Structuring investments to be tax-effective

Making the most of now

When it comes to investing for the long term, there's no time like the present to start. Markets move up and down, and can look a little scary when investors are panicking and running for the exit. However, that is the nature of markets and, over time, the swings in the market even out.

Demonstrating the value of time to investing, Figure 7-2 shows how two investors fare in their investing careers. Julie has the self-discipline to start investing $2,000 a year in managed funds at the age of 25. I didn't know what savings were until about the age of 28! More like me, Jack starts investing at the age of 35 and puts in $3,000 a year. Both keep investing until they're 55. The average annual return from the managed funds is 7 per cent, excluding costs.

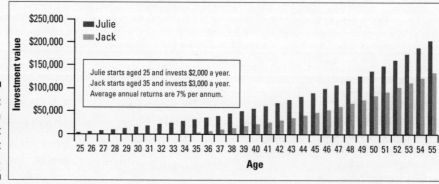

Figure 7-2:
No time like
the present
to start
investing.

Taking the example of Julie and Jack once again, Table 7-2 shows that, over the life of the investment, Julie invested a total of $70,000 while Jack invested $75,000. Although Jack invested more money, the value of his managed fund is more than 50 per cent less than Julie's.

REMEMBER

Jack and Julie's experience demonstrates the compounding effect of regular investing. *Compounding* is when investments earn a return on previous returns. Over time, this compounding is a major advantage of setting up a regular savings plan for any investment, but especially managed funds.

Table 7-2	Starting Early: The Effect on Investments			
Investor	*Annual Amount*	*Length of Time*	*Total Invested*	*Value, Aged 55*
Julie	$2,000	30 years	$70,000	$204,000
Jack	$3,000	20 years	$75,000	$135,000

Timing the market

The general rule is that you shouldn't try to time the market. *Timing the market* means trying to buy when the market is cheap, usually when it's gone down, and selling when it's looking expensive, usually after big moves up. This dipping in and out of the market, or *switching*, can add to your costs of investing. You could also miss out on some big moves up in the market. Transaction fees can also quickly add up as investors are charged for each transaction. Switching in and out of the market is also not that practical with managed funds. The effort in contacting the fund manager and filling in the forms, although not difficult, can be cumbersome if done regularly.

Potential tax implications crop up each time investors sell an investment for more than it was bought. Holding investments for less than 12 months can attract a higher rate of capital gains tax and can hit an investment's overall returns. Check with the Australian Taxation Office (ATO) at www.ato.gov.au for the latest tax rates on capital gains.

Investors want a good start for their money. Few things are more challenging for an investor than putting money into a fund only to see the value fall during the coming months. Don't time the market but be aware of what the market is doing. If the market looks uncertain and could lose value, then don't put all your money in at once. Plan to drip-feed your money into the market so that you're not stuck paying too high a price for your investments. This technique is called *dollar-cost averaging*, which allows you to buy units at strategic intervals, when the price drops, decreasing the average cost per unit. You can read more about this technique in Chapter 19.

For example, John has $90,000 to invest in a managed fund but he's unsure which way the market will go. John decides to invest one-third of the money in the fund, buying 30,000 units at $1 a unit. After a month, the value of the fund has fallen to 90 cents and John buys another $30,000 worth of units in the fund. After another month, the market has settled down and the price of the fund has increased to 95 cents a unit. John decides to invest the remaining $30,000. The average entry price of John's investment works out at 95 cents a unit, clearly better than his initial purchase at $1 a unit.

Drip-feeding money into the market is a simple but effective plan when markets are moving quickly up or down. Investors don't have to try to time the market with this strategy and don't commit all their money at once. Setting up a regular savings plan to feed into a managed fund has the same effect and helps to smooth out the price an investor pays to enter the market.

A little guidance can go a long way

For many people, seeking financial advice may seem like something people do only if they have a lot of money. For others, financial advice means paying big commissions for little return. Then again, for people running their own businesses or with family trusts, financial advice becomes a no-brainer. Setting up the right structures to make sure tax is kept to a minimum is as important as deciding where to put their money.

Complex financial situations aside, most people can benefit from some advice at some point in their investing careers, regardless of how much money they have. At certain life stages, such as marriage, children, redundancy, separation or various stages of retirement, financial needs can change. Whether or not you retire when the government says you can, legal structures are in place to help retirees minimise tax. Not to take advantage of these structures would be madness.

The types of questions that investors should have in mind are:

- For a certain level of income in retirement how much savings do I need to have in my superannuation account?

- When I know how much I need to retire, how much do I need to contribute to my superannuation to reach that amount?

- How can I do all of this in the most tax-efficient way possible?

- Do I have enough insurance, both life and income protection insurance, to pay me an income if I become ill and can't work? Insurance is particularly important for people with dependants and/or debt, such as a mortgage.

The strategies available to build up superannuation savings depend on so many different things — how much money you have now, how much time you've got until you want to retire and how much risk you're prepared to take. Part of my planning for retirement also involves asking how long the kids are going to be at home! A financial adviser can help you calculate what you need to do and how you should do it. Advisers cut out the noise that investors are bombarded with every day from the press and television, and focus on what's important for them.

Personally, I use a financial planner as a sounding board, asking questions either because I don't know the answer or because I want to confirm my understanding of something. Yes, it does cost a bit of money each time you talk to a financial planner, but I have found, to my own cost, that a little money upfront can save you a bomb later on.

Simple things, like changing jobs and moving your employer superannuation account, have potential tax implications. A bit of advice can help you make the move efficiently, keeping tax to a minimum. Similarly, a financial planner can advise on how redundancy payments can be used to boost super savings or what contributions you can get from the government for your super. All of these things can affect investors at so many different life stages.

So don't be afraid to ask. A visit to a financial planner shouldn't be like a visit to the dentist to have your teeth pulled out but more like a regular health check-up with the doctor — or being vaccinated before going for a trek in the jungle!

Chapter 8

Understanding Research and Ratings Agencies

*R*atings agencies are the movie reviewers and restaurant critics of the investment world. Just as a critic's review can turn a movie into a blockbuster, or make or break a restaurant, so too ratings agencies can affect the success of managed funds.

The content of this chapter is not for the faint of heart but is important. Agencies may have their critics but managed fund investing without third-party research can be like throwing a dart at a dartboard while blindfolded. The agencies provide another point of view and an unbiased opinion on an investment. In a way, ratings agencies keep managed fund providers honest. This chapter explains how the agencies do what they do, as well as how the agencies themselves rate.

Sufficient research can be accessed at no cost from some research houses, specialist fund brokers or financial planners. Pay a little money and the doors open to the research houses' premium services, which include recommendations on managed funds. Here, I explain the difference between ratings and recommendations.

This chapter also looks at how to read and understand the ratings agencies' research. The services the agencies provide are full of bells and whistles that can seem a little overwhelming. I help you to cut through the noise and discover which bells and whistles are worth using and which ones are 'nice to have' but not vital.

Discovering How Ratings Agencies Can Help

Ratings agencies examine a wide range of products, from bonds to equities and managed funds, acting as a guide for investors or buyers of financial products. Each agency has its own ratings system, typically based on a star system. When investors are familiar with how each agency rates its funds, the standardised ratings make for quick and easy comparison. Pictures of stars certainly make it easier to scan a list of funds!

Learning who provides the ratings

In Australia, several suppliers of managed fund research are available to retail investors. The main providers are Morningstar Australia, Standard & Poor's and, increasingly, Mercer. These agencies are all global players and have developed sophisticated ways of rating managed funds, adapted for use in Australia.

Here's a little more detail on the global research companies operating in Australia:

- **Morningstar Australia:** Part of the global Morningstar organisation, the Australian business is the largest provider of managed fund research in the local market. Managed fund research and ratings are available to both finance professionals and retail investors.

- **Standard & Poor's (S&P) Australia:** Part of the global Standard & Poor's organisation and perhaps better known for its credit ratings business, S&P Australia also provides ratings on managed funds. Managed fund research and ratings are usually available only to finance professionals.

- **Mercer Australia:** Increasingly popular, Mercer provides managed fund research aimed at industry professionals such as investment consultants who advise some of the large superannuation funds, trustees of managed funds and financial planners.

Smaller agencies such as Van Eyk, Lonsec and Zenith Partners provide research to financial planners, as well as tailored research to fund managers to distribute with their products. Some local agencies provide research on funds in certain sectors of the market, such as agribusiness, property and structured products. For more on agricultural investments, see Chapter 15.

Some of the agencies investors may come across are:

- ✔ **Van Eyk:** Specialist provider of a range of consulting and research products and services for financial planners. Research is generally not available to the public but, if you use a financial planner, there's a good chance she uses Van Eyk research at www.vaneyk.com.au.

- ✔ **Lonsec:** Provides a wide range of managed fund research, as well as specialist research on property, infrastructure and agribusiness funds. Lonsec provides fund profiles of over 7,700 funds and carries a recommended list of over 850 funds. Research is generally available only to financial planners at www.lonsec.com.au.

- ✔ **Zenith Investment Partners:** Provides specialist research for managed funds, as well as sector, market and economic reports to financial planners and their clients at www.zenithpartners.com.au.

- ✔ **Adviser Edge:** Specialist provider of structured product, property and agribusiness research, generally available only to financial planners at www.adviseredge.com.au.

- ✔ **AusAgriGroup (AAG):** Specialist provider of agribusiness managed investment scheme research available at the website www.ausagrigroup.com.au. Research is available via subscription and is primarily directed at financial planners and the agricultural sector. However, the research can be purchased by anyone who registers with the website.

Much of the research on managed funds produced by the local agencies is generally only available to financial planners. However, investors will come across research reports from all these agencies, as managed fund providers do use the research to sell their products.

Understanding what the agencies do

Ratings agencies look to provide a consistent way for investors to measure and compare managed funds. This all sounds very noble but, like all businesses, the agencies are not charities and are out to make money. Research is therefore targeted at those willing to buy it. In the past, research tended to be written for the big institutions that could afford to pay the big dollars. Over the years, some of that research has trickled down to a much broader public and, for the most part, is now generally available.

So, who pays the ratings agencies' bills? Ratings agencies have three main types of clients for their research:

✔ The financial intermediary market such as financial planners and other consultants who advise managed funds or trustees of managed funds

✔ The institutions that provide managed funds to investors — fund managers like to be able to point to third-party research when selling their products to investors (assuming it's favourable!)

✔ The retail investor market — the average person in the street who is looking to make his own investment decisions — although the retail investor doesn't feature high on the list of target clients

Agencies do their best to provide objective views on managed funds. With so many funds in the market, the agencies have developed sophisticated ways of managing all the data from funds and collating it meaningfully.

The agencies use questionnaires designed to cover a range of different aspects, such as how a manager invests the fund's money, what staff are on board and how skilled they are, how the fund is administered and the stability of the parent company. From this research, agencies build up a picture of how well a fund is managed. Ultimately, the huge amount of information collected is distilled into a rating and/or a recommendation.

Ratings agencies may be paid to write a research report on a particular fund, usually ones that aren't run of the mill. These types of funds can include agribusiness schemes that may be promoting timber plantations or funds that have capital guarantees built into them to protect your investment. Agencies must declare that they have been paid to write the research.

Getting hold of research

Getting hold of research is fairly easy. The agencies offer access to their research through their own websites, as well as making it available to the public through the financial press. As with many things in life, you get what you pay for. The information available to the public for the cost of a newspaper or a magazine is going to have certain limitations.

You can get hold of the research in all its forms in many ways, and visiting the websites of the research houses is a good first step:

✔ **Morningstar Australia:** The website at www.morningstar.com.au allows users to register at no charge to access basic research and ratings but not recommendations. A four-week free trial enables access to full research reports as well as recommendations. If you can access only one research provider then Morningstar is the one.

- ✔ **Standard & Poor's (S&P):** The website at www.standardandpoors. com.au requires registration to access research. However, to access the managed fund ratings, you also have to declare that you are a wholesale investor (refer to Chapter 3) with an income of $250,000 or $2.5 million of investable assets. Interestingly, though, the S&P ratings are freely available through some managed funds brokers (read on).

- ✔ **Direct managed fund brokers:** These brokers offer nil entry fees on funds, along with a range of research and tools. They include CommSec Direct Funds at www.commsec.com.au, which provides access to Morningstar fund sheet research and ratings; InvestSMART at www.investsmart.com.au, which gives access to both Morningstar and Standard & Poor's research and ratings; and 2020 DirectInvest at www.2020directinvest.com.au, where you can also access both agencies' ratings. FundsFocus at www.fundsfocus.com.au rates a limited number of funds with research from Standard & Poor's, and RaboDirect at www.rabodirect.com.au rates a limited number of funds with Morningstar ratings and fund sheets.

Alternatively, you can access fund research and ratings through a financial adviser or from specialist media:

- ✔ **Financial planners:** If you decide to use a financial planner, most have access to the premium research offered by at least one of the ratings agencies. Planners restrict the research they show their clients to any funds they may recommend as part of a client's investment portfolio.

- ✔ **Financial press:** A few publications regularly list a selection of funds and their ratings, usually provided by Morningstar. Weekly, the *Australian Financial Review* publishes Morningstar ratings in its 'Portfolio' liftout section and on its website — if you have a subscription — at www.afr.com.au (click on the Markets Data link and then Managed Funds). *The Australian*'s 'Wealth' liftout and monthly magazine *Smart Investor* also publish the Morningstar ratings (not online).

Try to get hold of the research that carries an agency's recommendations. This is the true value of the research. The ratings from Morningstar are a measure of past performance, whereas its recommendations are Morningstar's opinion, or forward-looking view, of the prospects for the fund. Morningstar recommendations are available to premium subscribers to its website (www.morningstar.com.au), along with the research, or from InvestSMART's website (www.investsmart.com.au). InvestSMART lists only the Morningstar ratings and recommendations and S&P's ratings, but not any of the detailed research. S&P's star ratings are a mix of both how the fund has performed in the past and its view of the fund in the future.

Rating the ratings agencies

The global financial crisis exposed some weaknesses in agencies and the way they work. Some agencies had given high ratings to funds that subsequently failed, with investors losing a lot of money. So it's appropriate to ask: Who rates the ratings agencies? Does anyone produce research to say that the agencies are doing their job right? These are reasonable questions, especially given the reliance investors can place on the agencies' ratings of managed funds. Finding out whether the agencies are worth listening to is important. There's no point using the research if it's as useful as a chocolate teapot, which promises a lot but is of no practical use.

Ratings should be seen as a starting point, a guide and a means of narrowing the field of managed funds rather than giving you a definitive yes or no on a fund. If that's the case, then investors may not feel the need to dig too deeply into how agencies work. That being said, investors should feel comfortable about what the agencies do.

Not much research has been conducted on how the agencies perform, but one recent survey by *Money Management*, a publication for financial planners, does give some insight into what fund managers think of the ratings agencies. The publication's 'Rate the Raters' survey, published in June 2010, asked fund managers what they thought. Overall, the agencies came out of it okay. No one agency was marked as outstanding, with all agencies having some good and some bad points. However, bear in mind that this is a survey asking fund managers what they think, not a study on how ratings agencies actually perform.

The following tables show the responses to two of the questions in the survey. The responses show that the fund managers rate the local, independent research houses as providing better research than their bigger, global cousins, although Lonsec and Mercer come out of the survey quite well.

'Looking at the firms that rated your fund, how would you describe the rating they gave you?'

Agency	Excellent	Fair	Poor
Lonsec	50%	45%	5%
Mercer	42%	50%	8%
Morningstar	23%	65%	12%
S&P	24%	52%	24%
Van Eyk	23%	65%	12%
Zenith	16%	84%	0%

'How did you rate the research methodology of these firms?'

Agency	Excellent	Good	Average	Below Average	Poor
Lonsec	36%	50%	9%	5%	0%
Mercer	8%	67%	17%	8%	0%
Morningstar	6%	56%	25%	0%	13%
S&P	0%	52%	24%	14%	10%
Van Eyk	16%	47%	21%	16%	0%
Zenith	21%	68%	5%	5%	0%

Understanding the Ratings

This section focuses on the two main providers of managed fund research in Australia, mainly because the headline ratings are available online in one form or another to the general public. Most of the other agencies only like to let financial planners and fund managers access their research. Morningstar Australia is the largest provider of research in terms of the number of clients it has. Standard & Poor's is arguably the nearest rival to Morningstar in the provision of managed fund research in Australia.

Morningstar ratings

Morningstar splits its ratings on managed funds into two — Morningstar ratings, which measure past performance, and Morningstar recommendations, which give an opinion of how the fund is expected to perform in the future. This section deals with the Morningstar ratings.

What are the star ratings?

The Morningstar ratings are made up of a five-star ratings scale from one star (the worst) to five stars (the best), designed to help investors easily compare managed funds and fund managers. A star rating is worked out by measuring how well a fund has done in the past, then making an adjustment for how risky that fund is and, finally, comparing it with similar funds.

A high star rating is not a guarantee that a fund will continue to perform well in the future, relative to its peers. Past performance does not predict future returns — see Chapter 9 for the perils of chasing returns. The star ratings are a great tool but investors should be aware of the limitations.

Importantly, though, the ratings are based on a fund's ranking among its peer group of funds. Morningstar calls the peer group the fund's *category* and it is a fundamental part of how the ratings are calculated. Categorising funds makes for easy comparison between funds. Also bear in mind that a fund may not be rated because it doesn't have at least a three-year track record of performance or because it has fewer than ten funds in its category of funds. Morningstar needs ten funds or more to make meaningful comparisons.

How are the ratings worked out?

Morningstar calculates its ratings for funds using three elements — past performance, riskiness and which category the fund is in. The way the first two elements, performance and risk, are used may seem tricky at first but bear with me on this. Morningstar looks at how a fund has performed over both three and five years and then asks how much risk that fund took on to generate that return. The greater the risk taken by the fund, the greater the penalty that Morningstar applies when calculating its rating. This method makes sense — risky funds can make great returns but the risk of poor returns also increases.

Adjusting for risk is like the task of horserace handicappers, whose job it is to make sure the horses all have an even chance of winning. The handicappers do this by adding weight to the faster horses. If the handicappers do their jobs correctly, all horses will cross the line at the same time. Morningstar adopts a similar principle in penalising funds for taking greater risks and so looks to neutralise the effects of risk on its ratings. So a fund that has great performance, better than most other funds, could be awarded a low star rating because it's deemed very risky. After deducting the risk measure from the total performance numbers, the result is what is called a Morningstar *risk-adjusted return*.

Morningstar's risk penalty is based on *utility theory*. In a nutshell, the theory assumes investors are more worried about unexpected losses than unexpected gains, and investors are prepared to give up some gains in return for more certainty of returns. I hope your eyes haven't begun to glaze over at this point!

For example, Kim finds a fund with 12 per cent returns per annum over several years and likes the idea of a healthy return. But, in some years, the fund has lost money and in other years returns have been 20 per cent. Kim decides peace of mind and steady returns are more important than the chance of outstanding returns. Kim settles for a fund with returns of 8 per cent per annum and a much lower risk of losing money.

A fund's overall Morningstar rating is a 60:40 combination of five- and three-year Morningstar ratings. This 60:40 mix rewards a fund for consistent performance. The mix ensures that funds with consistently good performance over the longer term end up with better ratings than those funds with mixed performance results.

Morningstar places a lot of emphasis on the importance of categories. These categories are based on the Morningstar style box that classifies funds according to the *market capitalisation* (how big they are) of the stocks they invest in and the investment style of the fund manager.

Figure 8-1 shows how fund ratings are distributed across a particular category. Morningstar deducts the Morningstar risk score from the Morningstar return score (producing the risk-adjusted return) and plots the results along a bell curve to get a star rating. The top 10 per cent of funds in a category are rated five stars; the next 22.5 per cent of funds receive four stars; after that, the middle 35 per cent receive three stars; the next 22.5 per cent receive two stars and the bottom 10 per cent are rated with one star.

Figure 8-1:
Morning-
star's
risk-
adjusted
return for
a fund
determines
the fund's
rating.

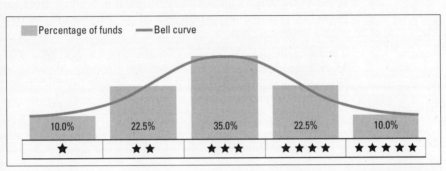

Source: Morningstar Australia.

Not all five-star rated funds are created equal. Funds are rated according to their relative performance among funds in their category. Funds that have a five-star rating in one category, such as international emerging market funds, may also have a much higher risk profile than, say, Australian equity funds. You can find out more at www.morningstar.com.au. Click on the Funds tab and choose Ratings Limitations from the left-hand menu.

Morningstar recommendations

Morningstar recommendations are a five-point scale from Highly Recommended, down through Recommended, Investment Grade, and Hold, to Avoid. The recommendations are Morningstar's views on the expected effectiveness of a fund manager's investment strategy. A recommendation by Morningstar is saying how it believes the fund manager will perform through different economic conditions and in comparison with similar funds. The recommendation is based on:

✔ Interviews with fund manager staff, both those making the investment decisions and those administering the money, using standard questionnaires

✔ Analysis of the information gathered in the interview process

✔ Consultation and debate with Morningstar analysts globally and locally to understand industry trends and the views of the fund manager being reviewed

Specifically, Morningstar takes into account four key areas:

- ✔ **People:** An assessment of the quality of the people making the investment decisions includes the mix of skills, how long the team has been together and what would happen if a key member of the team left.

- ✔ **Investment philosophy and process:** Morningstar looks at how the team comes up with its investment picks and the process behind those decisions, including what research is done. It looks for a clearly thought-out investment strategy that all members of the team can talk about knowledgably.

  The investment process also dictates how the portfolio is made up. Morningstar marries up the investment process with what stocks are in the portfolio and whether or not the portfolio makes sense, given the investment philosophy.

- ✔ **The fund manager's parent company:** A whole range of factors are considered here, including the stability of the ownership structure, the administrative functions, the other funds managed, the level of fees and tax considerations.

- ✔ **Other considerations, such as performance track record:** Performance is rated directly in the Morningstar ratings. The track record looks more at how the fund manager's philosophy has translated into performance.

Each of the key issues Morningstar assesses, shown in Figure 8-2, counts for a different percentage of the total mark awarded in coming up with a recommendation for a managed fund. The people running the strategy account for 40 per cent, processes account for another 40 per cent and issues relating to the parent company and the fund track record account for 20 per cent. A lot of judgement or opinion is used to come up with a recommendation. To be fair, the process is made as transparent as possible and the same questions are asked of all fund managers.

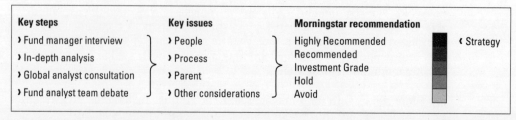

Key steps	Key issues	Morningstar recommendation	
❯ Fund manager interview	❯ People	Highly Recommended	❮ Strategy
❯ In-depth analysis	❯ Process	Recommended	
❯ Global analyst consultation	❯ Parent	Investment Grade	
❯ Fund analyst team debate	❯ Other considerations	Hold	
		Avoid	

Source: Morningstar Australia.

Figure 8-2: Morningstar uses a number of steps to analyse the key issues when making a recommendation.

Standard & Poor's ratings

The Standard & Poor's (S&P) ratings system is a little different from that of Morningstar, though it still uses risk-adjusted returns to calculate its ratings. S&P's ratings are what it calls a forward-looking view of the fund manager's abilities. The view is qualitative so, in effect, an opinion of what S&P believes the manager is capable of achieving.

Ratings are awarded from five stars, being the highest rating, to one star, being the lowest rating. The star rating reflects S&P's view of how likely a fund manager will produce consistently better returns than similar funds and a comparison benchmark index. S&P also issues an On-Hold rating when changes are made to a managed fund, such as an individual manager leaving the business, and a Sell rating if S&P truly thinks investors should steer clear of a fund.

Standard & Poor's describes its star ratings according to how well the risk-adjusted returns bear up against investment objectives and similar funds. Essentially, anything rated two stars or less is going to struggle to perform.

Standard & Poor's doesn't give much away on how it works out its ratings. S&P says it adopts a 'forward-looking qualitative assessment of a manager's ability to consistently generate superior risk-adjusted fund returns, net of fees, relative to relevant investment objectives and peers'. S&P classifies all funds so that funds with similar characteristics can be compared and rated accordingly.

Standard & Poor's interviews all fund managers on a regular basis, using a standard set of questions to ensure consistency across the ratings. S&P also looks at the track record of the fund manager's performance. The S&P rating that emerges from this process is a mix of S&P's judgement of the fund manager's staff, processes and investment strategy, as well as past performance.

Digging into the Research

Ratings are the easy-to-use star system that most agencies use to rank managed funds. The *research* is the in-depth commentary that backs up the ratings, covering a host of different items such as the management team, performance and the outlook, among others. The most readily available research for investors are the Morningstar research reports. Research from other ratings agencies are available from financial planners. For that reason, this section concentrates on the Morningstar research that is generally available.

Reading the research reports

Morningstar produces two types of report for each fund it assesses. The Fund Report is essentially a one-page summary of the key pieces of information about the fund that includes the Morningstar rating. Fund Research is a more in-depth view of the fund and includes the Morningstar recommendation.

Morningstar Fund Report

The Morningstar Fund Report is the most readily available of all managed fund research. This report is where investors find the Morningstar rating as well. The main pieces of information included in a typical report are listed as follows:

- **Fund name:** Self-explanatory!

- **APIR code:** This code is a unique identifier for each managed fund in the Asia–Pacific region.

- **Legal type:** What type of fund it is, such as an investment trust or superannuation fund.

- **Status:** Either open or closed; open funds are able to take new money, whereas closed funds no longer accept new investors.

- **Category:** This is the Morningstar category in which the fund belongs.

- **Performance:** Shown at a particular date, the chart shows the growth of $10,000 over a particular time period of at least three years. The chart shows how the fund has performed compared with other funds in its category, such as large Australian growth funds, as well as a broader market index such as the S&P/ASX 200 Accumulation Index. For more on benchmarks and the different ways to measure performance, see Chapter 9.

- **Current investment style:** Uses the Morningstar style box to show the category of the fund.

- **Financial year returns:** Shows the returns for a fund for each year over at least the last three years and a year-to-date (YTD) performance. The returns are also shown in comparison with the fund's category and against the index. A minus sign against the comparative numbers means the fund has performed worse than the index or category.

✔ **Trailing year returns:** Shows the fund's returns over one month, three months, one year, three years and five years. Again, the returns are compared with the category and the index. The fund is also given a ranking in its category, such as 3 out of 76.

✔ **Asset allocation:** Shows what percentage of funds is invested in what asset class, such as domestic equity, cash or listed property.

✔ **Entry and exit price:** The price that an investor has to pay to buy units in the fund and the price she receives when selling units back to the fund manager. The entry and exit prices are valid only for a certain date and change on a regular, sometimes daily, basis.

✔ **Spread:** The difference between the entry and exit prices. For example, the entry price of a fund may be $1.00 and the exit price $0.9960, so the spread is $0.004, which is usually shown as 0.4 cents. The fund manager effectively keeps the spread to cover buying and selling costs.

✔ **Fund details:** Includes the date the fund started (inception date), who the fund manager is, the minimum investment in the fund, when cash distributions or income from the fund is paid and if the fund offers a regular savings plan.

✔ **Net assets:** Shows how much money is invested in the fund in millions of dollars.

✔ **Fees:** Includes entry or contribution fees and exit fees. For more on fees, refer to Chapter 5.

✔ **Indirect cost ratio (ICR):** Cost of administering the fund, shown as a percentage of the total fund value, such as 1.85 per cent, and includes the annual management fee. For more on the indirect cost ratio refer to Chapter 5.

Morningstar Fund Research

The Morningstar Fund Research is a summary of Morningstar's views of the manager. The reports give an overall view of the fund manager, noting strengths and weaknesses, and an assessment of the strategy of the fund manager and the processes used to put the strategy into practice. The reports discuss the personalities involved in managing a fund and provide commentary on the performance. The reports also show the recommendation.

Furthering your research

The research and ratings from the agencies are good pointers for which funds to look at. However, don't stop there. Here are some of the other places to conduct research before investing your money:

- ✔ **Advisers:** If in doubt, seek advice from a qualified financial planner. Remember, you want independent advice. Make sure the financial planner isn't just selling a particular fund because it happens to come from a different part of the same organisation that the planner works for.

- ✔ **Australian Securities and Investments Commission (ASIC):** A quick check of ASIC's consumer watchdog FIDO at www.fido.gov.au is a must before you invest. Check to see if the fund manager you plan to use has any outstanding problems with the regulator.

- ✔ **Fund manager:** Always call the fund manager's call centre or visit the fund's website to see what further information on a fund may be available.

- ✔ **Press:** Read the financial press, such as the *Australian Financial Review* and specialist magazines, to check on managed funds. Don't bother with the sponsored editorial stuff, though, where fund managers pay journalists to write nice things about their funds. Read the views of independent experts to get a different perspective on a fund.

- ✔ **Product disclosure statement (PDS):** Read the PDS and understand what you're exposing your money to if you decide to invest in that particular fund.

Chapter 9

Making Sense of Performance

Managed funds aren't allowed to sell performance but performance sells.

—*Anon.*

Performance is what investing is all about. Investing is ultimately about how much money ends up in an investor's pocket. In the good times, performance is about how much money you make and, in the bad times, about how little money you lose.

However, performance can be more than just about how much money is made or lost. Funds management is such a competitive industry and performance is the lifeblood that sustains it. Measuring performance can be relative, comparing against other similar funds and the market, or absolute, looking at just how much the fund makes or loses in dollar terms. In this chapter, I explain the finer points of difference between the two measures.

Comparing how funds perform helps investors decide which funds offer the potential for better returns. However, measuring how much is made or lost can be tricky, as costs and tax can affect the final outcome. So, in this chapter, I also look at how the performance of managed funds must take account of costs.

Although past performance is a good indicator of where to invest, you also need to be aware that chasing historical returns can be disastrous. Here, I show you how to gauge past results, as well as how to look at market timing to help guide your investment decisions.

Understanding That Past Performance Is No Guide to the Future

'Past performance is no guide to the future.' What a great get-out line for fund managers when talking about the performance of their funds. But, in truth, investors should never judge a fund solely on past performance. Very few fund managers can consistently produce great returns year after year.

The financial regulators that police the investment community have learned from bitter experience that shonky performance promises have been the downfall of many retirees and investors. The regulators are at pains to make sure fund managers don't make promises they can't keep. Fund managers must follow a set of rules that dictate how they calculate returns and how they show performance to investors.

Whether a fund manager sends an email to a client or publishes performance details in advertising, the rules aim to make sure all fund managers calculate and report performance the same way. Being able to compare the performance of similar types of funds is a crucial part of investors making informed choices.

Learning from history

If history does show anything, it's that performance is not a reliable indicator of the future. Looking at the performance of the various asset classes — cash bonds, property, Australian shares and international shares — over the ten years to December 2009 shows how returns can vary hugely year to year.

Figure 9-1 shows how the returns of the various asset classes can vary over a 20-year period and that a previous year's amazing performance won't necessarily be repeated the following year. Starting with the early 1990s, Australian shares topped the charts in 1991, but was the only asset class to record a negative return the following year. The pattern was repeated for Australian shares in 1993 and 1994. International shares bucked the trend a little in the late 1990s with three years as the top performer in 1997, 1998 and 1999. However, the outperformance came to a shuddering halt over the next three years, when international shares were the worst performing asset class. Likewise, property had an amazing year in 2006. Contrast property's result with that in 2007 and what a disaster!

Predicting which asset class is going to be top of the class next year is near impossible. Spreading, or diversifying, your risk by investing in different asset classes may help you lessen the pain and still make a gain.

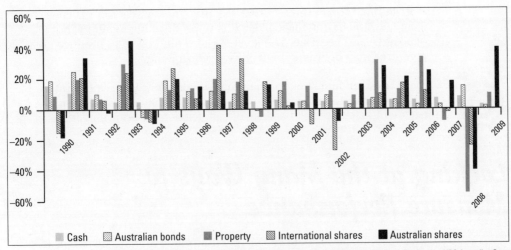

Figure 9-1: Asset class performance, 1990 to 2009.

Source: IRESS. Returns are based on the following indices: Cash = UBS Australian Bank Bill; Bonds = UBS Australian Comp Bond All Maturities; Property = S&P/ASX 200 Property Accumulation; International shares = MSCI World, Net Dividends in A$; Australian shares = S&P/ASX 300 Accumulation.

Buying into past performance

Everyone loves a winner and funds are no different. Investors are naturally inclined to follow the money, and why not? Looking at past performance is a great starting point, but you also need to be aware of the shortcomings of past performance. A fund may be a one-hit wonder; last year's shooting star could be this year's damp squib.

Looking at the history of top-performing managed funds can give investors pointers. Here are the aspects you need to check:

✓ **Expectations:** Don't be drawn into a great set of results from one year's worth of results from a managed fund. Funds that are top performers one year can set an unrealistic precedent for investors.

✓ **Fund type:** What type of investments are in the fund and how they are managed influence the returns. A fund that invests mainly in growth assets such as big mining companies produces different returns and at different times than a fund investing in property projects.

✓ **Longevity:** Funds don't last and may not be around in five years' time. Consistently poorly performing funds lose money and are likely to be closed down or sold off by the managers. My own research, using publicly available information, shows that more than 25 per cent of funds around ten years prior to December 2009 have since closed.

> ✔ **Risk:** Don't forget the role that risk plays in a fund's return. The riskier an investment, the more likely it is to produce big numbers, both positive and negative. The level of risk a fund takes to produce great returns may be way outside your comfort zone.

Do your research and stick to your guns. If you know what you want to achieve, over time, performance does even out to some extent. Don't be persuaded to change tack because of last year's top-performing funds.

Looking at the Many Ways to Measure Performance

To most people, performance is simply how much money is made or lost on an investment. Investors may want to measure the gain or loss either in dollar amounts or as a percentage of the original value of the investment. The finance industry, not known for doing things simply, has devised a number of ways to measure performance. The two most common methods of performance measurement are known as relative performance and absolute performance.

The Australian Securities and Investments Commission (ASIC) regulates the calculation and presentation of performance by fund managers. Guidance is also issued by the managed funds industry body, the Financial Services Council (FSC). If that isn't enough, a global body, the Chartered Financial Analyst (CFA) Institute, which the FSC aims to replicate in Australia, issues standards for performance reporting.

Performance figures presented by fund managers must not imply that they can be reproduced in the future and all relevant information must be disclosed. So, if the performance was due to the fund taking on higher risks such as borrowing to enhance returns, this must be disclosed.

Performing relatively

Relative performance means how an investment has done compared with other similar investments. For example, a managed fund may show growth of 15 per cent per annum. Not bad growth, but shown by itself the performance doesn't mean a lot. Place the fund next to similar funds or a market index and its performance begins to make sense. Showing performance compared with its peers or, for example, the S&P/ASX 200 index is known as *benchmarking*.

Table 9-1 shows how a fund manager typically reports the performance of a managed fund relative to a benchmark.

Table 9-1	Reporting Relative Performance						
As at 31 May 2010	**1 month**	**3 months**	**6 months**	**1 year**	**3 years**	**5 years**	**Since Inception (31/12/03)**
XYZ Australian Share Fund	−7.34%	−2.67%	−3.69%	+17.42%	−7.20%	+76.15%	+125.77%
All Ords Accum. Index	−7.57%	−3.33%	−3.91%	+21.41%	−20.12%	+35.10%	+75.57%
Relative performance	+0.23%	+0.66%	+0.22%	−3.99%	+12.92%	+41.05%	+50.20%

The performance of the XYZ Fund in Table 9-1 is shown in Figure 9-2.

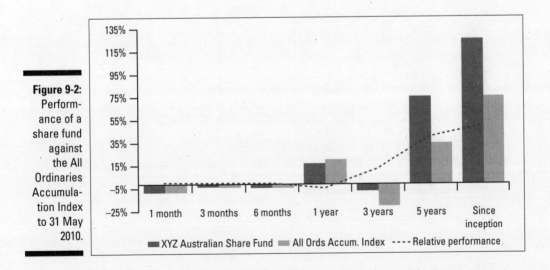

Figure 9-2: Performance of a share fund against the All Ordinaries Accumulation Index to 31 May 2010.

Alpha and beta: It's all Greek to me!

Investors are likely to come across several performance measures that have been given letters from the Greek alphabet to identify them. Two of the more commonly used measures are alpha and beta, which are used to split a managed fund's performance — yet another way of measuring the success or otherwise of a managed fund. The Sharpe ratio, which doesn't have a Greek letter attached, is another commonly used ratio, especially for comparing hedge funds.

Simply put, the *beta* measures the return *from* the market and the *alpha* is the return *above* the market. For example, say a managed fund returns 15 per cent in a year and the market or index returned 10 per cent over the year. The beta is the market return, or 10 per cent, and the alpha is 5 per cent.

Alpha is especially important when working out how well active fund managers are doing. By their very nature, active fund managers should aim to beat the index. Now, I know I'll get into trouble with fund managers for saying that. Their argument is that fund managers have a bias towards an investing style, whether it be value or growth or somewhere in between. This bias means a fund manager won't outperform the index all the time. Value managers do better than growth managers in flat and falling markets but are beaten by growth managers in rising markets. But active fund managers charge investors for the privilege of their experience and a better than market performance, or alpha return, is not unreasonable.

The beta return is the return that you get from the market and is usually measured by a benchmark index, such as the S&P/ASX 200 Accumulation Index in Australia. By definition, the market has a beta measure of 1.0. Any fund with a beta of 1.0 means that its returns match the performance of the market index. Index managed funds or exchange-traded funds are funds that typically match the returns of the market.

Alpha returns are those returns over and above the returns of the market, or above beta. Alpha is ultimately the return that a fund manager either adds or subtracts from the performance of a managed fund.

Conservative investors looking to preserve capital should focus on securities and fund portfolios with low betas, whereas those investors willing to take on more risk in search of higher returns should look for high beta investments.

The *Sharpe ratio* shows whether a fund's returns are due to clever investing or a result of taking on too much risk. The ratio is also a simple way to measure one fund against another.

The ratio calculates what is known as the risk-adjusted return and is typically shown as, for example, 1.0 or 1.55. The greater a fund's Sharpe ratio, the better its risk-adjusted performance has been. So, a ratio of 1 or more is considered good, 2 or more is very good and 3 or more is fantastic. I don't think I've ever seen a 3 but I'm sure they must be out there! A negative Sharpe ratio means that you'd be better off putting your money in the bank than in the fund.

How does it work? Say Fund A returns 15 per cent in one year while Fund B has a return of 12 per cent. However, as it turns out, Fund A has taken on more risk achieving the return and has a Sharpe ratio of 0.95 while Fund B has a Sharpe ratio of 1.45. Fund B has produced a lower return for a much lower risk. Going forward, Fund B is likely to produce more consistent returns, around the 12 per cent mark, than Fund A.

Performing absolutely

Absolute performance is the actual return an investment makes. Say you invest $10,000 in a managed fund and after three years your investment is worth $13,000. The fund has increased in value by $3,000, or 30 per cent, over those three years. That 30 per cent return is what is known as the absolute performance of your investment.

For many investors, the absolute performance is all that matters, regardless of the performance of the rest of the market. After all, the amount of money made, after expenses and tax, is what ends up in the investor's pocket. As an example, absolute performance may be a key measure for retirees who are dependent on a regular income from investments.

Some fund managers avoid comparison with benchmark indices such as the S&P/ASX 200. These types of fund managers are called *index-unaware* or *absolute-return* funds because they make investments without trying to beat a particular index. Absolute-return funds aim to make a certain percentage return and adopt a range of strategies to do that, some riskier than others. For more on absolute-return funds, see Chapter 16.

Splitting performance into income and growth

Most funds split the total performance number into income and growth. The *income* return is the proportion of the return that has been earned from income received from the underlying investments, such as dividends. The *growth* part of the performance number is how much of the total return is due to the increase in value of the underlying investments. Table 9-2 shows a typical layout of how a managed fund reports performance, showing the split between income, or in this case *distribution*, and growth.

Table 9-2	Income and Growth Performance to 31 May 2010					
APIR Code: BTA0021AU	*Fund Name: BT Australian Share Fund*			*Inception Date: 25/6/1986*		
	1 Year	*3 Years*	*5 Years*	*7 Years*	*10 Years*	*% p.a. Since Inception*
Distribution	2.45	8.84	9.85	8.14	7.45	8.12
Growth	14.14	−14.79	−3.21	2.94	−1.32	4.70
Total	16.59	−5.96	6.64	11.08	6.13	12.82

Source: BT Financial Group.

All income received by a managed fund must be paid out to investors, usually once a year, known as the distribution. Tax on distribution amounts is likely to be payable by investors. The end-of-year statement from the fund manager shows what income received attracts tax. Growth returns are made up of *realised* gains (money made from the fund selling investments during the year) and *unrealised* gains (how much the retained investments have gone up in value). Again, investors may have to pay tax on some of these gains.

When a fund pays a distribution, the price of the fund reflects the drop in asset value caused by the distribution. So, if the price is $1.00 and the distribution is 10 cents, the price of the units drops to 90 cents after the distribution to reflect the fact that money from the fund has been returned to all of the unit holders.

Allowing for tax and expenses

Tax is the hidden cost of investing. For non-superannuation managed funds (normal everyday managed funds to you and me), performance figures are shown before tax and before transaction fees, but after fund expenses.

- ✔ **Before tax:** Managed funds, in general, don't pay tax, and investors are left to pick up the tax bill. For that reason, performance figures are shown before tax.

- ✔ **Before transaction costs:** The performance figures also don't take into account some fees, such as entry and exit fees, that the investor may have to pay. These fees should be relatively small compared with other fees but are worth remembering.

- ✔ **After expenses:** However, performance figures are shown after expenses, including the annual management charge, investment fees (the charge for buying and selling investments), administration fees and discretionary fees.

Complicating things a little, superannuation funds display performance numbers differently from non-superannuation funds. These performance numbers must be shown after tax because tax is paid by the super fund. Tax for superannuation funds is, at the time of writing, a flat 15 per cent. Performance figures for superannuation funds must also be after investment fees but before administration and discretionary fees.

The costs of investing in a managed fund can impact on the long-term returns. Figure 9-3 shows what can happen when investing in managed funds with different management fees. For both Fund A and Fund B, $20,000 is invested for 20 years with an average annual return of 8 per cent. Fund A charges 1.95 per cent in annual fees and Fund B charges 0.75 per cent fees. With over a $16,000 difference after 20 years, even apparently small differences in fees can have a big impact.

Figure 9-3:
Value of a $20,000 investment in two funds with different annual fees after 20 years. Shows growth in value only and does not include income or distributions.

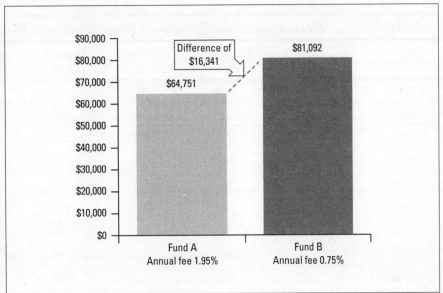

Applying Performance Results to Investment Choices

When quoting performance numbers in any advertising, fund managers must say that investors should not rely on past performance as a guide to future returns. This section sets out why chasing last year's best performing funds may not lead to next year's standout performer. More important than being a top-performing fund is being a fund that can demonstrate consistently good performance over time.

Avoiding the chase for returns

Few investors can judge what's going to be the next hot sector for making money. Table 9-3 shows the performance of the main asset classes over the 20 years to December 2009. The shaded areas show the top-performing sector of the year. The results show that chasing the best performing sector of the previous year is unlikely to produce the same top performance.

Table 9-3	Worst versus Best Performing Asset Classes, 1990–2009				
	Cash	Australian Bonds	Property	Australian Shares	International Shares
Dec 90	16%	19%	9%	−18%	−15%
Dec 91	11%	25%	20%	34%	21%
Dec 92	7%	10%	7%	−2%	6%
Dec 93	5%	16%	30%	45%	24%
Dec 94	5%	−5%	−6%	−9%	−8%
Dec 95	8%	19%	13%	20%	27%
Dec 96	8%	12%	14%	15%	7%
Dec 97	6%	12%	20%	12%	42%
Dec 98	5%	10%	18%	12%	33%
Dec 99	5%	−1%	−5%	16%	18%
Dec 00	6%	12%	18%	4%	2%
Dec 01	5%	5%	15%	10%	−10%
Dec 02	5%	9%	12%	−8%	−27%
Dec 03	5%	3%	9%	16%	0%
Dec 04	6%	7%	32%	28%	10%
Dec 05	6%	6%	13%	21%	17%
Dec 06	6%	3%	34%	25%	12%
Dec 07	7%	3%	−8%	18%	−2%
Dec 08	8%	15%	−55%	−40%	−24%
Dec 09	3%	2%	10%	40%	0%

Source: IRESS. Note: The shaded areas show the top-performing asset class for that year. Returns are as follows: Cash = UBS Australian Bank Bill; Bonds = UBS Australian Comp Bond All Maturities; Property = S&P/ASX 200 Property Accumulation; Australian Shares = S&P/ASX 300 Accumulation; International Shares = MSCI World, Net Dividends in A$.

For example, in 1993, Australian shares were the best performer, with an average return of 45 per cent, but dropped to minus 9 per cent the following year and were the worst performing asset class. If any trend can be identified, the worst performing sector (apart from cash, which remained relatively stable over the period) appears often to be the sector that makes the strongest recovery in the following year.

The table shows that a good performance one year won't necessarily lead to a follow-on performance the next. However, international shares bucked the trend from 1997 to 1999, as did property from 2000 to 2002 with successive years of top performance. Why one particular segment of the market does better (or worse) than another is largely down to value and what investors believe is the growth potential. Perhaps it then stands to reason that, once a sector is regarded as fully valued (or overvalued), it won't necessarily repeat a good year of performance.

Warning: Last year's standout, this year's disaster

A fund that produced fantastic results in the past won't necessarily reproduce them going forward. In fact, if a fund has produced fantastic returns in the previous year, investors should be wary of its prospects. History shows that the funds that have performed well in the last 12 months haven't necessarily done well over a longer period.

Table 9-4 shows the five top-performing funds for the 12 months to 31 May 2010. Table 9-5 shows the top-performing funds over the five years to 31 May 2010. Performance for the five-year funds is shown as average annual returns.

Table 9-4	Five Top-Performing Funds for 12 Months to 31 May 2010, Measured against the S&P/ASX 200	
Rank	**Fund Name**	**12-Month Return**
1	CFS FC Inv — CFS Colliers Geared Glob Property Sec	82.1%
2	CFS FC Pens — CFS Colliers Geared Global Prop Sec	81.6%
3	Optimum Corp Super — AMP Capital Global Property	75.5%
4	Optimum Pers Super — AMP Capital Global Property	75.5%
5	Naos Small Companies Fund	74.5%

Source: Morningstar Australia/IRESS.

Rank	Fund Name	12-Month Return	3-Year Return	5-Year Return
	Table 9-5 Five Top-Performing Funds for the Five Years to 31 May 2010, Measured against the S&P/ASX 200			
1	Baker Steel Gold Fund	48.99%	7.04%	18.78%
2	Stockland Direct Office Trust No. 1	−28.23%	−4.78%	17.68%
3	BlackRock Wholesale International Gold (Class D)	17.54%	4.25%	17.5%
4	ING OA IP ING Small Company Growth	31.36%	−4.46%	15.96%
5	Challenger China Share Fund	9.39%	−0.16%	15.69%

Source: Morningstar Australia/IRESS.

The tables show that the funds that have performed well over the 12 months to 31 May 2010 don't feature in the top-performing funds over the longer term. There is a good chance these funds will also not be in the top performers in five years' time. Research by Morningstar shows that, of the five top-performing funds, only 22 per cent were likely to repeat the performance in the following year. In fact, 18 per cent of funds in the top five ended up near the bottom of the pack the following year.

Looking for consistent performance

Very few fund managers can consistently be the best performer. Some funds are shooting stars one year and fade very quickly the next year. Searching for funds that produce good, reliable returns may seem dull and boring to some. But, with managed funds, it really is 'slowly wins the race'.

Consistency is the best indicator when looking at past performance. Funds that are always in the top half of the league tables for their sector are worth considering. Consistency is also about how funds do in the bad times. Compare the fund in down markets with the rest of the market. Generally, the more a fund loses relative to the market, the riskier it is.

Watch out for the headline performance return and always dig a little deeper to understand the numbers. A fund's average annual performance can be underpinned by one fantastic year followed by mediocre returns.

Timing the Market

It's not timing the market but time in the market.

—Anon.

This well-worn quote is trotted out by many a fund manager and investment expert. Like a tune that you can't get out of your head, it can drive you nuts after a while. But the message is spot-on. Unless you're an investing freak of nature, trying to time when a market is at the bottom or the top is exceptionally difficult and, invariably, more down to luck than skill.

Polishing your crystal ball

So what does timing the market mean? *Timing the market* means buying a fund or investment when the market is usually at a low and selling a fund when the market is at a high. Sounds straightforward, but very, very few people manage to time the market. To predict exactly when a market is about to turn up or down, you may as well use a crystal ball. Most experienced investors avoid trying to predict such movements.

On the other hand, *time in the market* means not trying to guess when the market will turn. Leaving your money in the market to ride out the highs and lows is what most commentators suggest. The natural reaction is to pull your money out when the market falls. But history shows that markets recover and can turn rapidly, taking investors by surprise. If your money is out of the market you could easily miss a good chunk of the recovery.

Learning what history shows about timing the market

History shows that trying to time the market — selling at the best price and buying at the lowest price — can be a risky strategy. Get it right and you'll have every fund manager in town offering you a job. Get it wrong and you can miss out on some great returns.

The chart shown in Figure 9-4 neatly sums up what might have happened to your investment returns if you'd missed the best performing days on the Australian market over the ten years to December 2009. At the top of the chart is the performance if your investments had stayed in the market for the whole period. Next is the performance if you'd missed the best 10 days of the market, sliding down to missing the best 70 days in the market. You would have been desperately unlucky to miss the best 70 days but, if you had, your portfolio would have been well into negative territory by the end of the ten years, down nearly 11 per cent. Leaving your money in the market for the whole period would have seen your money increase by almost 10 per cent.

Figure 9-4:
Effect of taking your investments out of the market — the risk of missing the best performing days!

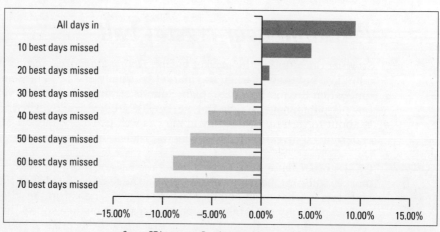

Source: BT Investments. Based on annual returns to 31 December 2009 compared with the S&P/ASX All Ordinaries Index to April 2000 and S&P/ASX 300 thereafter.

Part III
Choosing, Buying and Selling Managed Funds

Glenn Lumsden

'I wish he'd just go see a financial planner.'

In this part ...

Part III starts off with a beauty parade of fund managers. Far from wanting to travel and meet people, and having a desire for world peace, these fund manager beauties just want your money. I list the main players and what you need to know about them. Most fund managers keep a low profile but inevitably you find some rock-star managers who are worth following. You may even end up buying tickets to their concerts.

A big consideration for any investor is whether to take advice or go it alone. I set out the pros and cons of both in this part. Going it alone can save you money, and the sense of freedom from flying solo can be a big buzz. On the other hand, working with a financial planner can be a rewarding experience if you get the right one.

Oh dear! Investing in managed funds isn't all rock-star buzz and excitement — you also have to fill out the forms. Plain English struggles to put in an appearance on many of the forms, so having a guide to what's what is worthwhile. After you've filled out the forms and paid your money, you need to know how to monitor your funds. You may also want to buy more funds and at some point you'll need to sell them. Last but not least, I talk about buying, selling and monitoring your funds in this part as well.

Chapter 10

Discovering Who's Who in the Managed Funds Zoo

To the average investor, fund managers can seem a little scary. Many managers appear to be naturally shy and retiring, and highly protective of how they do business, which means getting to know them can seem daunting. On the face of it, fund managers are powerful players in the investment sector — they control staggering amounts of money, own decent chunks of large public companies and are courted by companies and governments alike. So, understanding why fund managers can come across to investors as intimidating isn't all that hard.

Regardless of how much you're investing, you need to be comfortable that the fund managers are looking after your interests, not just theirs. You want to be sure that your money isn't invested in riskier instruments than you're comfortable with — and that you're able to get the money back when you need it.

This chapter covers who the key players are in the world of fund management in Australia, as well as the benefits of choosing big rather than boutique-sized funds (and vice versa), and provides tips for choosing your personal fund manager.

Uncovering Australia's Key Players

Controlling some of the biggest fund managers in the Australian market are the big four banks. If you grudgingly put up with the big banks for your everyday banking, then chances are you're likely to only grudgingly give the banks more money when you invest in their managed funds. Outside of the banks, the large insurance providers make the list of Australia's key players in fund management, along with a handful of powerful overseas managers.

Competition for your money between the big fund managers is strong and, consequently, they place a lot of emphasis on advertising to sell their wares. You're likely to be introduced to who the main players are in Australia through advertising. With a decent chunk of money to spend on advertising, the big fund managers are ever present in the mainstream and investment media. Understanding and interpreting what the adverts mean then becomes an important part of the fund manager selection process.

Selecting a fund manager is an integral part of the investment process. Trusting a fund manager with your money means not leaving it to chance or blind trust, or, indeed, simply being impressed by jazzy advertising. Giving the fund manager the once-over (even twice) is vital. As when buying a second-hand car, kick the tyres, look under the hood, check the log book and go for a test drive before you commit yourself. You can even ask an expert to give you a second opinion if you're still not sure.

The biggest and the best: Getting to know Australia's top fund managers

Money that is managed comes from two main sources. *Retail money* comes from individual investors like you and me, either directly or through intermediaries like financial planners. *Institutional money* is typically from the large superannuation funds with big blocks of money for the fund managers to invest on their behalf.

This section introduces the key fund managers that investors can expect to encounter in the Australian market, both retail and institutional. The ranking and inclusion of fund managers in the lists of top fund managers is based purely on their size, measured by the amount of money they manage on behalf of investors. Also included here are some of the industry awards that give merit to the best fund managers.

The retail top ten

About 90 per cent of retail money managed in Australia is concentrated in the hands of ten players. Inevitably, when selecting a fund manager, the odds are that you're most likely to end up selecting one of these major players, purely because of their market share.

Based on amount of assets under management, Table 10-1 shows Australia's top ten managed fund administrators and the amount of money they run for retail investors in Australia.

Table 10-1 Top Ten Fund Managers and Total Retail Assets under Management, 31 December 2009

Rank	Manager Name	Assets under Management ($m)	Market Share (%)
1	Westpac/BT Financial (www.bt.com.au)	92,622	18.00
2	National Australia Bank/MLC (www.mlc.com.au)	78,261	15.20
3	Commonwealth Bank/Colonial (www.colonialfirststate.com.au)	75,432	14.70
4	AMP (www.amp.com.au)	52,229	10.10
5	ANZ/OnePath Australia (www.onepath.com.au)	46,343	9.00
6	Macquarie (www.macquarie.com)	37,572	7.30
7	IOOF (www.ioof.com.au)	25,921	5.00
8	AXA Australia (www.axa.com.au)	25,657	5.00
9	Mercer (www.multimanager.mercer.com.au)	14,113	2.70
10	Perpetual (www.perpetual.com.au)	9,910	1.90
	Others	56,565	11.00
	Total	514,625	99.9

Source: Plan for Life.

Following the institutional money

Include the institutional money (that is, the money invested through Australia's superannuation funds) in the funds' total assets under management, and the big overseas fund managers put in an appearance as some of Australia's key players. Information on the amount of money that the international fund managers look after is sourced from the fund manager and checked against Standard & Poor's (S&P) information (S&P is a global financial research business).

The big five international players in the Australian market, listed in order of total Australian funds under management, are:

- ✓ **Vanguard Investments** (www.vanguard.com.au): One of the world's largest managers of index or tracker funds, with approximately US$1.5 trillion in assets under management worldwide and A$80 billion in Australia.

- ✓ **State Street Global Advisors** (www.ssga.com/australia): Manages A$54 billion in Australian funds, with around US$1.4 trillion in total assets under management.

- ✓ **BlackRock** (www.blackrockinvestments.com.au): The world's largest fund manager after buying Barclays Global Investors in 2009. BlackRock manages around US$2.7 trillion globally and A$46 billion in Australia.

- ✓ **PIMCO** (http://australia.pimco.com): The world's fifth-largest fund manager and manager of the world's largest bond fund. In Australia, PIMCO manages around A$30 billion.

- ✓ **UBS Global Asset Management** (www.ubs.com): Looks after around A$25 billion locally and US$2.23 trillion globally.

The fund managers in the preceding list offer retail products in the Australian market. In most cases you can buy their funds directly, or via financial planners, who typically invest through administration platforms run by the major banks (see Chapter 17 for more on this investment process).

Note: Although not in the top five global players among Australia's institutional fund managers, Fidelity (www.fidelity.com.au) is perhaps one of the world's best known fund managers. It has around US$1.4 trillion of managed fund assets globally and has a growing retail and institutional presence in Australia through the inclusion of some of its funds on retail managed fund administration platforms such as Colonial First State's FirstChoice (see Chapter 17 for more on administration platforms).

Other major players

Other fund managers considered major players in the Australian industry include the following (listed in order of the amount of Australian funds under management):

- ✓ **Aberdeen Asset Management** (www.aberdeenasset.com.au): Manages US$232 billion globally and approximately A$16.5 billion in Australia (according to the company's marketing material). Aberdeen increased its growing presence in the Australian market even further when it purchased selected funds managed by Credit Suisse Asset Management Australia.

✔ **Platinum Asset Management** (www.platinum.com.au): Manages around A$16.5 billion (from company filings to ASX as at December 2009). Platinum is a classic example of a fund that established a solid reputation as a boutique (a small, independent fund manager — see the section 'Boutique managers may be better' later in this chapter), which allowed it to attract enough money to make it a serious player in terms of size.

✔ **Tyndall Investment Management** (www.tyndall.com.au): Co-owned by key staff and Nikko Asset Management, a major Japanese fund manager, Tyndall manages approximately A$10 billion in assets in its own right and $15 billion on behalf of Suncorp, its previous parent. Nikko manages around $125 billion globally.

✔ **Australian Unity** (www.australianunity.com.au): Manages around A$10.3 billion of Australian assets. Australian Unity partners with specialised fund managers that look after particular investment types — for example, Platypus Funds Management manages its Australian equities portfolios and Wingate manages its international funds (refer to Chapter 14 for more on types of funds).

✔ **Schroders Australia** (www.schroders.com.au): Wholly owned by the Schroders Group, which manages around A$266 billion globally. Locally, the group manages around A$9 billion across a range of funds and strategies.

Commending the best fund managers

Industry awards can be a good pointer for picking a fund manager. Like the Oscars, but without the fancy outfits, awards give industry recognition to fund managers. A plethora of awards are out there, but some of the better known ones (listed in order of ability to access by retail investors) are:

✔ **Morningstar's Fund Manager of the Year:** The winner of this award is the fund manager that maintained the highest overall level of fund management excellence during a calendar year. Previous winners include BlackRock, Perennial Investments and Schroders Investment Management.

✔ **Standard & Poor's (S&P) Fund Awards:** Touted modestly by S&P as the 'pre-eminent accolade in the funds management industry throughout the world', these awards began in Australia in 2004. Previous winners include BlackRock, BT Financial Group and Tyndall Asset Management.

✔ *Money Management/***Lonsec Fund Manager of the Year:** *Money Management* is an industry publication aimed at financial planners. Lonsec provides managed fund research and judges the awards. Previous winners are Integrity Investments, Patriot Funds and Schroders Investment Management.

- ✔ **SmartInvestor Blue Ribbon Awards:** Presents awards across a range of finance products and services. Past winners of its fund manager of the year include BT Financial Group, Colonial First State and Perpetual Investments.

- ✔ ***Money Magazine*** **Best of the Best:** Awarded annually to a range of financial services providers. The fund manager awards are made for best superannuation fund manager and cheapest fund manager.

- ✔ **Australian Fund Manager Awards:** These awards are made by the fund management industry to fund managers — in other words, they're a chance for the fund managers to give each other a pat on the back. Past winners of fund manager of the year include BlackRock, Challenger Financial Services, Perennial Investment Managers and Perpetual Investments.

Slicing through the advertising

Look at the advertising approach of any of the big fund managers and you quickly discover they use both brand and tactical advertising. But what does it all mean, and what are the fund managers trying to tell us about their companies and products?

Interpreting the double-speak

At its most basic level, advertising takes two distinct forms:

- ✔ **Brand or 'feelgood' advertising:** Aims to make people want to associate with a particular brand by using its products. A classic brand advert is the Qantas 'I Still Call Australia Home' series, with its stirring music and children's choir filmed in various locations around the world.

- ✔ **Tactical advertising:** Aims to sell a particular product or service. A master of this type of advertising is the electrical and household goods retailer Harvey Norman, with its hard to shake 'Go Harvey' ad jingle.

Advertising agencies regularly fall back on tried and tested means when it comes to selling managed funds. Often conservative, fund managers are reluctant to do anything radical for fear of offending. Occasionally, a company like Virgin Money challenges the status quo with edgy, funny adverts. Advertising agencies love this type of work but most fund managers would rather stick pins in their eyes than create controversy — in other words, most fund managers prefer to maintain a conservative approach to advertising.

Here's my (slightly tongue-in-cheek) interpretation of the underlying messages of some of the key themes that agencies use in adverts for the larger fund managers:

- ✔ **Customer-focused:** Customer-focused? More likely the fund has had a chronic problem in the past with customer complaints, and its market research tells management that its customer service is abysmal. So, the fund manager decides to spend up big on adverts to tell you how great the fund's customer service should be. Problem solved.

- ✔ **Innovative:** For some fund managers, being 'innovative' just means they've ditched some of their older funds because they weren't performing and replaced them with new funds, which are exactly the same. Hey, the names of the funds have been changed and that's pretty innovative!

- ✔ **Size matters:** The message that large fund managers would have you believe is that big doesn't mean lumbering and unwieldy. The fact that the advert sets out to tell you this 'news' probably means the fund manager in question is lumbering and unwieldy.

- ✔ **Think global, invest local:** This approach may mean the fund offers the potential for a diversified investment portfolio — or it just involves sending fund managers to obscure parts of the world to look at marginal mining companies, making sure a stopover in Paris or London happens on the way back.

- ✔ **We're different:** This message is a constant in fund manager advertising. However, if the fund manager looks like a large fund manager and smells like a large fund manager then it probably is a large fund manager; that is, no different from most of the others.

Especially in adverse times (such as during the 2008 global financial crisis), the message big fund managers like to project is that they offer longevity and a dependable safe haven from financial storms. The advertising is often akin to having a hot cup of cocoa on a winter's evening, only not as enjoyable.

Although managed funds can offer security and expertise, more important aspects need your attention than their latest advertising campaigns. See the section 'Choosing a Fund Manager' later in this chapter for more on what you should really be studying when you're assessing potential fund managers.

Examining the small print

Don't ignore the small print! Although it isn't going to get your pulse racing, you're best to always read the text at the bottom of an advert — even if you need a magnifying glass. The small print is where you find the important stuff.

Fund managers have to stick to certain rules or advertising codes of conduct. They mustn't make any claims that can't be backed up, and aren't allowed to bag their competitors. Australia's corporate, markets and financial services regulator, the Australian Securities and Investments Commission (ASIC), also gets jumpy when fund managers talk about performance in adverts, and provides more rules to cover its requirements here (refer to Chapter 9 for more on reporting performance).

An advert quoting performance numbers also has to show what's called a *benchmark* comparison — for example, the benchmark may be the S&P/ASX 200 index. Say a particular fund has returned 10 per cent per annum over three years. This may sound quite reasonable; however, if the S&P/ASX 200 index has returned 12 per cent per annum over the same period, the fund's return no longer looks so good. Only by seeing a fund's performance relative to the market can investors begin to make a judgement about a fund.

Be very wary of any advert or fund manager that offers a guide to future performance. This approach of looking into the future is a big no-no and you're best to treat such a guide with the utmost caution — ASIC really doesn't like this type of advertising and rightly so. Fund managers, despite what some of them may think, can't predict the future and certainly can't predict returns.

Although good performance sells a fund, fund managers can't sell performance (because ASIC doesn't like it much). Consequently, the standard advert disclaimer looks something like, 'Past performance is no guide to the future', which means something close to, 'We've done great things in the past but don't count on us to repeat it'.

The general rule to remember with any advert providing future performance numbers is this: If it looks too good to be true, then it probably is. As an example of this rule, many investors got burned using mortgage funds during the global financial crisis. These funds promised high returns to investors but, during the crisis, some stopped paying a return and froze their assets.

The Big Names versus Boutiques

People are easily put off by the thought of doing business with a big company. Large managed funds are easily accused of being bureaucratic monoliths, factories churning out standardised products or the 'McDonald's of the finance industry'. These accusations may even be appropriate for some big fund managers, and, for some investors, smaller boutique fund managers may offer the antidote. However, you're best to consider both types of fund manager on their merits and on your needs.

The pros of big managers

Let's face it, when it comes to everyday banking, the majority of people put up with mediocre service from the bigger banks because they think they're less likely to fail. Inevitably, you may also base a large part of any decision about which fund manager you use on its size.

Large fund managers offer compelling reasons to invest with them:

- **Breadth of experience:** Their size means the large fund managers can specialise across a variety of investment types, from local and overseas shares to commercial and retail property and bonds. They also have the experience to focus on a particular area of shares, such as small companies or mining stocks.

- **Longevity:** To have grown into a large fund generally means a fund has been in the game a long time, so it must be doing something right.

- **Money:** The big funds have the financial backing to meet their ongoing regulatory requirements, and run teams to administer their funds and marketing departments to sell the funds.

- **Range of funds:** With a large fund, you can set up a well-diversified portfolio across a range of assets, all with the one fund manager. This approach means you can keep the paperwork to a minimum, and keeping track of your investments is set to be a lot simpler too.

- **Support and administration systems:** Large fund managers spend a lot of money on making sure their support and administration systems work, because they're vital for keeping the funds operating. You can be sure — most of the time anyway — they're going to provide you the paperwork you need.

- **Top talent:** Big managers can attract the best brains in the business. They offer a wide range of employment options along with the opportunity to look after eye-popping amounts of money.

Boutique managers may be better

The sheer size of large fund managers creates advantages (see the preceding section), but size also creates disadvantages — which is where boutique managers come in.

The entrepreneurial spirit is alive and well with boutique managers, and nothing sharpens the mind more than putting money at risk. Freedom from the shackles of an investment giant does, however, bring with it the administrative and financial pressures of running a business.

Understanding boutiques

Don't be put off by the word *boutique*. Boutique fund managers are not the same as boutique clothing stores, with an expensive shopfront and staff who wear only black. Instead, 'boutique' for fund managers refers to the relatively small size and the select nature of the service and funds that this type of fund manager offers. Fees are also unlikely to be much more than the industry norms, unless the manager is an exceptional performer.

Boutiques can have tie-ups with or be part-owned by larger organisations. The impact of these kinds of arrangements is that some boutique fund managers may not strictly be independent from big investment organisations or banks. Boutique tie-ups with larger investor groups or banks are definitely not a bad thing and can provide the best of both worlds for smaller fund managers. The influence of the larger organisation is generally restricted to providing management support, systems, salespeople and occasionally money. The important part of the business, the investment decisions, remains with the boutique fund managers.

The following is what you can expect from a typical small or boutique fund manager:

- **Depth of experience:** The people running boutique or small managed funds tend to have worked for large fund managers at some point in their careers. For someone to have the wherewithal to start up a fund management business without first having built up the credibility that comes from working with a large firm is very rare. (Credibility is needed to attract money from day one — otherwise, it becomes a very expensive and short-lived business.)

- **Flexibility:** Boutiques are characterised as being more nimble than their larger brethren. Typically, they run smaller amounts of money, which means they can get into and out of the market quickly without affecting the price of a share too much. At its simplest, a company's share price is determined by the supply of and demand for those shares, as with any commodity bought and sold.

For example, a fund manager wants to buy a relatively large number of Company A's shares and places its order into the stock market. Sellers of Company A's shares, seeing a large demand for the shares, increase the price they're willing to sell their shares to the fund manager. The opposite is true when an investor sells a relatively large holding of shares. A big fund manager with large amounts of money to invest is like piloting an oil tanker — changing course can take days in order to avoid significant price movement in the shares.

✔ **Specialisation:** Smaller fund managers tend to specialise in a market segment or style of management, such as small-company funds. Using a specialised fund manager gives you access to highly skilled managers and focused funds, which may not be available through a large manager.

Small fund managers ordinarily have fewer resources than big fund managers, in terms of research teams, administration and marketing. Funds are also required to keep a certain amount of money aside — capital — to meet their licensing requirements (refer to Chapter 3 for more on the structure of managed funds).

Listing some of the boutique managers

Fund managers come and go, bought out by their bigger rivals or, less frequently, just by shutting up shop. Conversely, some fund managers regarded as boutique a few years ago have grown rapidly and are now major businesses.

Because of their small size, some boutique funds prefer to have a smaller number of clients investing larger amounts of money, as it's more cost-effective to administer. Minimum investment sizes with boutiques can vary anywhere between $1,000 and $50,000, but usually $5,000 (see Chapter 13 to find out more about minimum investments). However, if the boutiques have any of their funds listed with one of the major distribution platforms, such as Colonial First State or Perpetual Investments (see Chapter 17 for more on platforms), the minimum investment is typically between $2,000 and $5,000 but could be as low as $1,000 if you set up a regular savings plan with them.

Some fund managers close off funds to new investment when the funds reach a certain size. Occasionally the funds reopen to take new investment, so it's worth checking with the manager.

Here are some of the managers regarded as boutique players in Australia at the time of writing:

✔ **Ausbil Dexia** (www.ausbil.com.au): Established in 1997, this fund is an Australian equities specialist with around $11.5 billion under management. Minimum investment is $50,000 but funds are available through the platforms.

✔ **Australian Ethical Investments** (www.australianethical.com.au): Investing ethically since 1986, this fund has over $600 million under management. Minimum investment is $5,000, or $1,000 with a regular savings plan.

✔ **HFA Australia** (www.hfainvestments.com.au): A hedge *fund-of-funds manager* (meaning it invests in other hedge funds globally), this fund has more than $4 billion in assets. Minimum investment is $5,000. Funds are occasionally closed to new money. The main funds offered by HFA are managed by its wholly owned subsidiary, Certitude Global Investments.

✔ **Hunter Hall** (www.hunterhall.com.au): Specialises in ethical investing and manages around $2 billion. The standout performance of the fund is proof that you can invest ethically without sacrificing returns (see Chapter 15 for more information). Minimum investment is $10,000.

✔ **Investors Mutual** (www.iml.com.au): Set up by Anton Tagliaferro in 1998, this fund manages around $3.1 billion. IML is part-owned by the Treasury Group, which has investments in several fund managers. The funds are available through the platforms. A limited number of funds (its Sandhurst series of funds) are available direct from the manager with a minimum initial investment of $25,000.

✔ **Maple-Brown Abbott** (www.maple-brownabbott.com.au): Set up in 1984 by Robert Maple-Brown and Chris Abbott, this fund is privately owned and specialises in Australian and Asia–Pacific ex-Japan equity portfolios. It has in excess of $12.9 billion of funds under management. The funds are available through the platforms unless you have a minimum $500,000 to invest directly with them.

✔ **Perennial Investments** (www.perennial.net.au): Touts itself as 'Australia's leading boutique investment firm', with more than $20 billion in funds under management. The fund was founded by, among others, industry stalwart John Murray in 1999. Funds are available through the platforms.

✔ **Platypus Asset Management** (www.platypusassetmanagement.com.au): Don Williams established the company in 1998. Platypus is a 50:50 joint venture with Australian Unity Investments, the investment arm of Australian Unity, to distribute its funds. Funds are available from Australian Unity with a minimum investment of $1,000.

✔ **PM Capital** (www.pmcapital.com.au): Founded by Paul Moore (ex-BT Investments) in 1998 and remains privately held. PM Capital manages an absolute-performance fund available either direct or via Colonial First State.

✔ **Smallco** (www.smallco.com.au): Specialises in investing in small companies (as its name suggests). The fund limits the amount of money it manages — which is currently around $100 million. Minimum initial investment is $40,000. The company occasionally closes its funds to new investments when it reaches a certain size.

Watch out for management changes and how they may affect the running of the funds. For example, consider *key-person risk* when selecting a boutique fund manager. Having built reputations on the skills of one or two people, what happens if they leave? The expertise sitting with one person can potentially vanish overnight if that person were to leave or get hit by the proverbial bus.

Look out for boutique funds with other senior fund managers in the company with wide responsibility, because this kind of internal management structure helps to soften the blow of a key-person departure.

Choosing a Fund Manager

With so many funds to choose from, and so many specialty investments they can offer, making the choice can be tough indeed. But help is at hand.

In this section, I show you where you can find most of the information you need to help you choose a fund manager. I also explain how to sift out the important information you need to help you make a decision and how to interpret this information.

Doing your homework

When the time comes to shop around for a fund manager, you can get access to the information you need to make your selection in the following ways:

- ✔ The fund's websites and call centres (see the next section)

- ✔ The financial press (see the section 'Checking out magazines and newspapers' later in this chapter)

- ✔ The *product disclosure statement (PDS)*, which is a document that explains the features of the fund manager as well as the funds available from that manager (see the section 'Looking over the product disclosure statement' later in this chapter)

Starting at the source: Fund manager websites and call centres

Fund manager websites are the most obvious and easiest way to access information on the fund quickly. Have a wander around online to get a feel for the type of information available and a sense of how the information is presented. Is it written in plain English? If you need a business dictionary to interpret what the fund manager is saying online, then think carefully whether this manager is the organisation you want to be sending you a quarterly investment report.

Most fund managers have an About Us page on their websites and this is usually my first stop. First impressions count and the information displayed on the About Us page gives a good indication of what to expect. On this web page, you ordinarily find information about the company structure, history and personnel. Photos of key personnel are good, and not just for a giggle; they literally put a human face to the company. This web page also tells you about how the fund manager manages money, what it stands for and what investment methods it uses.

Don't worry if you don't immediately grasp some of the concepts listed on the website, such as value or growth investment styles (refer to Chapter 4 for more on investment styles). As you research, you quickly come to understand the differences in style and what such differences mean for you.

When researching fund managers, you're best to do some window-shopping. Speaking to the fund manager's call centre gives you a great insight into how it treats customers. Ask some basic questions such as 'What are managed funds?' and 'How do I invest in them?' Well-trained staff are able to give you reasonable answers or can tell you where to find the information you need. Think carefully about dealing with any funds where staff seem poorly equipped to do their jobs. In all likelihood, poor service isn't going to stop at the call centre.

Checking out magazines and newspapers

A number of magazines focus on personal investing. Usually produced monthly, these magazines cover a range of different investments, from shares and managed funds to cash accounts and contracts for difference (CFDs). The main personal investment magazines (all of which also have an online presence) are:

- *BRW* (formerly *Business Review Weekly*)
- *Money Magazine*
- *SmartInvestor*

Newspapers are also a good source of information. National daily newspapers, such as *The Australian* and the *Australian Financial Review*, carry specialist investment sections on a weekly basis. The weekend papers also carry personal finance sections. The articles in the print versions are, to a large extent, what you find in the online versions of the newspapers. Accessing these articles online is usually free, although you may have to pay for archived articles (check the newspapers' websites).

The best newspapers for topical information on managed funds are:

- **The *Australian Financial Review*:** Published by Fairfax, includes the weekly 'Portfolio' section, which is a useful guide to the latest trends in managed funds and includes performance tables from Morningstar, a company that provides research on managed funds (refer to Chapter 8 for more on Morningstar). You also find interviews with fund managers, which are a useful guide to discovering more about the companies they work for. Online, *AFR* is subscription only.

- **Fairfax newspapers:** Titles include *The Age*, *The Sydney Morning Herald*, *WA Today* and *Brisbane Times*. These newspapers are syndicated papers, which mean articles are shared across each of the publications.

- **News Corporation newspapers:** Titles include *The Courier-Mail* (Queensland), *The Daily Telegraph* (New South Wales), *Herald Sun* (Victoria), *The Advertiser* (South Australia), *The Mercury* (Tasmania), *NT News* (Northern Territory) and *The Australian* (national). Again, these are syndicated newspapers.

- **The weekend newspapers:** This group includes *The Weekend Australian*, *Sunday Age*, *Sun Herald* and the *Sunday Telegraph*. These newspapers have dedicated money sections that occasionally cover stories on fund managers.

- **The West Australian:** A Western Australian metro paper with a regular finance section.

Looking over the product disclosure statement

Everything you need to know about a managed fund is accessible from the organisation's product disclosure statement (PDS). Every fund manager must give you a PDS before you invest your money, or your financial adviser must give you a copy for every fund he recommends. The PDS is a legal document that must include a certain amount of information about the fund managers' funds as well as information about the fund managers, among other things. Most fund managers use the PDS as an opportunity to tell investors more about themselves, so it is a useful reference when it comes to selecting a fund manager. See Chapter 12 to understand more about what you can expect to find in the PDS.

Make sure you have the latest PDS for each managed fund you're considering. Each PDS is dated. Some PDSs have additional information appended to them in the form of a supplementary PDS that is usually issued to cover off any small changes to the PDS after its issue, such as a fee change. The fund manager or financial planner should give you the supplementary PDS with the original PDS and it's important you read them in conjunction with each other.

Seeking advice

Don't be afraid to ask for help. If you look at the fund manager's website, read the brochures, speak to the call centre and peruse the PDS, and you're still not sure, then a second opinion is called for. Speak to someone who can point you in the right direction.

Listening to first-hand experience of dealings with a particular fund manager can be invaluable. This could be as informal as talking to a relative or a friend who has invested in managed funds, to a formal arrangement with a financial planner. Find out more about financial planners in Chapter 11.

Going for CLASS When Choosing a Manager

CLASS is a quick guide to the main points you should cover off when looking for a fund manager. The CLASS qualities to look for are:

- ✔ Clear objectives
- ✔ Length of time in the industry
- ✔ A-grade performance
- ✔ Standout management
- ✔ Style

Clear objectives

Keeping business objectives clear and simple is one of the hardest goals to achieve for any finance company. For investors, getting sucked into the jargon and ending up confused easily happens. Good fund managers spend a lot of time making sure they communicate their objectives in an easily understood, clear and concise way.

Good fund managers need to be clear on two aspects of their fund management:

- ✔ **What their investment objectives are:** Fund managers need to be clear about their approach to managing money. This aspect of fund management is as fundamental to a fund manager as fins are to a fish. If they can't tell you what their investment objectives are and, more importantly, if you can't understand them, then chances are they're going to have problems managing your money.

✔ **Who they are:** This key element is obvious, really, and most fund managers are clear on this one. However, some fund managers still struggle to provide adequate information about their heritage. Think carefully about using any managers that won't tell you or don't provide information on their history. Understanding how fund managers got to where they are provides insight into how they manage money.

Some of the ways that managers describe themselves and their objectives are as follows:

✔ **'Active manager':** *Active* means these fund managers are proactively involved in managing money and not blindly following the market. These fund managers are telling you they don't sit on their hands. And so they shouldn't! You're paying them to perform better than the index so they'd better be active. An index measures investment performance on the stock market and many fund managers use various indices as a guide to measure their own fund's performance. The S&P/ASX 200, for example, measures the performance of the top 200 shares by size of company on the ASX.

✔ **'Strong corporate governance and socially responsible investing':** These two issues are fast becoming important themes. *Corporate governance* is a term that broadly refers to the rules or processes that a company uses to manage its business, ensuring that risks are appropriately managed and that executives do what they're supposed to do (in other words, making sure company directors don't rip off the shareholders). *Socially responsible investing (SRI)* makes sure companies aren't engaged in unethical practices such as using child labour. A growing body of evidence suggests the share prices of companies that are strong on corporate governance and SRI also perform better. Fund managers that highlight these issues as important to them are worth taking note of.

✔ **'Disciplined approach':** A favourite phrase with many fund managers, *disciplined* can mean not making an investment decision after they've been to the pub at lunchtime, or it can mean a full investment committee is involved in considering each investment proposal on its merits backed up by acres of research. Finding out which camp the fund you're looking at belongs to is important — refer to the section 'Choosing a Fund Manager' earlier in this chapter for tips on how to discover this sort of information.

Length of time in the industry

Fund managers wear longevity as a badge of honour — and usually for good reason. The importance of length of service in funds management ought never be underestimated. Why? Because track records of consistent performance over a long time can be a good measure of what to expect in the future.

Don't ignore recent entrants to funds management, such as new boutique fund managers (refer to the section 'Boutique managers may be better' earlier in the chapter). Chances are, the people behind the company have years of experience managing money at larger funds. If they performed well in the past, they have the credibility to replicate this performance in the new company. Although you may not want to jump in headfirst, keep an eye on these companies as they build up a track record.

A-grade performance

When the time comes to gauge a fund manager's performance, you only have the past to go on. The most important attribute of performance that you need to look for is consistency. Although every company has its bad years, and you have to take this into account, overall, a fund manager needs to show a record of doing well over a number of years. This expectation means that its funds perform at, or preferably above, the market across all asset types, from shares to bonds and property.

Be careful of fund managers with funds that have sharp ups and downs, or saw-tooth, movements in returns year after year, especially if this is out of tune with the way the markets have performed generally. These managers are most likely taking riskier bets with investors' money, leading to bigger swings in returns.

You need a strong stomach to ride out the bad years with risk-taking managers, and their approach may not be appropriate for your circumstances.

Standout management

Good management is as important as good performance. (By 'good management', I mean how the company is run, not just the management of the funds.) Getting a sense of how good management really is, though, can be tricky.

Looking at the available material, talking to people who use the services and reviewing fund performance can give you a good feel for a fund manager's approach to management. The fund research houses also make an assessment of management when rating funds.

Take the extra time to track down fund research from the research houses, which can be accessed in abbreviated form from some of the fund brokers and which should include the research house comments on management. Fund brokers that provide fund research include CommSec Direct Funds (www.commsec.com.au), InvestSMART (www.investsmart.com.au) and Funds Focus (www.fundsfocus.com.au).

Style can impact performance

A fund's investment style basically summarises how fund managers view the world and the type of stocks they invest in.

Value investors look at stocks that are undervalued compared with similar stocks. Value fund managers tend to do better in falling markets or markets that are only rising slowly, and underperform in strongly rising markets. *Growth* investors search for stocks that have the potential for strong earnings growth. These funds do well in strong bull markets but can do worse in falling markets. (Check out more on investment styles in Chapter 4.)

Be sure you understand what investment style the fund manager uses, because it can and does impact on performance.

Getting to Know the Person Looking After Your Money

Most fund management companies have a team of people managing your money. The fund managers are the individuals responsible for making the major decisions on how to manage the money within a fund. Yes, usually they're backed up by teams of research analysts who provide them with the information they need on companies. Ordinarily, they also have investment committees who provide guidelines that cover what fund managers can and can't invest in. Even with back-up support from analysts and committees, the individual fund managers are still the ones who win the plaudits and big pay packets when things go well. (When performance is terrible, fund managers either quietly slip away or get promoted to management positions where they can't do any more damage — and can perhaps put their skills to better use.)

So how do you find out about the people? The good fund management companies, with nothing to hide, provide bios of their key managers and information on the funds they manage. These companies also produce regular fund updates, usually every six months. Again, the good ones have the fund manager's name on the update, showing the manager is taking responsibility for the performance.

Try to get to know your fund manager, the person actually looking after your money. Treat it like a job interview and you're the interviewer. Go to the fund's website and look at all the available information on the fund and its manager. If available, have a look at the fund managers' résumés and get a sense of their commitment to the funds you're investing in. Examine their investment styles, their outlook on the markets and their track records.

Many of the big fund managers don't tell you who's managing the fund until you invest in it, which is a big help (not!). This scenario is like betting on a horse at the races but not being told who the jockey is until after the bet's been placed. This lack of information is a real shortfall in investor and client communications and very disappointing for investors. The boutique managers are much more cooperative. After all, they rely on the managers' reputations to attract funds, so it makes sense to spruik these drawcards.

At the risk of generalising, you're going to come across certain fund manager types — some you should seek out and some you should avoid. I group them as rock stars, gurus and vampires!

The rock stars

Rock star fund managers are high-profile managers well known for what they do. The media gives them idol status, and these managers are now legends who have become part of investing folklore, with the power to move markets. They make a comment in the press and investors hang off every word. The true rock stars of investing have global recognition and there aren't very many of them — no Australian fund managers have achieved rock-star status yet, although plenty of gurus (see 'The gurus' in the next section) meditate on their wares. The rock stars have got to where they are by being not just good but exceptional — and consistently exceptional.

The rock star of rock-star investors is of course, Warren Buffett. Even his nickname, the 'Oracle of Omaha', anoints him with foresight beyond normal. Keeping company with Warren Buffett are the likes of:

- **Anthony Bolton:** UK fund manager who managed the Fidelity Special Situations fund for 28 years to 2007, with an annualised return of 19.5 per cent, far greater than the 13.5 per cent of the broader UK market.

✔ **Bill Gross:** Up there as founder of PIMCO, the world's fifth-largest fund manager, and manager of the world's largest bond fund, the PIMCO Total Return fund. The old adage that, if you want to know what's going to happen in the stock market, first look at the bond market, has meant that when Bill Gross comments, not just investors but governments pay attention.

✔ **Peter Lynch:** Another legend from the Fidelity Investments stable, Lynch is best known for growing Fidelity's Magellan fund from US$18 million in 1977 to US$14 billion when he retired from full-time investing in 1990. Lynch averaged an annual return of 29.2 per cent in the Magellan Fund, beating the S&P 500 Index (the index that measures the performance of the top 500 listed companies in the US) for 11 out of 13 years. Although not actively managing money, Lynch continues to advise Fidelity.

✔ **Jim Rogers:** Made his name as one of the great contrarian investors, putting his money where others feared to tread. Rogers is also well known for going against the grain when investing in commodities. Rogers also is no longer actively managing but is an adviser to one or two funds.

✔ **George Soros:** The hedge-fund supremo who made his name betting against the Bank of England in the early 1990s — and winning over US$1 billion.

The gurus

Closer to home, finding legendary rock-star fund managers (refer to the preceding section) with the global recognition of someone like Buffett is a little harder. Australia does have some exceptional investors, though, who've taken on 'guru' status. Guru fund managers have an innate sense of where value lies in the market and a great sense of timing. Some guru-type fund managers have changed the way we invest or have made a significant contribution to how we invest in managed funds. (See 'Listing some of the boutique managers' earlier in this chapter for more on some of the funds set up by these gurus.)

The Australian gurus of funds management include:

✔ **Robert Maple-Brown (Maple-Brown Abbott):** Set up his company in 1984 and developed a reputation as a value investor, with the fund outperforming its peers over a number of years. Maple-Brown is no longer involved in the day-to-day running of the funds.

✔ **Kerr Nielsen (Platinum Asset Management):** Built his reputation at BT Funds Management. Kerr famously predicted the market sell-off in October 1987 and made a substantial amount of money for his funds. Platinum was set up in 1994 and floated on the ASX in 2007, making Kerr and his co-founders immensely wealthy.

✔ **David Paradice (Paradice Investment Management):** Set up his company in 1999, focusing on investing in smaller companies. The company's solid investment returns help to solidify this guru's reputation as one of the best in the sector.

✔ **John Sevior (Perpetual Investments):** Head of Australian equities since 2002 at Perpetual and regarded as one of the market's best stock pickers. Outspoken, Sevior is prepared to use his funds' equity stakes to enact corporate change and can make or break deals.

✔ **Anton Tagliaferro (Investors Mutual Ltd — IML):** Regards himself as a value investor never afraid to speak his mind on shareholder matters. IML was founded in 1998 after this guru's stint at Perpetual.

Three elements have made these gurus successful and are worth considering when you're looking for someone to manage your money — longevity in the industry, consistency of performance and specialisation, whether it be in a particular market sector or with a certain style of investing (see Chapter 4 for more on investment style). On top of these three elements, each guru has had the occasional flash of brilliance, adding zing to his performance and helping to cement his reputation in the marketplace.

The vampires

After dealing with fund managers for more than 20 years, in my experience the overwhelming majority of these managers are smart — they have a passion for the markets and a genuine commitment to what they're doing. But it doesn't necessarily follow that they're all good at what they do. You find some exceptional individuals in the Australian fund management market, just as you find managers who consistently underperform their benchmarks.

Then you come across a small number of fund managers who make you really wonder why they're in the job at all. Year after year they consistently underperform the market and fail to add any value for investors. Yet they happily keep charging 1 per cent or more for the privilege of giving investors these mediocre returns. These fund managers are the vampires.

Some are just not good at their jobs, regardless of how hard they work. And, like the mythical vampires, a lot of them work after dark — but in the case of vampire fund managers, such after-hours 'work' is at the expense of stockbrokers.

You're unlikely to get to know the names of vampire fund managers unless they do something really wrong and end up in the papers. As always, consistent performance is a good pointer — where these managers hang out is in the consistently poor fund performance region. If you're unlucky enough to end up with a vampire fund manager, over time you're going to feel like you've had the blood sucked out of your investments. After a few years, you're then likely to compare your investment against some of the better performing funds and you begin to realise that, rather than good results, your fund gets the award for anaemia. Avoid!

Following the leader who makes money

The larger fund managers offer a wide range of funds, good administration and, if you're selective, funds that offer reasonable long-term performance. The stability and security offered by big fund managers is appealing to a lot of investors.

On the other hand, you can't go past many of the boutique funds, especially those that have a proven track record. Don't forget, many of these managers have been around for more than a decade. Often these managers were the smartest guys in the room at the big funds until they decided to strike out on their own to manage money outside of the constraints of some of the bigger organisations. Researching a boutique fund manager may take a little more time before you're comfortable investing but you can find getting to know the people managing the money easier. Boutiques are not as faceless as some of the bigger managers.

Follow the money and invest with the managers who make money. With just a small amount of time and effort, you can find out who the successful managers are and which companies they work for, whether that company is a large fund manager or a boutique.

The power of one

Most people outside of the cloistered world of the investment professional had never heard of fund manager Paul Fiani before 2008. That was until a takeover bid was launched for Qantas. The headlines Fiani made in early 2008 were ones fund managers tend to avoid like the plague. And the deal he helped topple is the stuff of novels, although perhaps not as exciting as some of the 'bodice-ripper' novels available for sale at airports.

As head of UBS Global Asset Management's Australian Equities team, Fiani controversially used his fund's 6.5 per cent stake in Qantas to block a takeover bid from consortium Airline Partners Australia (APA). Members of the consortium included some of finance's big names, led by private equity firm Texas Pacific Group, Macquarie Bank, Allco Finance (which has since gone bankrupt) and Onex Partners.

The controversy was that UBS's investment bank was advising the APA consortium during the deal and stood to make millions in fees if it went ahead. This takeover was the deal of the year and people's careers were going to live or die by its success or otherwise. APA needed more than 50 per cent of shareholders to agree to get the deal across the line. Fiani objected to the deal all along but was constrained from talking publicly. Infamously, US billionaire Samuel Heyman overslept and, reportedly, faxed his acceptances for his 4.9 per cent stake in Qantas a few hours too late. In the end, APA had acceptances from only 45.6 per cent of shareholders and because of this, Fiani's no vote was seen as crucial to the failure of the deal.

The writing was on the wall for Fiani and his days with UBS were numbered. There was a collective drawing of breath as finance professionals imagined the firing squad lining up to take aim. Needless to say, Fiani left a short time after the vote. For all the talk of 'Chinese walls' between related companies, the true reason for Fiani leaving — whether he walked or was encouraged to leave — has yet to emerge. But I'm sure you can guess at how uncomfortable Fiani's position must have become.

Note: *Chinese walls* are the imaginary but legally binding barriers separating related investment businesses to prevent the sharing of market-sensitive information so as to avoid any potential conflict of interest and breaches of the law.

In the event, the global financial crisis quickly followed the collapse of the deal and, soon, what became starkly apparent was that the APA consortium and the banks financing the deal had had the luckiest of escapes. Share prices dived, the cost of debt went through the roof and Allco, which would have owned close to 30 per cent of Qantas, went bust, unable to finance its already heavy debt burden. (To underline how bad the operating environment for airlines had become, in early 2009 Qantas shed 1,750 staff in a bid to cut costs.)

The postscript to the story is that Paul Fiani went on to set up his own successful fund management company, Integrity Investments. The name says it all and sums up Fiani's investing philosophy. The episode is just one example of the power of fund managers to influence. This story is also an example of an experienced fund manager leaving a large fund to set up his own boutique shop, driven by a desire to do his own thing.

Chapter 11

Looking At Your Options: Taking Advice or Going It Alone

. . . .

In This Chapter

▶ Working out if you need advice

▶ Dealing directly with fund managers

▶ Using a managed fund broker

▶ Taking advice from a financial planner

. . . .

A s with all investing, you have choices as to how to go about investing money in managed funds. You can make use of an adviser, typically a financial planner or a stockbroker, or you can invest yourself, either direct to the fund manager or via a specialised managed funds broker.

Figuring out how you should invest, by either using a financial planner or doing it yourself, should be more than just a result of trial and error. How much time, money, experience and investing confidence you have all play a part in making the right choice. The complexity of your financial situation may also determine how you deal with your money. Generally, the more complex your affairs, for example, when family trusts, self-managed super funds or business ownership are involved, the more likely that professional advice is appropriate.

You'll find occasions, such as investing on behalf of a grandchild or saving to buy a house, when taking a DIY approach may be right. With a little planning and careful research you can end up with the investments you want and you can save money on fees, if you know how. This chapter explains the benefits and pitfalls of all the choices you have over how to go about investing in managed funds, and how and where to use each of them.

Examining the Best Route for You

Deciding how to go about putting money into a managed fund can be similar to the way people like to travel. Choosing the convenience of booking a tour where accommodation and the like is all laid on is one option. Another is independent travel. Researching your trip, booking accommodation and flights online and arranging your own sightseeing is part of the fun for many.

Investing in managed funds offers similar options — using a professional or going it alone. Both methods have their pluses and minuses. Much of the choice boils down to how much confidence you have as an investor and, also, how complex your finances may be.

Looking at your options

You can choose from three main ways to invest in managed funds, with different levels of service from each and, of course, different levels of fees:

✔ **Fund manager:** You can deal directly with a fund manager. Investors can call the office or visit the manager's website and deal direct. If you can work out what fund you want and you're happy with the manager, this is a good option.

✔ **Managed fund broker:** Most of these brokers generally offer a rebate of some of the fees charged on managed funds. Usually, managed fund brokers rebate the contribution fees — which can be anywhere up to 4 per cent or more of your investment — charged by fund managers. A great option if you want to invest yourself and are looking for the lowest fees.

✔ **Financial planner:** The bulk of managed funds are sold through financial planners. The industry is set up to make it easy and rewarding for financial planners to sell managed funds. A great option if you need help understanding what funds suit your circumstances. Expect to pay for the service though.

 You can always mix and match the way you invest. For example, you might want to use a financial planner to help you set up your superannuation arrangements. For your investments outside of super, you may want to take a more hands-on approach to reduce costs. You may even want to pay an hourly rate to a financial planner to draw up a plan for you and then go off and do the transactions yourself to save money.

Getting what you pay for

Whichever way you decide to put your money into managed funds, you generally get what you pay for. Table 11-1 shows the main differences between going direct to the fund manager, using a direct broker or using a financial planner.

Table 11-1	Comparing the Different Investment Avenues		
Feature	*Fund Manager*	*Direct Broker*	*Financial Planner*
Financial advice	No	No	Yes
Contribution fee rebate	Depends on the fund manager	Yes, generally rebated in full	No, unless a rebate is negotiated
Ongoing commissions	Yes	Yes, some brokers rebate a percentage	Yes
Fee for service	No	No	Yes, unless commissions received from fund manager
Managed fund research	Generally no	Yes, Morningstar and Standard & Poor's are the more popular providers	Yes, a range of research is available to financial planners
Choice of funds	Limited to manager's funds or menu of funds available on its administration platform	Yes, typically between 1,000 and 3,000 funds	Yes, but may be limited by what has been approved by the planner; perhaps 500-plus funds

Buying a luxury car doesn't always mean great after-sales service. The same goes with using a professional for financial advice. To my mind, half the value in using a professional is the initial advice. The other half is the service you receive after you've made your investments. If you're not getting after-sales service, you're probably not getting value for money.

Dealing with a stockbroker

Many full-service stockbrokers also provide access to managed funds. A full-service broker is one that provides advice as well as share-trading services — usually over the phone, not online! Some stockbrokers can be a bit touchy about clients using managed funds. They believe their stock recommendations can outperform fund managers, so why use managed funds? Some stockbrokers do better than many fund managers, whereas others can be mediocre, to say the least.

In my experience, some stockbrokers don't even know how to fill in a managed fund application form. I'll be giving them a copy of this book! Many stockbrokers, however, take a more holistic view of their clients' investments and recommend clients have a portion in shares, some in cash and the rest in managed funds. Managing risk is easier with this type of portfolio; the stockbroker can also potentially give better advice because they have a full view of the portfolio.

Dealing Directly with Your Fund Manager

Developing a relationship with a fund manager may be a stretch of the imagination. Big fund managers are like banks in that they have thousands of customers, and investors talk to people in call centres. Dealing with them can seem a little impersonal. The biggest challenge can be finding a fund manager that you like in the first place. Refer to Chapter 10 for more on selecting a fund manager. Service from a fund manager can make or break a relationship with investors, perhaps even more so than the performance of its funds.

Dealing direct can work well

Dealing direct saves fund managers money so they can market their products and services directly to investors and cut out the intermediary (the financial planner). But, because financial planners play an important part in selling managed funds, fund managers have to be careful not to get planners offside. If you do go direct to a fund manager, knowing which one to deal with is half the battle. Once you've decided that, you need to get the right information from the manager:

✔ **Access the website.** Visiting the fund manager's website, you should be able to find out about the fund manager, the funds on offer, costs, application forms, fund updates and performance figures.

✔ **Call up the call centre.** Giving the fund manager a call is an excellent way of assessing the level of service you're likely to receive if you decide to use that fund manager. Ask for a product disclosure statement (PDS) to be sent to you and also ask about the policy on fee rebates.

Not all fund managers want your money, especially if you have only a little to invest. Some managers prefer to take big chunks of money from a few large investors. For them, managing $1 million from one investor is a lot more cost-effective than, say, managing 100 investors with $10,000 each. These fund managers are after what is called the *wholesale* money. Refer to Chapter 3 for more on wholesale investing.

Wholesale managed funds generally have much lower ongoing management fees. To get access to wholesale fund managers, use the administrative platforms offered by some of the big fund managers such as Colonial First State, BT and Perpetual. Going direct to a wholesale fund manager generally means stumping up $500,000 just to get through the door. Platforms let you invest from as little as $2,000. RaboDirect has a limited choice of wholesale funds from $250 — check out the website at www.rabodirect. com.au. Chapter 17 explains more about platforms and other administrative structures such as wraps and master trusts.

Making sure you understand the costs

Fund managers are obliged to disclose all the fees of a managed fund, whether or not you invest direct. Fees don't vary, regardless of the investment route taken. Investors are likely to have to pay an entry fee of up to 4 per cent of the initial amount invested, as well as ongoing commissions of around 0.3 per cent per annum on the value of the investment.

Cutting out the middleman, such as a financial planner, doesn't mean you won't pay the ongoing commission. Sounds odd, certainly, but these commissions are usually built into a fund's ongoing management costs and are difficult for fund managers to cut out. So, lucky old fund managers — they end up keeping the fees.

Investors may be able to negotiate a rebate of some or all of the commission-type fees, typically the contribution fee and the ongoing trail fee:

✔ **Contribution, or upfront, fee:** Some fund managers are happy to rebate the 4 per cent upfront fee. The manager either doesn't charge the fee or rebates it as additional units. Either way, the investor should not be out of pocket. So $100 initially invested stays as $100. You may have to ask for this fee to be waived or rebated.

✔ **Ongoing commissions:** Investors are unlikely to avoid this fee of usually 0.3 per cent per annum of the value of the investments. Investors should certainly ask for a rebate but most fund managers aren't set up to make a rebate.

Fund managers are legally allowed to rebate commissions only to entities that have an Australian Financial Services Licence (AFSL); that's to say, financial planners, stockbrokers and managed fund brokers. Legal ways around this exist, such as waiving fees, but fund managers can be hamstrung when it comes to giving rebates to individual investors.

Investing through a Managed Fund Broker

If you can't negotiate rebates on fees with your fund manager, then the next best option is to use a managed fund broker. Managed fund brokers, sometimes known as *discount brokers* or *direct brokers*, are the industry's best-kept secret. They're only barely tolerated by the financial planning community. But, for investors looking to save costs when investing, managed fund brokers are ideally set up to help investors.

Finding out what services are offered

Fund brokers account for only a small percentage of the managed funds sold in Australia, but investors and fund managers alike can't ignore them. Fund brokers generally offer the following services:

✔ **Choice of managed funds:** Investors can peruse a range of managed funds from a number of different fund managers. Comparison tables allow investors to rank funds by performance, fees, size of fund and research star rating. (Refer to Chapter 8 for more on research and ratings agencies and Chapter 9 for the lowdown on performance.)

✔ **Fee rebates:** Fund brokers rebate most or all of the upfront or contribution fees and some brokers rebate a portion of the ongoing fees. (Check out Chapter 5 for more on fees.)

✔ **Fund research:** Most fund brokers offer research from Standard & Poor's and/or Morningstar Australia. Research is provided free.

✔ **Newsletters:** Fund brokers provide subscribers with regular updates on new funds, market commentary and other investing articles, such as on superannuation.

Managed fund brokers don't give advice. Most are not licensed to give advice. Fund brokers provide a range of tools to help investors find and compare funds. But, essentially, investors are left to their own devices when it comes to selecting investments.

Direct brokers are paid by fund managers to advertise their funds but most brokers do not disclose this. Although a fund manager doesn't pay to have its fund listed on a direct broker's website, it does pay to have the fund included in email or printed newsletters. A managed fund being promoted by a fund broker should never be taken as a recommendation.

Reducing your costs

Investors can reduce their costs by using direct fund brokers. In fact, that is their reason for being — to rebate as much as possible of the fees and keep enough to make a decent living, as follows:

✔ **Fee rebates:** Fund brokers rebate the entry or upfront fees charged on managed funds. The rebate is done in agreement with the fund managers.

✔ **Ongoing or trail commission rebates:** A few brokers reduce the amount of ongoing commissions by offering a rebate of some of the fees.

Finding a fund broker

Managed fund brokers run most of their business online. A search for managed fund brokers on the web throws up a number to choose from. The two largest online stockbrokers in Australia, CommSec and E*Trade Australia, both offer direct managed fund businesses. However, the services are quite different. CommSec's service is fairly straightforward — you request or download a PDS, fill in the application form and send it to the fund manager with your money. E*Trade's service is a little more complicated — you sign up for an account and effectively trade your managed funds online through E*Trade's service.

Table 11-2 shows the main managed fund brokers in the market.

Table 11-2	Major Managed Fund Brokers in Australia				
Fund Broker	**Research**	**Entry Fee Rebate**	**Ongoing Fee Rebate**	**Number of Funds**	**Ultimate Parent**
CommSec Direct Funds www.commsec.com.au	Morningstar	100%	No	1,000+	Commonwealth Bank of Australia
InvestSMART www.investsmart.com.au	Morningstar and Standard & Poor's	100%	50% of trail in excess of $300 p.a.	2,000+	Fairfax Media
2020 DirectInvest www.2020direct invest.com.au	Morningstar and Standard & Poor's	100%	No	2,000+	Independent
E*Trade Australia www.etrade.com.au	None	Nil fee	No — 0.66% p.a. fee	500+	ANZ Bank
Funds Focus www.fundsfocus.com.au	None	100%	100% of trail in excess of $400 p.a.	100+	Independent
RaboDirect www.rabodirect.com.au	Morningstar	Nil fee but 0.75% brokerage fee, not rebated	No	65+	RaboBank
Westpac Online www.westpac.com.au	Morningstar	100%	No	950	Westpac Banking Corporation

E*Trade and RaboDirect offer online investing in managed funds so you don't need to fill in forms every time you want to buy and sell. However, to offer this service, the managed funds are not directly owned by the investor but by E*Trade or RaboDirect on behalf of the investor. Therefore, you usually can't transfer your funds to another provider, if you want to. Not unless you sell your investments first, potentially triggering capital gains tax liabilities.

Using Financial Planners and Advisers

Financial planners sell the bulk of retail investment in managed funds in Australia. The fund managers have geared up their businesses to support financial planners. Commissions and fees are skewed to rewarding the financial planners for recommending managed funds. To find out how commission payments are changing, flick back to Chapter 5.

Making the decision to seek advice

My advice is, if in doubt, seek advice. The great thing about taking advice is that you can always choose to ignore it. You may end up paying some money for advice you don't use but at least you've explored the option.

Investing can be complex, with different structures such as superannuation and pensions, as well as the vast range of funds available. Finding out what investments are right for you, as well as the tax consequences of investing, can be a challenge. Seeking advice can help you cut through all the options.

Fund managers provide a lot of support to financial planners, such as educational and marketing material. Golf days and conferences in exotic locations are a part of the relationship between fund managers and financial planners. Although these exercises may not persuade a financial planner to recommend a particular product, investors need to be aware of these links.

Working out what service you need

Not all planners are created equal. Different types of planners include:

- **Bank or insurance company planners:** Typically employed by banks such as the Commonwealth Bank of Australia or insurance companies such as AMP. Planners may be paid a mix of salary and commission, and offer advice on superannuation, managed funds and insurance. These planners typically only recommend products and funds run by the organisation they work for.

- **Group-affiliated planners:** Work independently but are part of a larger group that provides administration, legal and compliance support to the planners. The group also provides the licence necessary for the planners to operate. The group may be independent or attached to one of the larger banks or insurance companies. These planners may have a bias towards the products recommended by their group.

✔ **Independents:** These planners run their own businesses and are not tied to any particular planning group, bank or insurance company. They have their own licences and can choose which administration platforms or products to use.

Finding a financial planner

You can find a financial planner in a number of different ways:

✔ **Financial Planning Association (FPA):** The FPA website at www.fpa.asn.au has a Find a Planner feature to help search for a planner in your area. When using a planner, make sure that she is a member of the FPA, as the organisation sets minimum standards of education, operation and ethics.

✔ **Banks:** All the major banks in Australia have in-house planners to assist their clients. Pop in to your local branch for an initial chat with the planner.

✔ **Referral:** The best place to start when looking for a financial planner is friends and family. A referral from someone who has used a particular planner can be invaluable.

Don't be afraid to give the financial planner a hard time when you first meet with him. Have a range of questions in front of you to find out how he works, how he's set up, what products he uses, who owns the business and what fees are charged. Also explore the fee-for-service options, where you pay a set fee for the advice and aren't charged commissions by the fund manager that are usually paid to financial planners.

Chapter 12

Filling In the Forms

Managed fund investors must deal with at least three documents before they can invest. The first document is the product disclosure statement (PDS); the second is the application form; and the third is the financial services guide (FSG). Unfortunately, you can't get around the forms. Although fund managers would love to get hold of your money as easily as possible, they must follow certain rules when collecting personal information and, ultimately, your money. The PDS also covers who can and can't invest in the product. Rounding out the application process is what is known as anti-money laundering.

In this chapter, I cover all three of these forms, including how to complete them and make that first transaction, and how anti-money laundering measures affect your investment in managed funds. I also look into taking out investments on behalf of children, which can be tricky.

Getting Your Head around the Product Disclosure Statement

The term 'product disclosure statement' doesn't exactly roll off the tongue. At first glance, you'd be forgiven for thinking that legislators dreamed it up solely to baffle investors. And perhaps they achieved their aim! Thankfully, the law acknowledges that sounding it out is a mouthful and allows the industry to shorten it to PDS, also adding to the financial services industry's love of abbreviations.

The PDS is a legal document that tells investors what they need to know about a company's managed funds. Whenever an investor wishes to invest in a managed fund, whether through an adviser or direct with the fund manager, she must be given a PDS. One of the main reasons people lose money in managed funds, apart from the funds going down in value, of course, is that they don't really know what they're getting themselves into. Investors need to understand what product they're buying, and the PDS should cover most of the information they need.

The rules say that fund managers must issue a PDS if they sell funds to the general public, so you'll get one whether you want it or not. A PDS is a comprehensive guide to any financial product a fund is selling; in this case, managed funds. This section explains what a PDS is and how to not throw your hands up in horror when faced with one. The law says every part of a PDS is important — and I'm not going to disagree with the law — but certain sections need extra attention and I set these out.

You shouldn't need a PhD to read a PDS

A product disclosure statement is like a property inspection report and an estate agent's marketing material all rolled into one. The inspection report tells you of all the nasties lurking beneath the floorboards and the estate agent tells you how wonderful the house is. The PDS, however, is not an independent document. The fund manager puts the PDS together but follows strict rules on when one must be issued, and what can and can't be included in the document.

A product disclosure statement should be straightforward. Any reasonable person reading a PDS should be able to understand what's being said. A large amount of information needs to go into one of these documents and the trick is keeping it simple. Over the years, fund managers have grown wise to investors' complaints and have ditched the jargon. Most PDSs are now much easier to read, although some PDSs may as well have been written in another language for all the sense they make. Fortunately, these horror PDSs are few and far between.

The purpose of a PDS

A PDS is designed to give potential investors all the information they reasonably need to make a decision about an investment. A PDS covers a range of subjects, from legal information to what the fund is about and how you can make a complaint if you're unhappy with the fund manager.

Fund managers also use the PDS as a chance to roll out some marketing. The fund manager uses the PDS to showcase itself and the work it does but must be able to back up any claims it makes. A PDS should contain the following information:

- ✔ **Benefits and risks:** As much as fund managers love to tell you all the good news about their funds, they also have to point out that you might lose money.

- ✔ **Commissions:** All commission payments to financial advisers or brokers must be disclosed. Some of these fees are openly disclosed, such as the typical 4 per cent fee paid on buying a fund. Other fees, such as ongoing trail commissions, are usually included in the annual management fees.

- ✔ **Complaints procedures:** Aggrieved investors should know who to complain to if they're unhappy with the fund manager. If the fund manager can't sort out the problem, then the Financial Ombudsman Service is the next step. For more on complaints, see Chapter 20.

- ✔ **Fees:** If investors are to complain about anything, fees are at the top of the list. A PDS must set out all fees and also give examples of how fees work in practice.

- ✔ **Legal requirements:** Sets out which company does what when managing the money and who looks after the funds when they're invested. Refer to Chapter 3 for more on the structure of managed funds.

- ✔ **Product details:** Provides a detailed run-through of the managed fund or funds that are being sold in the PDS. More detail on what must be included is covered in the section 'Too much information! A typical PDS layout' later in this chapter.

Investors can ask for information from the fund manager that may not be in the PDS. However, the fund manager is only obliged to provide information that is already publicly available and can charge for providing additional information.

A PDS does not need to be submitted to the financial watchdog, the Australian Securities and Investments Commission (ASIC). Only if the investment is to be listed on the Australian Securities Exchange (ASX) does ASIC need to see a copy of the PDS. Even if a PDS is submitted, ASIC is at pains to stress it does not recommend or guarantee any products.

Superannuation PDSs

A product disclosure statement that promotes a superannuation fund has the same information as a PDS for a standard managed fund, plus a bit more. The PDS includes information on insurance as well as the services offered by the fund to its members. The main additional elements found in superannuation PDSs include:

✔ **Insurance:** As a major part of superannuation, information covers death and disability benefits as well as insurance premiums.

✔ **Investment strategies:** Again, strategies are an integral part of superannuation funds. Investors usually have standard options based on an investor's risk profile, be that conservative or aggressive, for example. A menu of funds an investor can mix and match their money across may also be offered.

Superannuation funds have a different structure than that of managed funds in order to comply with superannuation law. Super PDSs have more information about their role as trustees in managing the investments. For more on superannuation, refer to Chapter 3.

Shortening super PDSs

Providers of superannuation funds are now required to produce what is known as a *short-form* PDS. At the time of writing, providers have a transition period until June 2012, by which time they must comply with the changes. So what has changed? In theory, it should be simpler, substantially shorter and make it easier to make investment decisions.

The size of the new superannuation PDS is limited to 8 pages rather than the usual 80-plus. Standard headings that need to be in the new-style PDS include:

✔ About the fund

✔ How super works

✔ Benefits of investing

✔ Risks of super

✔ How your money is invested

✔ Fees and costs

✔ How super is taxed

✔ Insurance in super, if applicable

✔ How to open an account

Another key part of the new PDS is that providers must give easier-to-understand labelling of the investment options available. The idea is to make it easier for super fund members to understand the key characteristics of different funds. Comparing funds should be simpler with the use of labels such as 'balanced', 'conservative' or 'growth'. The new PDSs should also make it straightforward for super fund members to compare investment performance.

Superannuation funds offered by employers usually have a financial planning contact if investors need advice. If unsure of what to do, use this contact — you're paying for the service! Industry funds can't offer advice unless they're specifically licensed to give advice.

Too much information! A typical PDS layout

As always, the law governs what goes into a PDS. Fund managers generally add a few nice photos and other feel-good marketing messages to soften the blow of having to include the legal stuff.

The rules say that PDSs must be up to date. But chances are a PDS is going to be out of date as soon as it's published. For example, any information on performance numbers, where a fund invests its money and in what proportions, dates quicker than fish left in the sun.

Keeping the PDS fresh and relevant means fund managers are allowed to publish the PDS as one document or to split it into two or three different documents. Splitting out the information makes sense. One document can contain the information that remains the same for a while — most of the legal stuff — and other documents can contain information that needs regular updating — the managed fund information. PDSs can run into a hundred pages or more in length, so splitting the PDS keeps the cost down for the fund manager.

If the manager is publishing a single PDS, then documents 1 and 2 here will be together:

✔ **Document 1:** This first section deals with all the information that is fixed and unlikely to change anytime soon. So here you find the legal information, the fees and costs, any tax consequences that need to be considered, terms and conditions and the like. It may also include the application form, direct debit forms and so on.

✔ **Document 2:** Generally includes a menu of funds that the manager is offering. As a menu in a restaurant tells you the name of the dish and the main ingredients, so too does a managed funds menu. Each fund usually has a page showing what the fund invests in, possibly the name of the actual fund manager running it, along with a bio (though this is rare), the related fees and costs, and possibly performance numbers.

✔ **Supplementary PDS:** Sometimes changes to important information in a PDS can't be avoided. For example, the law might change, especially with superannuation funds, and that may affect the tax situation of a fund or an investor. Rather than rewrite the whole PDS, a supplementary PDS can be issued, noting the changes and saying which sections of the original PDS are affected.

When a supplementary PDS is issued it must state that it is a supplementary PDS, must be read in conjunction with the PDS it is supplementing, and must identify the name and date of that PDS.

If an investor makes a managed fund application using an out-of-date PDS, the issuer must carry out one of the following actions:

✔ Repay the money invested.

✔ Give the investor a supplementary PDS and the opportunity to withdraw his application.

✔ Still sell the managed fund to the investor but give him a supplementary PDS, as well as the opportunity to cancel the application and be repaid.

If the fund manager does not give the investor one of these options, the investor has the right to cancel his investment and have his money refunded.

Discovering the main parts of a PDS

A PDS has about five or six standard parts that can be split across one, two or even more documents. More complex PDSs selling a range of different investments and services, including cash deposits, for example, may have up to ten parts.

Laying out legal information and disclaimers

The first items you're likely to come across in the PDS are the legal points, invariably in small print. The PDS does not usually have a section called 'Legal information' or the like but it is easy to find. Usually this information is in the small print on the inside front cover. This section is important because it tells you who is actually managing the money. It includes:

✔ **Name and date:** Usually found on the front cover, the PDS must state the fund's name, such as the Perennial Tactical Income Trust, the date the PDS was issued and the name of the issuer, usually the name of the fund manager. The number of parts (documents) the PDS has must also be noted.

✓ **Legal information:** The important pieces of information are who the issuer is (usually the fund manager or a related company) — this information is usually stated on the front cover as well — its Australian Financial Services licence number and its tax number or Australian Business Number (ABN). Other information is what the responsible entity for the fund or funds is. The responsible entity makes sure the fund is administered properly and in accordance with the law. For more on responsible entities, refer to Chapter 3.

✓ **Validity:** The PDS also says who can use the PDS. Usually a PDS is only valid if received by a person in Australia. This statement doesn't mean you have to be a resident; it just means you have to physically be in Australia to receive the PDS — it's the law! You can't be overseas and download a PDS, which you then use to invest, even if you are Australian.

✓ **Disclaimers:** Where would any legal document be without a get-out clause! Quite rightly, PDSs are not a recommendation for a managed fund and a PDS must say this. A licensed financial adviser can only make a recommendation after she's found out about your personal financial situation. A quick chat at a barbeque doesn't count though! Fund managers don't make recommendations and they encourage investors to take advice before investing.

The information contained in a PDS is only ever general information and does not take individual investors' personal circumstances into account. If in any doubt, take advice from a qualified professional.

Introducing the fund manager

The next section of the PDS typically introduces the fund manager, giving a summary of the main points an investor needs to know about, all wrapped up in a little marketing spin. Here you find:

✓ **Fund manager information:** After setting out legally what the company is, the fund manager then tells investors what it does but without all the legal jargon.

✓ **Marketing:** Inevitably the fund manager tells you why you should choose it to manage your money and why it's different from its competitors.

✓ **Summary:** A good PDS has a brief summary of the main points of interest, including the minimum amount that can be invested in a fund, minimum ongoing contributions and minimum withdrawals, if any (you can usually withdraw all your money if you want, but not, say, $100 at a time, which is expensive to administer). The summary also gives an overview of the fees, such as the entry fee, management cost per annum and transaction costs. Transaction costs are usually the *buy–sell* *spread*, or the percentage difference in price that you buy a fund and sell a fund, and are typically about 0.3 per cent — refer to Chapter 5 for more on costs.

✔ **The cooling-off period:** Sometimes known as *buyer's remorse*, the *cooling-off period* is how long an investor is given to go back to a fund manager after making his investment and say he's changed his mind and wants his money back without incurring any costs. Typically, the period is 14 days after the investment is made.

Understanding risk

All PDSs must explain what risk is and what types of risk are involved in the fund. Most PDSs I've seen go through every risk that every academic has ever identified in relation to investing. In this section PDSs typically include:

✔ **A basic explanation of the concept of risk:** Risk comes with any investment and investors need to feel comfortable with taking on risk that matches their objectives.

✔ **Information about asset classes:** The PDS sets out which asset classes, such as cash, shares, property or bonds, are included in the fund and should explain that each class carries a different level of risk. Each asset class also has a different investment timeframe to help smooth out the levels of risk. The riskier the investment, the longer you need to hold it for. For more on risk and asset classes, refer to Chapter 6.

✔ **Types of risk:** All sorts of risk can threaten your investments, such as movements in the stock market (market risk) or the fund manager not doing a decent job (management risk). Another risk is that you may not be able to sell your managed fund when you need to (liquidity risk) and, of course, each asset class carries its own level of risk. Refer to Chapter 6 for a full list of risks.

Potentially, investment involves a lot of risk! Don't be put off by the long list of potential risks included in a PDS. All managed funds have some risk but most are impacted only by some of the risks mentioned.

Setting out the fees and costs

Knowing what fees and costs an investor is likely to pay is one of the more important parts of the PDS. Refer to Chapter 5 for more on fees and costs.

The fees and costs section typically starts with a consumer warning that paying too much for a managed fund can make a big difference to investment returns over a long period. The warning encourages investors to think about what they're paying for and suggests negotiating better rates where possible.

Here are the fees and costs this section usually covers:

- **Adviser fees:** The PDS should set out in detail the money it pays to professional financial advisers that investors may use. These fees include the contribution fees and what's called *adviser trail fees*, or ongoing fees paid to advisers. Adviser trail fees can be anywhere between zero and 0.50 per cent or more per annum.

- **Adviser service fee:** Investors may also negotiate an additional fee with the financial planner, which can be deducted from the investments and paid to the adviser.

- **Management fees:** The annual costs of managing the investments are quoted as a percentage of the money invested. These fees are usually between 0.50 per cent and 2.50 per cent per annum.

- **Transaction fees:** These are typically paid when moving money into and out of a fund. The fees include:

  - Contribution fees, also known as entry fees, which can be up to 4 per cent each time you put money into a fund

  - Buy–sell spread, the difference between the buy price and the sell price of a fund (for example, if the buy price is $1.002 per unit and the sell price $0.998 per unit, the spread is 0.4 per cent), is money kept by the fund manager to pay for the transaction costs

  - Other transaction fees, including establishment fees, withdrawal or exit fees for taking money out of a fund, switching fees for transferring money from one fund to another and termination fees; fund managers rarely charge any of these fees but list them anyway.

- **Other fees:** These can include a performance fee. This fee is usually charged as a percentage of money the fund manager makes over and above a previously set return. So, if the manager says it aims to make 15 per cent per annum and actually achieves 20 per cent, the performance fee is charged on the difference between the target return of 15 per cent and the actual of 20 per cent, so 5 per cent. Performance fees can be anywhere up to 20 per cent of the overperformance.

A PDS must give an example of how the fund's main fees work in practice. For example, if an investor were to invest $50,000, how do the standard fees impact the investment? The example usually presented is the difference between annual management fees of 1 per cent and 2 per cent over 30 years. Your investment returns can be reduced by up to 20 per cent over the period by paying the higher rate (for example, from $100,000 to $80,000).

Setting up an account and managing your money

The next section of a PDS explains how investors can set up an account, how to manage their account once invested and how to transfer money into and out of managed funds. The information provided in this section includes:

- ✔ **Access:** After they've invested, investors may be able to access their account information securely online. Investors may even be able to transact online, such as withdrawing money or changing funds.

- ✔ **Contact:** Shows the various ways investors can deal with a fund manager, such as through the internet and email, by fax, phone or by mail.

- ✔ **Income, or distributions:** Most funds pay an income to investors called a distribution. Income can either be reinvested in additional units in the fund or credited to the investor's bank account. You need to nominate what you want to do with your distributions.

- ✔ **Payment:** Fund managers can receive investors' monies in a number of ways, from a simple cheque to convenient BPAY, direct debit or electronic funds transfer (EFT) from a bank account.

- ✔ **Reporting:** Sets out when investors can expect regular reports, including the annual report, from the fund manager.

Investors electing to reinvest their fund distributions in additional units may still be liable for tax on those distributions. Timing when you invest in a fund is also important. A distribution sees the price of the fund go down by the amount of the distribution. Investing just before a distribution is effectively the same as having a portion of your investment returned. There may also be tax implications on that distribution — refer to Chapter 5 for more on tax and distributions.

Listing other information

The PDS should also cover some, if not all, of the following:

- ✔ **Auto-rebalancing:** Some fund managers offer a service to rebalance your portfolio. Like rebalancing the wheels on a car to keep it driving straight, rebalancing a portfolio keeps your investment profile on track. For more on rebalancing your portfolio, see Chapter 13.

- ✔ **Borrowing in funds:** The PDS states if the managed funds are allowed to borrow to invest. A fund borrows, or gears, so as to magnify returns. Borrowing also increases the risk and can magnify losses as well, which is why a fund needs to declare whether it borrows or not. See Chapter 18 for more on geared funds.

✔ **Checklist:** Helps you to make sure you've completed all the boxes and included all the relevant information.

✔ **Ethical or environmental investing:** Fund managers usually say whether or not they take ethical or other standards into account when investing. For example, some funds only invest in clean fuel companies rather than coalmines, or don't invest in gaming or tobacco stocks. See Chapter 15 for more on ethical investing.

✔ **Fund constitution:** Every managed fund has a constitution that sets out how the fund is managed and the investor's rights as a unit holder. These stock standard documents aren't usually included in the PDS, but the PDS should state how investors can get hold of the constitution.

✔ **Personal information:** Explains how investors' personal information is stored and used. Fund managers also include a section about using your information to tell you about other products; in other words, marketing.

✔ **Taxation:** The PDS provides general pointers when it comes to tax. The fund manager doesn't know an investor's financial position so can't be specific when it comes to tax, as every investor is different.

✔ **Terms and conditions:** Sets out the terms by which you use the services of the fund manager, how much the fund manager is liable for if you suffer a loss from using the service, and your rights and responsibilities as an investor.

✔ **Transactions:** Sets out how transactions are processed and the cut-off times for them to be processed the same day. Cut-off is usually 3 pm each business day. Transactions such as buying, selling or switching units use the unit price set that day. After 3 pm the unit price used is calculated the following day.

✔ **Unit pricing:** A managed fund issues units (not shares) and the price of each unit represents an equal portion of the value of the fund. This part of the PDS explains how the unit prices are calculated. For more on pricing managed funds see Chapter 13.

Let the fund manager know as soon as possible if you don't want to be inundated with marketing material after you've signed up. Some fund managers assume you don't want to be marketed to unless you tell them but these managers are in the minority.

Who Can and Can't Invest

Most people can invest in a managed fund, as can various legal entities such as superannuation funds, charities, companies and family trusts, among others. The requirements of a company when completing the application form are different from those of an individual. Investing for children or minors also has certain rules, and overseas investors have to jump through hoops to get their applications approved.

Individuals and entities

You can invest in a managed fund by a range of methods, as an individual investor or by using a particular legal structure such as a family trust or company. The application form caters for all legal structures:

- ✔ **Individual:** Individuals can apply in their own names, as a joint account or as a sole trader.

- ✔ **Partnerships:** A partnership's name, country of formation, place of business and ABN must be supplied.

- ✔ **Companies:** A company's name, country of incorporation, place of business and ABN need to be provided.

- ✔ **Trusts and superannuation funds:** The full name of the trust or superannuation fund, the type of trust, country of establishment and ABN or ARSN must all be supplied on the form.

Much of the information provided in the application form is also used to meet anti-money laundering regulations. (See the section 'Anti-Money Laundering: How It Affects You' later in this chapter.)

Non-residents can invest in Australian managed funds but need to bear in mind a couple of points:

- ✔ PDSs usually stipulate that the PDS must be received by the investor in Australia. So it can't be posted to an investor overseas and neither can it be downloaded from a website while overseas.

- ✔ Funds may be obliged to withhold tax on earnings, currently at 7.5 per cent for certain countries on the Australian Taxation Office (ATO) approved list (called the Exchange of Information, or EOI, countries). If the country of residence is not on the list, then the withholding tax is 30 per cent (at the time of writing). Investors may need to complete an Australian tax return and reclaim the tax withheld as a refund. Check the ATO website for up-to-date rates at www.ato.gov.au.

Investing for children

Investing on behalf of children can be tricky, especially when it comes to tax. Some investments can't be held in the name of a minor, whereas others can. In general, managed funds don't accept investments in the name of anyone below the age of 18 years. Investing in managed funds on behalf of children is possible, however, and here I explain how.

An adult can invest on a minor's behalf and *designate* the account in the child's name. But you may need to consider tax consequences when investing on behalf of a child. Other investments, however, such as shares, can be held in a child's name. Children of any age can also be issued a tax file number (TFN) by the ATO to help manage their income and tax affairs.

Children and managed funds

Many people invest on behalf of their children or grandchildren. Most managed funds make investing on behalf of minors possible on their application forms, with some conditions, such as:

- ✔ **Through designation:** Anyone over the age of 18 years, such as a parent, grandparent, guardian, uncle, aunt or godparent, can designate to invest on behalf of a child. The person investing does so in his name and includes his own TFN. Some fund managers provide a box on the application form to include the name of the minor on whose behalf the money is being invested.

- ✔ **Through a family trust:** Family trusts have the flexibility — depending on how they're set up — to invest in many types of investments, including managed funds. Again, depending on how a trust is set up, the distribution of income from investments can be managed in the most tax-effective way for beneficiaries. For example, monies can be distributed to beneficiaries with the lowest marginal tax rates before any remainder is distributed to those with higher marginal tax rates. Check with a qualified professional for the best way to set one up.

Education savings plans

Education savings plans are specially designed as a managed investment plan to pay for school fees and the like. Parents or grandparents can set them up for a nominated child to pay education expenses. The product has some tax-smart features that allow the fund manager to claim back the tax paid on investment earnings. Plans are set up as *scholarship plans* in accordance with the relevant tax law. The manager is then entitled to obtain a special tax benefit that is passed on to the investor. The tax benefit is worth up to $30 for every $70 worth of earnings used to pay education expenses. Investors must use any money withdrawn from the fund to pay education expenses. If not, the withdrawals may not qualify for the tax benefit and the proceeds could be assessable as investment income.

For example, Steve sets up a plan for his son and contributes $20,000. Earnings from the investment over 12 months are $1,400, resulting in an education tax benefit of $600 against the tax charged on the earnings. So the total benefit available to fund Steve's son is $22,000. If Steve doesn't use the money to pay for his son's education, then he loses the tax benefit.

Some plans are set up in a similar way to master trusts (see Chapter 17). The plans offer a choice of funds from a range of fund managers across different asset types and risk levels. Plans can be started from $1,000. Some may place a limit of around $350,000 on contributions. Fees are virtually the same as standard managed funds.

The two main providers of education plans are Lifeplan at www.lifeplan. com.au (part of Australian Unity Investments) and Australian Scholarships Group at www.asg.com.au. Both are *friendly societies*, which are investment bodies set up to be owned by and for the benefit of their members, and both offer slightly different products. As always, if in doubt seek financial advice.

At the time of writing, the ATO's rules for the withdrawal of money from a fund to pay for anything other than education expenses are as follows:

- ✔ If you hold a plan for ten years or more, withdrawals are not taxable.

- ✔ If money is withdrawn within eight years, it is fully assessable for income. The amount assessed is reduced to two-thirds for a withdrawal in year nine and to one-third for a withdrawal in year ten.

Finding other investments for children

Other investing options for children include:

- ✔ **Family bonds:** Family bonds are available for children under the age of 16 years. Similar to managed funds, they allow investors to choose from a range of asset types. The difference is that, unlike managed funds, which don't pay tax on earnings (the investor does), the fund manager is taxed on earnings at 30 per cent. The investor pays no further tax as long as the investment is held for the minimum ten years.

- ✔ **Investment bonds:** Another tax-advantaged investment available for children aged between 10 and 16 years in their own names. Income bonds have a minimum term of 10 years but can be as long as 40 years.

Bonds that are available include those offered by Lifeplan at www.lifeplan. com.au, CommInsure's Investment Growth Bond at www.comminsure. com.au, OnePath's Investment Savings Bond at www.onepath.com.au (choose from the options under the Investment tab at the top — note that OnePath is the new name for the former investment division of ING, now owned by ANZ.) and IOOF's Wealth Builder at www.ioof.com.au (click on the Investments tab and then scroll down the investment products list under Wealth Accumulation).

Sealing the Deal

The application process, assuming you have all the relevant documentation, usually takes a week or so. Any more than a couple of weeks and you want to be on the phone seeing if your application got lost in the mail.

The application form is usually found at the back of the product disclosure statement. A managed fund application form generally has four main parts to collect the following information:

✔ Personal details such as name, address, contact numbers and tax file number (TFN) — if you don't provide a TFN or proof of an exemption, the fund manager is required to deduct tax from all earnings due to the investor

✔ Choice of funds and, if selecting more than one fund, how you'd like the money to be split across each fund

✔ Bank account details for a regular savings plan and the direct credit of distributions if investors decide not to reinvest income from the fund

✔ Proof of identification if investing with a manager for the first time, including forms and certified copies of identification documents

A section for financial advisers to complete is usually included, if investors choose to use one. Advisers fill in their details, mainly so they can receive the commissions on offer or to note any changes to the standard commission arrangements.

If any information, such as bank account details, name and address, is incorrect, chances are you'll receive a call from the fund manager to provide the correct details. Fail any of the ID checks and you'll be asked to send in more information. If you can't provide sufficient ID, your application won't make it past the fund manager's front door and your cheque will be returned.

Information you need before you start

Investors need to gather a certain amount of information to complete the application forms. Here's a checklist of the information you typically need:

✔ **Personal details:** This is the obvious stuff — name, date of birth, address and other contact details.

✔ **Tax file number (TFN):** You need your TFN or a letter showing why you may be exempt from providing one, such as being a not-for-profit organisation or non-resident. No TFN means the fund manager must withhold tax on any income at the highest rate.

✔ **Income or reinvest:** You need to decide whether you want to reinvest your income from a fund in more units or to take the income as cash.

✔ **Bank account details:** These details are only needed if you're making payments as part of a regular savings plan or wish to receive distributions of income from a managed fund rather than reinvest. Some funds allow for regular withdrawals of capital also.

✔ **Investment options:** Investors may wish to invest across a number of different funds with the same fund manager. The application form lists the funds available and investors need to indicate what percentage of their money they wish to invest in each fund. You need to decide beforehand what funds suit your needs. See Chapter 14 on choosing a managed fund.

✔ **Adviser service fee:** Investors using a financial planner may agree to pay the adviser an ongoing service fee. The application form may allow for the fee to be deducted from your account by the fund manager and paid direct to the planner.

✔ **Power of attorney:** If an investor is signing under a power of attorney, then a certified copy of the relevant power of attorney document must be attached.

Proving your identity is crucial to having the application accepted by the fund manager. The fund manager is obliged under anti-money laundering and counter-terrorism financing laws to make sure that investors are who they say they are. Financial planners can verify some of the documents required by the fund manager but you still need to complete some or all of the ID forms.

Investors need to provide the same identification documents anyone needs to open an Australian bank account, usually one primary document or two secondary documents:

✔ A copy of either your driver's licence or passport, known as a primary ID document

✔ Alternatively, a Centrelink card or birth certificate *and* a copy of a notice that shows your name and address, such as an electricity bill, known as secondary ID documents

All identification documents sent to the fund manager must be certified copies. This means an approved individual has seen the original document and signed the copy saying that it's a true copy. The list of approved people who can certify copies is included in the application form, such as justices of the peace, post office workers, accountants, doctors and the like.

Transferring your money

After your application is completed and approved, transferring money across to a fund manager is straightforward. Fund managers have made it as easy as possible for you to give them your money. The typical methods available are:

- ✔ **BPAY:** Funds can be transferred from your bank account using this method.

- ✔ **Cheque:** The good old-fashioned cheque is still very much in fashion with fund managers.

- ✔ **Direct debit:** Investors can set up a direct debit for regular payments such as a monthly savings plan. The application form contains a direct debit authorisation form that you need to complete.

- ✔ **Electronic funds transfer (EFT):** The fund manager needs to give you its bank account details before you can make an electronic funds transfer from your own bank account.

Knowing What Else to Look Out For

Reading product disclosure statements and dealing with application forms can seem overwhelming given the amount of information included. Some PDSs contain only one fund. Other PDSs are split into two parts and contain hundreds of different funds, such as the Colonial First State FirstChoice or Perpetual WealthFocus Investments.

On top of the multitude of funds on offer in the PDS, the fund manager may also cram other services, as well as other legal documents, into the PDS. The amount of information needn't be overwhelming if you know what else to look out for.

Look to open up an account with any financial services company and your letterbox will groan under the weight of documents the law insists you are sent. Apart from the marketing documents and application forms, the other document that must be sent is a financial services guide, or FSG. And this is *before* you even become a client. The FSG is one of the more important documents a fund manager may include in the PDS.

The law stipulates that the financial services guide must be sent out to each new prospective retail client, as well as when it must be sent and what information must be included. The FSG sets out the services the fund manager offers, the costs and who to complain to if something goes wrong. Some managed fund product disclosure statements may include the FSG as part of the PDS. If not, you should be given the FSG at the time you are given the PDS and certainly before you invest. For more on the definition of a retail client, refer to Chapter 3.

The difference between the *financial services guide* and a product disclosure statement is that the FSG tells investors what *service* they'll be getting, whereas a PDS tells investors what *product* they're buying. The FSG is meant to give retail clients enough information to decide whether or not to use whatever company is providing the managed fund.

The information that must be in the FSG includes:

- **Provider:** The name and contact details of the entity providing the financial service

- **Services:** A list of the services that may be provided to all clients, not necessarily just to you

- **Remuneration, commission and other benefits:** Information about all of the relevant commissions, fees and costs involved in providing the financial services to clients

- **Complaints:** Details of how clients can register a complaint

- **Compensation:** Outline of the arrangements in place for paying compensation to clients, such as insurance policies the entity may have to cover claims

The FSG is another way the law tries to protect the interests of investors. Needless to say, the document must be clearly written and up to date. The document is a great way to home in on the things that matter, such as fees and costs, without having to wade through pages and pages to find what you need.

ASIC, Australia's corporate watchdog, sets the rules that all financial services companies must comply with when it comes to the financial services guide.

Including other products and services

The bigger fund managers have cottoned on to the idea that the product disclosure statement can be a great way to sell other products and services. It's the equivalent of the 'do you want fries with that' school of selling more products. The two most common products you find in a PDS are margin lending (borrowing to invest) and cash services such as deposit accounts.

Both cash and margin lending services are financial products so can only be sold via a PDS. Including these products with managed funds makes sense for the fund manager. The application forms generally include a section to complete on each of these separate products and services.

Anti-Money Laundering: How It Affects You

The introduction of the anti-money laundering and counter-terrorism laws has meant a huge change to the way financial services companies look at clients. Some businesses in the financial services sector may become unwittingly involved in helping *money laundering*, when criminals use the legitimate financial system to hide their ill-gotten gains.

Anything to do with laundering the proceeds of crime to fund lavish lifestyles or finance terrorism is stern stuff. The federal government takes its international obligations seriously and the finance companies have had to invest millions to make sure they comply with the law. The body responsible for managing the anti-money laundering rules is the Australian Transactions and Reports Centre (AUSTRAC).

What does it mean for the fund manager?

Fund managers have to make sure they know who their clients are and that they report any suspicious transactions. Sounds simple but companies have had to radically change how they collect and store client information. The onus is on fund managers to make sure they're comfortable with every transaction that goes through their books. They also have to be comfortable that their clients are who they say they are.

Fund managers also have to report the following:

- Cross-border movements of cash over $10,000

- Movements of bearer-negotiable instruments if asked by police or customs

- Transactions of $10,000 or more in cash or e-currency, such as electronic funds transfers

- Suspicious matters, such as people they suspect are not who they say they are

- The fact that they are complying with the law

As you can see, the fund managers are ultimately responsible for policing their clients' transactions. For more information on anti-money laundering you can visit the federal attorney-general's website at www.ag.gov.au (scroll down the list titled Crime Prevention and Enforcement and click on Anti-Money Laundering).

What does it mean for the investor?

In practical terms, the anti-money laundering requirements mean providing detailed and verifiable information. Here are the three main types of entities typically used to open managed funds and the information they need to provide:

- **Individuals:** Must provide name, address and date of birth, and provide proof of name and proof of date of birth or residential address

- **Companies:** The full name of the company as registered by ASIC, address of the company's registered office and place of business, ACN, the name of each director, if applicable, and the name and address of any beneficial owner of the company

- **Trusts:** Full name of the trust (as per the trust deed or schedule), type of trust, country established, names of beneficiaries, whether it's an ASIC-registered company, its registered office and place of business, ACN, directors, if applicable, and names of beneficial owners

Completing the application forms for managed funds can seem a hassle. You have to give certified copies of your identification information or a financial planner must certify he has seen the original documents. But managed funds are not alone in this, as all financial products need the same information to meet the anti-money laundering requirements.

Chapter 13

Buying, Selling and Monitoring Your Investments

*B*uying and selling managed funds sounds like it could get complicated, but knowing how a fund is priced in the first place can help to make buying and selling easy as pie, if not cheap as chips. Ultimately, the market sets the value of a fund but the fund manager is the one that calculates what a managed fund's unit price is.

In talking about how a fund's price is worked out, I explain how income paid to investors by a fund, the distribution, can affect the price of the fund. Buying a fund at the wrong time before a distribution is paid could land you with an unexpected tax bill. So beware!

After you've bought a fund, making sure it stays on track is vital. Managed funds may have a reputation as set-and-forget investments but they shouldn't. Managed funds should be treated like any other investment. Keep an active interest in your funds. If a fund is performing badly, review why — if you're not happy, think about switching to another. Switching funds can be straightforward without having to sell up first. As long as both funds are either managed or administered by the same fund manager, switching is possible.

This chapter explains the practicalities of buying and selling managed funds and looks at the documentation involved, as well as how the buy and sell prices of managed funds are worked out.

Calculating the Price You Pay

Understanding how the price of a managed fund is worked out can give you a better idea of when to buy or sell managed funds. Managed funds must follow some strict rules when working out the price of a fund. But you don't need to be a maths genius to understand the process; far from it. Understanding the basics of how a fund is priced can help you make better decisions about when to buy and sell units in a managed fund.

Understanding how units are priced

Buying and selling managed funds is slightly different than say, buying or selling shares on a stock market. The price of a share on the stock market is, by and large, determined by the demand and supply for that share. If lots of people want the share and holders of the shares don't want to sell, then the price of the share goes up until sellers are tempted. This process happens in reverse when demand is low and a stock price goes down.

The way managed funds are priced is a step removed from the normal supply and demand that shares experience. The important thing to note is that the fund manager calculates the price of a managed fund. The calculation is based on the value of the underlying investments in the fund divided by the number of units on issue. So, if the fund's investments are valued at $100 million and it has 100 million units on issue to investors, the price of the managed fund is $1 per unit.

The value of a fund's investments is the starting point for setting the unit price of a fund. The value of a fund is calculated by taking the value of the investments held, subtracting the manager's costs and adding income due from the investments. The effect of costs and income on a fund is covered in more detail in the sections, 'Learning how dividends can affect price' and 'Making sense of management expenses' later in the chapter.

Issuing and redeeming units

Buying and selling units in a fund is a straightforward process that involves filling in a form either online or in print. Investors wanting to buy into a managed fund have units in the fund issued to them by the fund manager. When an investor sells, the manager redeems units in the fund, meaning that the units are cancelled.

Like a balloon being pumped up with air or deflated, the number of units expands and contracts as people buy or sell units in the fund. This buying and selling of units does not affect the price of the fund. Only a change to the value of the investments held by the fund changes the unit price.

During any particular business day, a large fund receives requests to buy and sell many thousands of units. The result may be that a fund could have greater or fewer units at the end of the day than when it started.

Valuing a managed fund's investments

Managed funds can potentially hold a wide range of investments. A fund needs to value these investments on a regular basis in order to work out the value of its own units. Investments held are generally valued as follows:

- ✔ **Cash:** The value here is the balance in the bank account.

- ✔ **Listed investments:** These are investments, such as shares or bonds, that can be bought or sold. The value is usually easy to work out as it is based on the last quoted price available from the exchange.

- ✔ **Unlisted investments:** Valuing these investments, such as direct property or shares in privately held companies, can be tricky. Funds that hold property investments like shopping malls or office towers only value these occasionally, typically every three years.

The value of the fund also takes into account what are known as *realised* and *unrealised* gains and losses. A realised gain or loss is the money made or lost on selling an investment. An unrealised gain or loss is the difference in value between what an investment was bought for and its current value.

Most managed funds that invest in listed investments value their units and set a price daily. Investors can work out an up-to-date value of their investment in a fund by multiplying the daily unit price by the number of units they have.

Managed funds that invest in direct property or other unlisted or illiquid assets rely on their assets being valued on only an occasional basis. Most funds set a daily price for the fund, taking into account any income received or due and any expenses. However, the value of the assets used in that pricing are based on values that are potentially up to three years old. Property fund managers can use some discretion when it comes to valuing buildings, but whatever number they come up with must be able to be independently verified.

How can you tell at first glance if a fund is investing directly in property or in property shares? A fund investing in listed property shares usually has the word *securities* in its name. A direct property fund usually has the word *trust* in its name. But always check the product disclosure statement!

Learning how dividends can affect price

Managed funds are likely to earn an income from some or all of the investments held. At the end of the financial year, the fund manager must gather up all of this income and distribute it to the unit holders. Distributing the income will hit the value of the managed fund.

Managed funds can receive income from their investment in a number of different ways:

- **Cash:** Money in the bank pays interest on deposits. Fund managers may hold cash as part of their investment strategy or may be waiting to buy shares.
- **Bonds:** These investments pay regular dividends or coupons, which are similar to interest payments from a bank.
- **Property:** Rental income is the main source of revenue for those managed funds holding direct investments in property.
- **Shares:** Companies pay dividends to shareholders, generally twice a year. Dividends are typically a percentage of the company's profits after the tax office has taken its cut.

Fund managers can't hold on to this income after the financial year end. When the managed fund distributes the income, it effectively takes out some of the fund's value and gives it to investors. For example, say a fund is trading at $1.00 a unit and has received income during the year equivalent to 5 cents a unit. After the year end, giving the income to the investors means the units are worth 95 cents each.

You may want to avoid buying units in a managed fund just before it pays a distribution to investors. Taking the preceding example, say you buy 10,000 units in the fund at $1.00 a unit, or $10,000 worth. The next day the fund distributes 5 cents a unit in income. You receive $500 and your units are now worth 95 cents each, or $9,500 in total. At this point you're no worse off. However, you'll now very likely have to pay tax on that $500 of income. If you're a top-rate taxpayer, you lose almost half of that income (or $232.50 at the 46.5 per cent tax rate, including the Medicare levy) to the tax office. If you had waited a day or so, you could have avoided the tax, bought 526.32 additional units and had all your money working for you in the fund from day one.

Making sense of management expenses

Management expenses, the cost of running the fund, also affect its unit price. Management expenses are shown as a percentage of the average value of a fund, such as 1.35 per cent a year. These expenses include administration costs, audit fees, legal fees and a range of other costs. For more on what makes up management expenses, refer to Chapter 5.

The calculation of the unit price of a managed fund takes into account the management fees. Although the unit price of a managed fund is usually worked out daily, the fund generally takes the money for the management expenses only once each month.

Taking a look at price spreads

A price spread is the difference between the price an investor buys units in a fund and the price an investor sells units in a fund. Price spreads are a way for fund managers to earn a little extra income or to cover their costs when investors buy and sell units. Table 13-1 sets out an example of how investors may see a fund manager quote the price of a fund.

The entry price is what you pay to get into the fund and the exit price is what the fund manager pays you when selling your fund. The difference, or spread, of 0.4 per cent in the example in Table 13-1 is what the fund manager keeps. The spread is designed to cover any costs incurred by the fund manager for administering the transaction.

The price spread can vary between funds. The spread is usually around 0.3 per cent to 0.4 per cent but can be over 1 per cent, depending on the type of fund. Funds that borrow to invest, or geared funds, typically have spreads greater than 1 per cent.

Table 13-1	Buy and Sell Prices		
XYZ Managed Fund			
Effective Date	*Entry Price*	*Exit Price*	*Spread*
29/07/2010	$0.6225	$0.6200	0.4%
28/07/2010	$0.6124	$0.6100	0.4%
27/07/2010	$0.6175	$0.6150	0.4%
26/07/2010	$0.6163	$0.6138	0.4%
25/07/2010	$0.6104	$0.6080	0.4%

Buying a Fund

As you may imagine, fund managers make it as easy as possible to get your money through the door. For most investors, buying is usually a case of filling in the forms and/or instructing an adviser to buy on your behalf.

Instructing your adviser or going direct

Using a financial planner to buy managed funds is usually the result of an ongoing dialogue between the investor and the planner. Buying managed funds through a planner should only happen after the investor has agreed to a plan of action that must be covered off in a *statement of advice*, where the main dealings between an investor and the financial planner are laid out. The investor still needs to sign the application forms for the funds, unless she has given the financial planner a limited power of attorney to sign on her behalf.

A statement of advice states that the financial planner has taken into consideration an investor's financial situation and goals. Through the statement of advice, the financial planner also recommends what investments to use, including managed funds. Investors also agree on the fees they pay the financial planners through this document.

If you don't want to use a financial planner, then you can buy managed funds direct. The obvious place to start is the fund manager. If you know what fund you want, then simply visit the fund manager's website and download the product disclosure statement (PDS) or call the contact number and have one posted. If you're unsure which fund you want, visit a managed fund broker website (refer to Chapter 12). Here you have a choice, usually of more than 1,000 managed funds, along with research to help you decide. Most managed fund brokers also offer to rebate some or all of the contribution fee (entry fee) of 4 per cent (refer to Chapters 5 and 11).

What happens when you buy?

Buying units in a managed fund is generally straightforward, and this section takes a look at the mechanisms involved. Sometimes, however, if using a master trust service that lets you invest in several different fund managers through the one product, you may want to transfer units into that service. I look at how that can be done.

Buying units in a managed fund

Say you have $10,000 to buy units in a managed fund. If you take the pricing from that shown in Table 13-1 for 29 July 2010, you can see that the entry price is 62.25 cents per unit. If you get your application in to the fund manager before 3 pm, you'll get the unit price set that day. If you don't, the entry price will be the one set the next day. Before 3 pm, your $10,000 buys $10,000 divided by 62.25 cents worth of units, or 16,064.257 units. The fund manager either gives you those units from another investor who is selling, or issues new units to you if no others are available.

Assuming that you're entitled to receive the 4 per cent contribution fee usually charged when investors buy into a fund as a rebate of additional units, your full $10,000 is invested. If you're not entitled to the rebate, then your initial investment is $9,600 and the other $400 is either kept by the fund manager or paid to a financial planner. Check out Chapters 5 and 11 for more about how to reduce your fees.

Transferring investments to a fund manager

Transferring existing investments to a fund manager is only really possible with the bigger fund managers that run master trust arrangements. These fund managers and their master trusts are the likes of Colonial First State's FirstChoice, Perpetual Investments' WealthFocus and MLC's MasterKey. A *master trust* is a single investment account giving investors access to a menu of different funds, including funds from other fund managers. For more on master trusts, see Chapter 17.

Say an investor has funds with Colonial First State's FirstChoice, which he bought through his financial planner. The planner decides to shift from using Colonial to using MLC's MasterKey. As long as MLC has the same funds (as identified by each fund's unique industry code, known as the APIR — the Asia–Pacific Investment Register) then the funds can be transferred across. *APIR codes* are a standard way of indentifying managed funds in the industry.

Transferring funds may cost you. Although fund managers do the paperwork for you to transfer the funds out, chances are they will charge you. A typical fee is around $75 a fund but this can vary. Check with the manager before you transfer.

Paperwork you can expect from your fund manager

Investors can expect to receive two sets of paperwork — one set of papers with each transaction and another set at least once a year, usually an annual statement. Here's what each set of documents shows you:

- **Transactions:** Each time you buy or sell units, you're sent a transaction statement from the fund manager setting out the fund name, the number of units bought or sold, the price and the date. You should also be told when funds will be transferred to your bank account if you're selling.

- **Statements:** The fund manager sends you a statement of your holdings at least once a year after the tax year end. Typically, this set of documents is posted by fund managers sometime in late September each year. As well as setting out your investments, the statements have a breakdown of the income distributions you've received from the fund. The important part is all the information about the income that is assessable for tax, split between income and capital gains. For more on what information you receive in these statements, refer to Chapter 5.

You should get regular updates from the fund manager, perhaps every six months, letting you know what's happening with the funds you've invested in.

Monitoring Your Investments

Managed funds have a reputation as *set-and-forget* investments. After investors have bought the funds, they tend to not worry about them for a long time into the future. But managed funds should be like any other investment, such as shares or property. Managed funds need to be regularly looked after, even if an investor has a 20-year investment strategy.

Like buying a house, you don't just leave it to the elements or you could find yourself with a leaking roof and rising damp. Houses need care and maintenance, and the same can be said for managed funds. So what should you be doing to manage your managed fund investments to avoid the leaks? Read on.

Rebalancing your funds

Building a portfolio of funds usually means putting together a mix of funds that match the level of risk you're comfortable with. Some investors use a financial planner to help them figure out how much risk they want to take for the returns they need. Other investors work it out themselves — in Chapter 6, I show how you can invest on your own and talk more about managing risk.

Over time, some of your fund investments may perform better than others, which can throw out of whack the level of risk in your portfolio. This situation is where rebalancing comes into play. Like riding a bike, if you lean over too far to one side you'll fall off. Same with a portfolio of funds — if one hugely outperforms or underperforms the others, the risk of falling over is magnified. A portfolio of funds is rebalanced to bring both the risk and returns back to your original target.

Each fund carries a certain level of risk, depending on the type of investments it holds. For example, international funds are generally riskier than Australian share funds. Figure 13-1 shows how relative risk of a portfolio can change as values change. Many investors can live with this change in the level of risk. For others, the need to stay on track and to avoid *portfolio drift*, as it's called, is important.

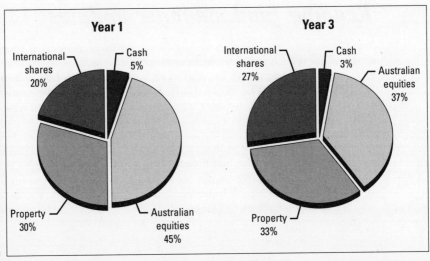

Figure 13-1: Asset allocations in different funds can shift over time, requiring rebalancing to bring them back into line with preferred risk levels.

Year 1
Cash 5%
International shares 20%
Property 30%
Australian equities 45%

Year 3
Cash 3%
International shares 27%
Australian equities 37%
Property 33%

Figure 13-1 shows the percentage holdings in a portfolio made up of four managed funds across different asset classes in its first year and again in its third year. After three years, international shares have done extremely well and now represent 27 per cent of the portfolio, having increased from 20 per cent. However, the risk associated with having more international shares in the portfolio could be too much for the investor.

The investor has two choices — do nothing and take a chance that the international fund continues to do well; or rebalance the portfolio to get the risk back to a more comfortable level. How is this done? In the example in Figure 13-1, the investor would sell off some of her holdings in the international fund and use the money raised to buy some more of the Australian fund.

Rebalancing a portfolio from a managed fund that has performed well to one that might not have performed so well may sound odd. But what you're doing is locking in some money you've made and putting it back into a fund that has the potential to recover. Importantly, you're getting the level of risk in the fund back to where you're comfortable.

How often you want to rebalance depends on how much your portfolio moves outside of your targeted mix. You may never have to rebalance or you may find you're tweaking your portfolio every six months.

Reading fund manager updates

Fund managers usually provide regular updates on how their funds are doing. This is a chance for fund managers to either say how great they're doing or offer sage words of caution to investors when funds aren't doing so well. Updates can be every quarter, some every six months and others once a year. The fund manager won't give too much away on how the fund is being run. An update gives details on the following:

✔ **Performance:** The fund manager should show you how the fund has performed over the last month, three months, six months, one year, three years and five years. Most also show how well the fund has done against a benchmark index such as the S&P/ASX 200. For more on fund performance, refer to Chapter 9.

✔ **Investment holdings:** Fund managers don't like to give away their secrets, and telling what investments they own is one of those secrets. That being said, fund managers usually show their ten biggest holdings in the fund, the five top-performing shares they own and possibly the five worst shares as well. The fund should also set out in percentage terms what sectors, such as banks, resources, cash and the like, the fund is exposed to.

✔ **Other factors:** The fund manager usually has a bit to say about how the fund has performed, what investment ideas have worked and even those that haven't. The fund manager may also have a word about the economy, an opinion on where the market is headed and what factors are likely to influence the performance of the fund in the future.

Selling a Fund

So, you're about to retire and you want to cash in your investments to buy that beach house. Or perhaps you spotted your dream home and need to raise some money for a deposit? Maybe you're just nervous about the market and want to put your investments into cash. Whatever your motives, this section covers the practical points of how to sell a fund, how to switch money between funds and what fees investors can expect to stump up. Yes, even when you sell a fund you may have to pay fees!

How do you sell managed funds?

Selling some or all of the units in a managed fund is a straightforward process. For investors who use a financial planner to make the initial investments, the instructions to sell should also usually be through the financial planner. However, investors may, for whatever reason, not want to use their financial planner, or have dealt directly with a fund manager or fund broker to buy their funds. In this case, the following options are generally available:

✔ **Online:** Most of the large fund managers have a secure internet facility available to let investors sell funds. The monies are paid into the bank account using details provided when the units were bought.

✔ **Phone:** Fund managers can accept instructions to sell over the phone. You may need to verify your identity in order to do so. The fund manager will tell you what you need to do.

> ✔ **Withdrawal form:** Fund managers also have a form available to let investors sell their investments. Complete the form with your account details and how much you want to sell. You may need to include bank details of where you want the proceeds sent after the sale.

It may take some time to get your money from the fund manager, from a few days to a week or more. When you get your money depends on the fund you have sold. Most funds should be able to get your money to you in a week but if you're invested through a master trust (such as Colonial First State's FirstChoice), this could take longer. Master trusts allow investors to buy funds from a range of fund managers and this adds another layer of administration, which can slow down your payment.

What happens when you sell?

Investors sell managed funds for two reasons — to take their money out of the investment to use for some other purpose or to move their money across to another managed fund. Both reasons involve slightly different processes and have potentially different costs associated with them.

Selling units in a managed fund

When the fund manager receives your instruction to sell some or all of your units, the fund manager either reissues your units to other investors looking to buy units in the fund or, if there are no buyers for your units, cancels those units.

Table 13-2 shows an example of a fund manager receiving an application to buy 1,000 units in an Australian equities fund and an application to sell 2,000 units in the same fund.

Table 13-2		Selling Managed Funds	
Investor	*Units*	*Price per Unit*	*Total to or from Fund Manager*
Buys	1,000	$5.00	$5,000
Sells	2,000	$4.98	−$9,960
Net	−1,000		−$4,960

From the example in Table 13-2, the fund manager is left with 1,000 units that are not needed and needs to give \$9,960 to the seller of the units. The fund manager has received \$5,000 from the buyer of units but needs to find another \$4,960 to make up the total to give the seller. The fund manager is obliged to keep a small amount of a fund's investments in cash, usually enough to see it through two to three months' worth of expenses and unit sales. The cash is used to pay the regular bills for management expenses and to give money back to those investors selling units (called *redemptions*). Most of the time, the fund has enough cash to manage these payments.

However, the market can change quickly and a big sell-off of stocks in the market can make investors nervous. Selling by a lot of investors can leave the fund manager short of cash. The only way the fund manager can raise cash is to sell off some of its investments in the market.

Switching investments to another fund

Switching an investment is when you sell some or all of your units in one fund and buy units in another fund with the same fund manager. Changing funds may be for several reasons, including poor performance of one fund or perhaps to take some profits and invest them in another fund.

Switching funds can be done in the same way as buying or selling a fund. A financial planner can instruct the fund manager on your behalf after you've given permission to do so. Otherwise, you may be able to go online and use the fund manager's website to switch, fill in a form (sent out to you or downloaded from the website) and send it to the fund manager, or talk to a staff member over the phone.

Investors should be aware of the following when switching funds:

- **Buy–sell spread:** The price points when you switch your units are based on the normal buy–sell spread that the funds quote. The fund is sold at its exit price and the new fund is bought at its entry price.

- **Fees:** Most fund managers don't charge you if you switch funds but some may charge an administration fee. Find out from your fund manager if there are any fees before you switch.

- **Tax:** If you sell your funds for more than you bought them, chances are you will have to pay tax on the gain that you made.

Trading funds through the stock market

The managed funds industry is heading for a shake-up, courtesy of the Australian Securities Exchange (ASX). Plans are afoot to build a system that will allow managed funds to be traded on the stock market, just as shares are bought and sold today. The system is expected to be launched in Australia sometime in 2011.

While the system for trading managed funds may not sound radical or even particularly exciting, it promises to revolutionise the way managed funds are bought and sold. Gone will be the days of having to deal directly with a fund manager or a number of fund managers if you want to invest in managed funds. Through a normal share-trading account with a stock-broker you'll be able to buy and sell funds at the click of a button or a call to your broker.

The new system will potentially change the way managed funds are currently sold. Fund managers currently rely heavily on financial planners to sell their products but, with the changes, will have to put more effort into marketing their funds directly to investors rather than focusing on financial planners. People will still be able to receive advice on which funds to invest in but, for many, the convenience of being able to trade through a broker will increase the appeal of managed funds.

The ASX tried to launch a similar system in 2000. The initiative failed due to a lack of interest from fund managers. The success of the new system will once again depend on fund managers supporting it and listing their funds. This time around, the support seems to be there and fund managers seem keen to expand the way they sell their funds.

Part IV
Determining How Funds Are Labelled

Glenn Lumsden

Funds tracking in the wild west.

In this part ...

*H*ere, I take a fine-tooth comb to how managed funds are categorised. Human nature loves everything well ordered and labelled. Categorising funds doesn't just give someone a job to do. It can also help investors compare like with like and to make sense of which funds might be the best for them. Standard industry categories are demystified and I summarise the different characteristics of each. For those funds that don't want to be labelled, 'resistance is futile!' I round up some of the other ways funds are grouped. Here I talk about ethical funds and agricultural funds.

And, just when you thought you couldn't get enough abbreviations, I introduce two more: exchange-traded funds (ETFs) and listed investment companies (LICs). These funds trade on the stock exchange but have all the hallmarks of managed funds.

In this part, I also delve into the world of what are known as administration services and managed accounts. These aren't managed funds but ways of keeping track of your managed funds. Most of the big fund managers offer administrative systems. Other than just another way to charge more fees, these services can be useful. Keeping track of your managed funds gets a whole lot easier using an administration system.

Chapter 14

Understanding Standard Fund Types

Setting off down the road of successful investing means knowing where you're headed and how to get there. Understanding what fund types you can meet along the way and which ones to catch a ride with helps you reach your destination.

Investing is a lot easier when the choices are simple and laid out well. Choosing a managed fund could easily fall into the too-hard basket given the sheer number of funds out there. Fortunately, someone a long time ago decided to lighten the load for investors and put the funds into neat boxes. Neat boxes are good; they help investors to compare similar funds, pick winners and avoid duds. Properly labelled funds also mean investors don't have to waste time looking at funds they're not interested in. In this chapter, I show you the eight ways Australian funds are labelled.

Pack your bags, because I also take a look at how funds investing in international markets are labelled. You find these funds have similar labels to those investing in Australia. However, throw into the mix different geographies as well as global sector funds (such as those investing in resources globally) and you have a whole new set of managed fund labels for your luggage.

I also go to opposite ends of the managed fund spectrum and look at concentrated funds and index funds. Think of concentrated funds as drinking neat lemon juice and index funds as a glass of lemonade. Concentrated funds don't mess about when it comes to investing and can deliver a real kick.

Considering Types of Managed Funds

Understanding what a managed fund does and the investments it holds is all part of the process. And by this I mean how a manager looks after the money. Fund managers tend to follow different investing styles. Some might look for shares with big growth potential, whereas others look for shares they think are undervalued. Some styles are riskier than others and some may produce better returns than others. Chapter 4 has more on investing style.

Ensuring you know what's in the box

So where does finding out what a fund does and the investments it holds fit into the investing process? Without wanting to oversimplify things, the following easy-to-use steps explain how a fund's type helps to decide what funds to use:

1. **Work out what you want to achieve from your investments.**

   Yes, making money is the ultimate goal but how much you need to make and how long you have to make it are the questions that need answering. For example, investing for retirement is a goal that should occupy investors for most of their working lives. Investing to save for a new car is much more short term, say two or three years.

2. **Decide what level of risk you're prepared to take, and over what period, to meet your goals.**

   Some people are naturally more conservative than others and the type of funds they choose reflects that attitude to risk. It follows that, with less risk, so the chance of making big returns diminishes.

3. **Match the managed funds with your goals, level of risk and timeframe.**

   All this sounds so easy! To find out more about choosing managed funds, refer to Part III.

Mismatching managed funds and investment goals can create headaches for investors down the track. Investors face a serious risk of missing out on their goals if they don't invest in the right funds. For example, a cash fund has lower levels of risk but potentially lower returns than, say, an Australian share fund that has higher risk and higher potential returns. Putting money into a cash fund lets you sleep well at night, but your returns aren't going to shoot the lights out.

Keep your investment goals realistic. Investing $10,000 and seeing it turn into $1 million in five years' time would be a fantastic result. Although not impossible, this result is also highly unlikely unless the investor takes on levels of risk similar to buying a lottery ticket.

Making it easier to compare

Managed fund categories are good when it comes to comparing like with like. Putting the performance of managed funds next to each other is a great eye-opener. After all, performance is what investing is all about and funds that show better performance than others do stand out. Even better yet is comparing the performance of funds over a number of years. Like moths to a flame, investors should be drawn to funds that do consistently well over a long period, typically five years or more.

Categorising funds helps investors to understand how funds make money and hopefully grow their investments. Classifying funds also helps investors to keep focused on what they're trying to achieve. Doing this means you can avoid chasing the latest best performing fund or latest investment fad.

Using research agencies to compare funds

The ratings agencies, such as Morningstar and Standard & Poor's, are in the business of comparing funds. Comparing funds — along with many other types of investments — and selling the information to investors and fund managers is how the agencies make money. The ratings agencies are massive data-collecting and sorting businesses.

Collecting a huge amount of statistics from the fund managers, the agencies sift the information through their databases and churn out easy-to-use fund comparisons. Morningstar highlights the importance of the way it categorises funds to make sure investors are comparing like with like. A system of star ratings from one star to five stars (being the best) makes it even easier for investors to scan a list of managed funds for the top performers.

Morningstar, in particular, gives investors the ability to search for managed funds across a wide range of criteria, such as star ratings, performance, size of fund and, importantly, category of fund. Visit www.morningstar.com.au to find out more about the fund-comparison tool available online.

Looking at Eight Ways Australian Funds Are Labelled

The range of managed funds is enormous and their performance can vary just as much. Labelling funds gives investors a pointer as to what to expect in terms of performance and risk. Cash funds are a lot less risky than Australian share funds but the returns are also lower. Armed with this knowledge, investors can mix and match funds to suit their needs.

The various managed funds are grouped according to a number of different criteria (I cover the first three of these criteria in more detail in Chapter 3):

- **Legal type:** Whether the fund has been set up as a unit trust, as a superannuation fund to help save for retirement or as a pension fund to pay an income to retirees.

- **Retail or wholesale:** Refers to the type of clients that can use a particular fund. Retail investors are typical everyday investors with $1,000 or more to invest. Wholesale investors have much larger amounts to invest, usually $100,000 or more, and can be individuals or corporations. Rules govern what type of fund can be offered to what type of investor.

- **Style:** The way fund managers select investments for their funds. Style can be growth, value or core; that is, a mix of both growth and value styles of investing.

- **Size:** In the context of classifying funds, size refers to the size of the companies that the managed funds invest in. So, some funds invest in large companies and some invest in small companies. You find some managed funds referred to as being 'large cap' or 'small cap', where *cap* is short for *capitalisation*, a measure of the market value of the companies the funds invest in.

- **Markets and sectors:** Funds can also be classified by the market or markets they invest in, such as Australia or China, and also by the sector, such as property or resources.

- **Multi-sector:** Funds that invest across a range of different asset classes, from cash to shares and bonds. These funds are classified by how much risk is in the fund from the underlying investment mix.

Making things interesting, managed funds can be categorised under a combination of any of the preceding groups. Ratings agencies like Morningstar have more than 40 different categories for managed funds. Most funds fit comfortably into the categories but many types of funds don't fit exactly. I've set out categories based on both the ratings agency classifications as well as other widely used classifications. For more on types of managed funds, see Chapter 15.

Cash funds

Cash funds are at the low-risk end of the investment spectrum. These funds can usually be identified by the inclusion of 'cash fund', 'cash management trust' or 'cash management fund' in the name. The aim of these funds is to provide stable and regular income with a low risk to investors. Cash funds achieve this aim by investing in the following mix of investment types:

✔ **Deposits:** Just like you or me putting money into a deposit account at a bank, so cash funds use deposits with banks and other licensed institutions. The difference is that cash funds should be able to get better interest rates because of the large amounts of money they put on deposit.

✔ **Money market:** These usually short-term investments are typically a form of debt issued by governments, banks and corporations to help them with short-term cash flow needs. The investments pay a regular income and are easily bought and sold by investors.

✔ **Fixed income:** These investments are the likes of government and company bonds or debt. Bonds are a form of debt issued by governments and companies to raise money. The bond has a set lifespan of up to ten years, sometimes more, and pays a fixed regular income over that lifespan. When the life of the bond is over, the initial amount it was issued for, usually $100 per bond, is paid back to the holder.

Looking at the make-up of investments in some of the cash funds, you'd be forgiven for thinking that these funds might be better described as bond or fixed-interest funds (read on for more on these funds). It seems that classifying these funds can be a grey area. Although cash funds do invest in bonds and fixed interest, the level of risk determines how the fund is categorised. The more a fund's investments are skewed to fixed-interest investments, the riskier it becomes. The more risk in the fund, the more likely it falls under the bond and fixed-interest banner.

Bonds and fixed-interest investments carry varying degrees of risk. Fixed-interest investments are usually given a rating by Standard & Poor's, with AAA being the highest possible. The lowest investment-grade rating issued is BBB. Any rating below BBB, such as BB, and the investment is regarded as a *junk bond*, or non-investment grade. Cash fund managers concentrate their investments on the higher investment-grade ratings of AAA to BBB.

Bonds and fixed income

Aiming to give regular and stable income at relatively low risk, bond and fixed-income funds don't register high up the investing excitement scale. Bonds and fixed income can be summed up in one word — debt. Bonds and fixed income are a way for governments and companies to borrow money without having to go to a bank. Usually not backed by any hard assets, investors rely on the good credit of the issuer to repay the debt. A whole ratings industry revolves around providing credit ratings for governments and companies (refer to Chapter 8 for more on these agencies).

Bonds are issued at a certain price, say $100 per bond, and then pay a regular income, known as a *coupon*. The coupon rate is usually shown as a percentage of the original price. So a $100 bond with a 6 per cent per annum coupon rate means investors get $6 per annum in income. Bonds are usually issued for a specific period, such as ten years. After ten years, the issuer of the bond pays back the original issue amount, such as $100 per bond.

These funds may also invest in what are known as *hybrids*. Not unlike a hybrid car running on both battery and petrol, hybrid securities are a mix of debt and equity. Hybrids start off like bonds, paying a regular income, but, at some point in the future, convert to shares in the issuing company. The risk in bond and fixed-income funds is usually low to medium. Morningstar classifies these as:

- **Short-term fixed interest and cash enhanced:** These funds invest in similar investments to the cash funds but with a little more risk in the form of greater exposure to bonds.

- **Bonds, Australian or global:** Funds of this type invest predominantly in local or global government and company bonds with different income, length of issue and risk.

- **High-yield credit:** Funds included in this category are likely to have in their name 'income', 'high yield', 'diversified income', 'credit income' or 'hybrid securities', to name a few.

- **Mortgages:** These funds invest in usually residential mortgages that have been bundled up and sold like a bond that pays a yield.

Large-cap equities

As the name suggests, large-cap (capitalisation) equity funds invest their money in large companies on the stock market. A company's size is worked out by multiplying the price of one share on the stock market by the number of shares the company has on issue. Conveniently for fund managers and investors alike, some stock market indices reflect the size of the companies that make up those indices.

For example, the S&P/ASX 50 is an average price of the biggest 50 companies listed on the Australian Securities Exchange (ASX) and includes companies like BHP Billiton, Telstra and Commonwealth Bank of Australia. The S&P/ASX 50 is generally regarded as the main large-cap share index in the Australian market. Managed funds investing in large-cap stocks tend to restrict their investments to companies that are included in the top 50 stocks by size.

Fund managers invest in large-cap stocks because they're less risky than investing in smaller companies. Large companies tend to have a long track record of making profits and may be less likely to fail. The shares of large companies may also be more liquid, meaning that fund managers can easily buy and sell large quantities of shares without the share price moving too much.

So what size is the right size of company for a large-cap fund manager to invest in? Large-cap companies are generally defined as stocks in the top 70 per cent of the capitalisation of an equities market. In Australia at the end of July 2010, the stock market was valued at around $1.3 trillion, according to the ASX. For a stock to be considered large cap it must be worth more than around $3.9 billion.

Mid- and small-cap equities

Mid- and small-cap managed funds invest in the shares of companies that are, not surprisingly, regarded as either medium or small sized. The main Australian stock market indices in Australia that fund managers use as a reference are the S&P/ASX Midcap 50 for medium-sized funds and the S&P/ASX Small Ordinaries Index for small companies. The S&P/ASX Small Ordinaries Index accounts for around 7 per cent of the total value of companies on the ASX, whereas the S&P/ASX 50 makes up about 63 per cent of the total value of the ASX. A big difference!

What size of company is too small for a small-cap fund manager? Many small-cap fund managers invest only in companies bigger than $500 million. Some have a lower limit on the size of the company. Anything below $100 million in value and investors enter the murky realm of what are known as micro-cap stocks. We're talking small fry here. These stocks can be highly speculative, with high levels of risk, but the potential for big returns is exceptional. Not many micro-cap funds exist. One that does is the Ausbil MicroCap Fund at www.ausbil.com.au.

Small-cap managed funds can be a lot riskier than large-cap managed funds but can show big returns if the manager picks the right shares. Because small-cap shares are just that — small — many investors just don't know about them. The big stockbroking houses tend not to research the smaller companies and many go undiscovered and undervalued for a long time.

Multi-sector equities

Also called *diversified* funds, the fund managers of multi-sector equity funds may invest in a diverse range of investment types, from large-cap stocks to small-cap stocks, property, cash and fixed interest. Multi-sector funds tend to be known by how risky the fund's investments are. The following is a general guide to multi-sector fund investments:

- ✔ **Conservative:** These funds tend to have less than 20 per cent invested in growth assets such as shares and property. The majority of funds are in bonds, fixed interest and cash investments.

- ✔ **Moderate:** Between 20 and 40 per cent is invested in growth assets.

- ✔ **Balanced:** Between 40 and 60 per cent is in growth assets.

- ✔ **Growth:** Now it's getting more exciting, with 60 to 80 per cent in growth assets.

- ✔ **Aggressive:** For those investors who get a buzz from the thrill of the ride, these funds have up to 100 per cent in growth assets. The risk of losing money in the short term can be high but over the longer term they may outperform other funds.

Multi-sector funds offer a quick and simple way to diversify your investments. Investors still bemused by the array of funds can easily match one of these funds with their preferred level of risk.

Single-sector and single-asset funds

Some funds may focus on one particular sector of the market or one particular type of asset. Property and infrastructure funds are perhaps the best example of these types of funds. Infrastructure assets are typically toll roads, bridges and tunnels, for example, that have a long expected life and hopefully produce a healthy income from toll charges. Property funds may invest in single office blocks or similar, although usually they invest in more than one property to spread the risk. Morningstar categorises property funds under 'Australian real estate', 'global real estate' and 'unlisted and direct property'.

Investing in infrastructure

Infrastructure was one of the darlings of the stock market for about eight years, until 2008, and the master of the infrastructure fund was Macquarie Bank. Long seen as a fairly dull segment of the market, infrastructure is the investing equivalent of watching paint dry. An asset such as a road is built and tolls are charged. Get the traffic forecasts right and income from the road can be forecast 20 to 30 years into the future. Fallen asleep yet?

However, these are great investments for investors needing a regular and growing income. Macquarie made infrastructure exciting and packaged up toll infrastructure projects, including airports, from across the globe into both listed and unlisted funds. Borrowing money was cheap and the money earned from investments produced a healthy profit. That was

until the global financial crisis hit in 2008. Income slowed as traffic using the roads declined. Debt became a lot more expensive and the economics of infrastructure funds was thrown into doubt. After much soul searching and revamping, the infrastructure funds that survived emerged from the crisis with less debt and lower revenues.

Infrastructure funds are back to doing what they do best — earning long-term income from their assets. Carefully researched, these funds may have a place in an investment portfolio. The infrastructure funds offered in Australia tend to invest in global assets or companies. The main players include AMP, Colonial Asset Management, Lazard Funds, RARE Infrastructure and of course, Macquarie. Magellan Funds, Mercer and Vanguard also offer infrastructure funds.

A way to quickly understand what type of property investments a fund holds is to look at the name of the fund. Generally a *property trust* invests directly in industrial, commercial and residential property. A *property securities fund* invests in the shares of stock exchange listed and/or unlisted property companies. The same is true of infrastructure funds. *Infrastructure trusts* invest directly in toll roads and the like, and *infrastructure securities funds* invest in the shares of listed companies.

Other single-sector funds include:

✔ **Resources funds:** These funds invest in mining, oil and gas companies, and related support businesses. Some funds focus on a single commodity, such as gold, but they're rare. Most funds invest globally across a range of mining and extraction companies. A better known fund is probably Colonial First State Global Resources Fund at www.colonialfirststate.com.au (click on the Find a Fund tab, select Investment Products and Global Shares and click on the search button, and then scroll down to find the fund).

✔ **Technology funds:** The funds available in Australia tend to invest in global technology firms such as Microsoft, Apple, Samsung and Google. The best known of these funds is perhaps the BT Technology fund at www.bt.com.au (to download a factsheet, type the name of the fund in the search window and scroll down to the fund).

Alternative investments

The alternative investments category is a dumping ground for funds that can't readily be classified with other mainstream funds. The term is a relatively loose one and covers a range of different funds that either invest in non-standard assets — those outside of cash, fixed interest, property and shares — or use non-traditional investment techniques like hedging or derivatives to enhance returns. These funds include:

✔ **Structured products:** These funds are usually quite complex and might invest in shares or an index of shares using derivatives. A *derivative* is a financial instrument; specifically, an agreement between two parties to buy or sell something at a particular price in the future, where the value of the derivative is based on something else, such as the price of a share like BHP. The funds usually have what is called a *capital guarantee* that protects the investor's initial investment — meaning, at the very least, you get your money back.

✔ **Hedge funds:** These funds, like conventional funds, aim to beat the market's performance. However, unlike conventional funds, they use a mix of different investment strategies and instruments, including derivatives, to beat the market.

✔ **Private equity funds:** These are funds that generally invest in unlisted companies and can be a great way for investors to get access to successful companies not available via the stock market. Private equity funds are usually the realm of the super rich but, increasingly, funds are being offered to a broader investor base.

✔ **Agricultural funds:** Investing in agricultural schemes such as forestry projects for pulp and timber, orchard fruits such as olives and almonds, and even crops such as ginseng, many of these funds may be driven by the 100 per cent tax deductions available to investors and not necessarily by the viability of the schemes.

Alternative investment managers sell their funds as offering superior returns not linked to the performance of the market. Some also offer a way to protect your capital. The risk across these investment types can vary enormously, so do your homework before committing yourself to alternative investments. See Chapter 15 for more on private equity and agrifunds, and Chapter 16 for structured products and hedge funds.

Fund-of-funds

Fund-of-funds are managed funds that invest in other managed funds, rather than holding direct investments in shares, property or cash. You sometimes see these funds also called multi-manager funds or strategies.

Fund-of-funds have made a splash in the world of alternative investments such as hedge funds, private equity funds and venture capital. Hedge funds use specialised techniques involving derivative products to enhance returns; private equity funds invest in private companies; and venture capital funds invest in companies that are at an early stage of setting up. All of these areas can be hard for the average investor to get access to if you don't have a big enough chequebook. Fund-of-funds tend to specialise in one of these areas, acting as expert investors in hedge funds, say.

For example, many hedge funds in Australia are open only to professional investors and have a minimum investment of $1 million. A fund-of-funds meets the criteria of professional investor. The fund-of-funds pools money from several investors enabling it to invest in the hedge funds on behalf of its client base. Here is what fund-of-funds offer investors:

- ✔ **Diversification:** By investing across a number of funds that already have some diversification, fund-of-funds can help to spread risk across a wider range of investments.

- ✔ **Knowledge:** Half the battle when investing in hedge funds or private equity funds is knowing what funds are available. Funds that aren't generally available to the investing public are hard to find. Fund-of-funds take some of the work out of finding specialist fund managers.

Following a Well-Travelled Path: International Equities

International investing gives investors exposure to different economies developing at different rates from the local market. Putting some of your money to work overseas gives you access to the big-name global companies like Microsoft and Proctor & Gamble, as well as the smaller, high-growth emerging economies in Asia, Latin America and Eastern Europe.

Bursting the dotcom bubble

Up until the early 2000s, international investing was a significant part of many Australian investors' portfolios, comprising up to 20 per cent of the value of their investments. All that changed as many local investors got burned in the dotcom crash of 2000. Hyperinflated internet stocks with no real means of making a profit drove global markets, and especially the US, to dizzying heights. Market commentators talked about a new investing paradigm — a new way of valuing stocks. No matter that some companies had no means of selling anything, let alone making a profit. This was the era of the internet and normal rules didn't apply.

Well, the rules did apply and reality eventually set in. Losses in the dotcom companies skyrocketed and the money ran out. Fitting out offices with trendy furniture, bringing pets to work and throwing off the suit and tie may have been cool, but businesses burned through the cash they had raised faster than throwing money onto a bonfire. Then everything came crashing down. The losses provided a salutary lesson that markets don't stay up forever and highlighted the risk of investing overseas. Aussie investors retreated home with tails between their legs, happier investing in what they knew — managed funds with big resources stocks and the big banks.

Going overseas? Fasten your seatbelt

International markets offer a huge diversity of ways to make — and lose — money. Get the right market at the right time and you can do very nicely. Get it wrong and you could lose a lot. The Asian financial crisis of 1997 and 1998 sent a warning to investors eager to jump onto the bandwagon of the tiger economies.

I was working in Hong Kong as a stockbroker at the time — the losses were very real and the hurt was extensive. I remember my boss having to get on a plane to New York to explain to a client why the US$60 million of Malaysian bank shares he had recommended the client buy a few months earlier were now worth only $5 million. These are some of the risks of investing in foreign markets.

Classifying international funds

International market managed funds can be classified as follows:

- ✔ **Single country:** Where the fund invests in only one market, such as the United States, Japan or China. Funds tend to focus on major world economies.

- ✔ **Regional:** Regional funds may focus on Asia, Latin America or Europe, to name but a few.

✔ **Global:** With global funds, selected investments are from a variety of markets but usually the major developed markets, which tend to have lower risk than emerging markets. Global funds can then be classified according to the types of investments they focus on:

- **Global asset funds:** These funds may have a particular theme, such as global brands, investing in the big names like Pepsi and Coca-Cola.

- **Global diversified:** These funds select the top stocks in certain markets, such as Google in the United States, HSBC Bank in the United Kingdom or BMW in Germany. They also invest across different asset classes such as cash, US Treasury bonds, property and shares. Many funds are classified according to risk, such as 'World — Conservative' or 'World — Aggressive', depending on the mix of asset classes they invest in. The more shares make up a percentage of the fund, the riskier it is.

Choosing between developed and emerging markets

Apart from the great beaches and cheap food of some emerging economies, clear differences exist between the developed, first-world economies of the United States, Europe and Japan and the emerging economies such as Brazil and South-east Asia. Like a good whisky, developed economies have had a long time to mature. These countries have well-developed legal systems and strong financial infrastructure in place. Growth in these economies — global financial crises excepted — can be solid if a little dull. Emerging economies, however, can offer more excitement. The earlier the stage of economic development of a country, the more exciting the ride can be, given the potential for break-neck growth as these countries gear up their economies from a low base.

Emerging markets, as a general rule, are riskier than developed markets. Like toddlers finding their feet, emerging markets can surprise by the speed at which they develop but can also bump into things along the way. The biggest differences between emerging and developed markets are:

✔ **Access:** Getting access to some emerging markets can be difficult, even for professional fund managers. For example, India has tight restrictions about how much of a company foreign investors can own. China is sometimes better accessed via China stocks listed in Hong Kong. Developed markets like the United States and Japan are relatively easy to access.

✔ **Liquidity:** Emerging economies don't have as many companies to invest in and those that are available aren't big compared with those in developed markets. Fund managers with a lot of money to invest may struggle to buy and sell shares in emerging market companies without significantly affecting the price they pay or receive.

- **Risk:** The risks of investing overseas are many, including political risk, economic risk, currency risk and regulatory risk (where laws are changed to favour local investors). Risks exist in all international markets but may be more acute in some emerging markets.

Emerging economies tend be grouped by region or by economies at a similar stage of development. Wrapping up the markets in an acronym is a neat marketing trick by economists and bankers, such as:

- **BRICs:** Brazil, Russia, India and China
- **CIVETS:** Columbia, Indonesia, Vietnam, Egypt, Turkey and South Africa

Other emerging markets are based on region and may share similar traits, such as being at a similar stage of development or having similar industries. Regional markets that managed funds typically invest in are:

- **Middle East and North Africa (MENA):** Egypt, Morocco, Jordan, Turkey, Algeria, Tunisia, Sudan, Saudi Arabia, Oman and United Arab Emirates, to name a few
- **North Asia:** Hong Kong, Taiwan, South Korea and China
- **South-east Asia:** Singapore, Thailand, Malaysia, Philippines and Indonesia
- **Sub-continent:** India, Pakistan and Bangladesh

Finding your way around the currency hedging maze

The effect of currency lurks in the background of all overseas investments. You may have made a bundle on the Shanghai stock exchange, but any movements in the exchange rate against the Australian dollar can affect your returns. Currency movements work both ways, either adding to or taking away from returns on an investment.

Say, for example, you buy A$10,000 of units in a fund that invests in US-dollar shares. Your A$10,000 is used to buy US shares with an exchange rate of A$1 to US 85 cents, so US$8,500 of shares. The shares go up 10 per cent over the year to US$9,350 and you decide to cash in your units. However, the exchange rate is now A$1 to US 90 cents. Your US$9,350 is worth A$10,388. If the exchange rate had stayed at US 85 cents your investment would have been worth A$11,000. The difference the exchange rate makes on your investment is A$412, or about 4 per cent.

Reducing or eliminating the effects of currency on returns is possible using hedging. *Hedging* is a method of locking in the price an investor pays for the foreign currency when he converts it back to the local currency. The way that this is locked in is by using derivatives; in particular, currency futures.

Managed funds can hedge against their foreign currency exposures but most don't. The cost of hedging is negligible, perhaps at most 1 per cent of the assets in a fund. But few funds actually hedge against currency, partly because fund managers don't think it's worth it. Also, funds benefit if the currency moves in their favour, adding to returns. Unsurprisingly, funds that don't hedge are called *unhedged*.

Managed funds that hedge against currency movements must distribute gains made by hedging to unit holders as income (not capital gains). Investors may have to pay income tax on those gains.

Weighing Up Concentrated Funds

Concentrated funds are like eating a whole lemon as opposed to having a slice of lemon in your drink. Rather than having an investing flavour running through a fund, the fund manager takes a big bite into a particular segment of the market to get the best possible returns. Most of the big fund managers offer a concentrated fund of some sort. For fund managers, concentrated funds are a way of highlighting how good they reckon they are.

Like your funds neat? High conviction may be your tipple

Concentrated funds tend to invest in a much smaller number of stocks than most conventional funds. A concentrated fund typically has between 15 and 40 stocks in a portfolio — 25 stocks is the average. A conventional fund can have 60 stocks or more. Also known as high-conviction funds, the fund managers take a view that the more funds you have in a portfolio, the less likely a fund is to perform better than the market. Concentrated funds look to beat a chosen index, such as the S&P/ASX 200.

Having a high conviction means fund managers are backing their skill and judgement to pick a fewer number of stocks that they think will outperform the market. High-conviction fund managers thumb their noses at conventional fund management styles and are prepared to put their reputations on the line to produce superior returns.

You may notice that concentrated funds say they use an 'active, bottom-up' approach to investing. Simply put, fund managers tend to ignore what's happening in the broader economy and focus on picking good companies.

Higher risk can pack a punch

By their very nature, concentrated funds look to significantly outperform the market. With higher potential returns come higher risks. The risk of losing money in the short term may be higher than for managed funds that hold a larger number of stocks. Managers who have cracked the concentrated investment formula do very well for the funds and their investors. Get it wrong and these funds show up at the bottom of the league performance tables.

Ratings houses like Morningstar and Standard & Poor's don't separately categorise concentrated funds. These funds are usually shown as part of a broader group of funds, such as Australian large-cap equities. Given these funds can be riskier than the average large-cap fund, they perhaps should be given a group of their own. These funds can be tricky to find. So, in Table 14-1, I list a selection of funds and fund managers that offer concentrated funds.

Table 14-1	Some Managers That Offer Concentrated Funds		
Fund Manager	**Fund Name**	**PDS**	**Number of Stocks**
Advance Asset Management www.advance.com.au	Advance Concentrated Australian Share Fund	Advance Alliance Investment Suite	15 to 25
Aviva www.avivainvestors.com.au	Aviva Elite Opportunities Fund	Aviva Investors Professional Selection Investment Funds	Up to 30
OnePath* www.onepath.com.au	ING Select Leaders	ING OneAnswer Investment Portfolio	15 to 35
Perpetual Investments www.perpetual.com.au	Perpetual Concentrated Equity fund	Perpetual WealthFocus Investment Funds	25 to 40

__Note:__ OnePath is the new name for the former investment division of ING.

Concentrated funds are likely to be volatile (read risky) in the short term, with the potential for prices to move up and down a lot. These funds are not for the faint-hearted and suit growth and aggressive-style investors. Over the longer term, say five years, fund managers figure that the volatility in the funds will smooth out and the funds will perform better than traditional funds.

Understanding Index Funds

Index funds are simple to understand. No, really, they are! Funds are designed purely to mirror a market index such as the S&P/ASX 200 or similar. Index funds are also known as having a *passive* investment style because no management of investments is involved. They just copy an index, typically using a computer program. On the other hand, funds with an *active* investment style look to manage the investments so as to beat the performance of a selected index.

An index fund invests in exactly the same stocks that make up the index, and in the same proportion, otherwise known as *weighting*. This way, the fund can copy the performance of the chosen index. Index fund managers argue you'd be nuts not to invest in an index fund, especially as the majority of active fund managers don't beat the index. In Chapter 9, I talk more about the performance of active managers.

Taking the stress out of decision-making

Index funds take a lot of the thinking out of investing. Giving instant diversification across the whole market, investors don't have to think too much about choosing the right fund. They only have to choose the right index.

When you've invested in these funds, you know what to expect. If the market goes down, so does your fund, and by the same amount. You don't need to rely on the skill of the fund manager to produce the returns. And the best bit about index funds is the cost. Annual management fees are usually a lot lower than traditional managed funds, anywhere from 0.4 per cent to 0.9 per cent per annum. You would use an index fund to help diversify a portfolio and to instantly get the market performance. Investors can then add a little zing to their portfolio by adding, say, a resource sector fund or some other specialist fund. For more on investing strategies with index funds, such as exchange-traded funds, see Chapter 15.

So what's the catch with index funds?

The catch with index funds is that there aren't any catches, or surprises, and no big shocks. Index fund performance is never going to shoot the lights out and investors know what to expect. Whatever the chosen index does performance-wise, the index fund should match that return.

Index funds are invariably cheaper than other actively managed funds for the simple reason that the fund manager doesn't have to do a great deal with an index fund. Most of what the manager does is automated, from pricing and valuing the fund through to buying and selling the underlying investments. Some human intervention may be involved when it comes to sorting out dividends and the like, but this is all administrative stuff. Not a lot of thinking goes into the make-up of the fund as it should mirror the chosen index.

Index funds are different from exchange-traded funds (ETFs), even though the investment strategies are exactly the same — to mirror the performance of an index. Index funds work just like any conventional unlisted managed fund and are set up as a trust, offering units to investors. ETFs, on the other hand, are listed on the stock exchange and are bought and sold as with any other share on the market. For more on ETFs, see Chapter 15.

Chapter 15

Examining More Ways of Classifying Managed Investments

. . . .

In This Chapter

▶ Finding out about listed investment companies

▶ Examining exchange-traded funds

▶ Investing with a conscience through ethical funds

▶ Growing wealth with agricultural funds

. . . .

*I*f you haven't looked at Chapter 14 yet, I suggest you do so. Then you can decide whether that chapter provides enough excitement about ways to classify managed funds. If it doesn't, this chapter certainly makes up for it! Hang on to your hats, as I take you on a ride through some of the more exotic managed fund categories, such as agricultural investments and private equity. I plunge headfirst into ethical, or values-based, investing, which is steadily gaining interest with investors.

I also dive into managed investments that look and feel like managed funds but can be readily bought and sold on the Australian Securities Exchange (ASX). *Managed investments* is a catch-all term for investments that have similar characteristics to managed funds but are set up differently. These investments include listed investment companies (LICs) investing in a range of different asset types both locally and abroad.

Other types of managed investments that look and feel like managed funds are exchange-traded funds (ETFs). ETFs are similar to index funds, in that they aim to mirror the performance of a listed market index such as the S&P/ASX 200. Investors serious about managed funds should also give ETFs a good look. ETFs and LICs are both ready alternatives to managed funds.

Listed Investment Companies

As the name suggests, *listed investment companies (LICs)* are specialist investment companies that trade on a stock exchange. The ASX has some 60 LICs listed, worth a total of around $19 billion as at the end of June 2010. When buying an LIC, investors are buying shares in a company. LICs are grouped with what the ASX calls *listed managed investments*, including Australian real estate investment trusts (A-REITs, which are listed property trusts), infrastructure funds (refer to Chapter 14), listed absolute-return funds (see Chapter 16) and exchange-traded funds (see the next section in this chapter).

LICs mimic managed funds in what they invest in across a range of assets, including fixed interest, property and shares. Sometimes seen as the poor cousin of managed funds, LICs have occasionally attracted bad press. LICs take some heat from critics because of their value — or lack of value — on the ASX. I cover value later on in this section, as well as some important differences between LICs and managed funds.

Understanding Listed Investment Companies

LICs are fairly straightforward investments with three points to understand — what they do, what to look out for in an LIC, and how to buy and sell them. Here, I take a look at each of these points and show how LICs stack up against managed funds — the two are closely related. You may also see listed investment trusts on the ASX. These are very similar to LICs except they issue units — just like a managed fund — rather than shares.

Finding out the differences between LICs and managed funds

The best way to understand what an LIC is and why investors might invest in one is to compare it with a managed fund. Table 15-1 shows the comparison.

Investors who like dealing in shares quite rightly sing the praises of LICs because of the convenience of being able to trade them on the ASX. Equally, investors buying LICs acknowledge the benefits of getting access to a professionally managed portfolio of assets.

Table 15-1   Listed Investment Companies versus Managed Funds

Feature	LICs	Managed Funds
Listed on ASX	Yes	No
Legal structure	Company	Trust
Type of fund	Closed end; the number of shares are fixed and investors trade those shares on the ASX	Open ended; units are issued or redeemed (cancelled) as investors put money in or take money out of the fund
Price	Quoted on the ASX during market open hours	Calculated by the fund manager, usually on a daily basis
Bought and sold	Via a stockbroker through the ASX	Direct with fund manager or financial planner
Investments	All types of listed investments, including shares, fixed-interest investments, property	Listed and unlisted investments across cash, fixed interest, property and shares
Income to investor	Paid as a dividend after tax; directors of the LIC not obliged to pay all income as a dividend and can keep some back	Paid as a distribution; by law the fund must pay all income received to investors at least once a year and investors pay the tax due
Franking credits	Yes, paid with dividends	Yes, paid with distributions
Invests overseas	Yes	Yes
Entry or contribution fees	Brokerage from 0.1% to 2.5% (depending on broker)	Up to 4%
Ongoing fees	Yes, deducted by the company and reflected in the price quoted on the ASX; Australian shares from 0.1% to 1.0% p.a.; international shares from 1.0% to 2.0% p.a.	Yes, deducted by the fund manager and reflected in the calculation of the daily unit price; fees between 0.6% and 3.0% p.a.

Some of the advantages of LICs are:

- ✔ **Closed end:** LICs are bought and sold as shares on the stock market. Unlike a managed fund, no money is taken from the actual underlying fund, just the shareholding changes hands. The LIC manager doesn't have to worry about selling any of the underlying investments to return money to investors wanting to sell.

- ✔ **Diversified:** Like a managed fund, investors can achieve instant diversification when buying an LIC. For a relatively small amount — the minimum trade order on the ASX is $500 (also known as a *marketable parcel*) — investors can buy into a mix of investments.

- ✔ **Low cash holdings:** LICs don't need to hold a lot of cash, only enough to meet day-to-day expenses. Investors rightly want as much as possible of their money in shares so as to get the best return. Managed funds need to keep a fair amount of cash handy to pay out investors who want to sell or redeem their units.

- ✔ **No commission payments:** Unlike managed funds, LICs don't pay ongoing fees to planners, or anyone else for that matter.

- ✔ **Traded:** LICs can be readily traded on the ASX so investors should be able to get their money out of the market fairly quickly — after the transaction has taken place, the investor receives the sale proceeds in three days.

Some of the disadvantages of LICs are:

- ✔ **Investment restriction:** LICs invest only in listed investments. These underlying investments can be easily bought, sold and valued, but investors can miss out on unlisted investment opportunities that some managed funds offer, such as direct property.

- ✔ **Liquidity:** LIC shares aren't always easily bought and sold on the ASX. Some LICs may not trade that often. If, say, you buy LIC shares and no-one wants to sell, you may have to pay a higher price or wait until someone is prepared to accept the price you're offering.

- ✔ **Pricing:** On many occasions, the price of an LIC quoted on the ASX may not reflect the value of the underlying investments held by the LIC. For more on LIC pricing see 'Valuing an LIC' later in this chapter.

Choosing an LIC

With more than 60 LICs listed on the ASX covering a range of different investments and markets, a good choice of investments is available. LICs range in size from the very large (those valued at more than $3 billion) to the very small (valued at only around $30 million).

The LICs are dominated by a very small number of large players; Table 15-2 lists the biggest nine.

Table 15-2	Top Nine Listed Investment Companies by Market Value and by Sector		
LIC Name	*ASX Code*	*Market Cap at 31 July 2010*	*Investment Focus*
Australian Foundation Investment Company Ltd	AFI	$4,679 m	Domestic — large cap
Argo Investments Ltd	ARG	$3,551 m	Domestic — large cap
Milton Corporation Ltd	MLT	$1,551 m	Domestic — large cap
BKI Investment	BKI	$479 m	Domestic — small cap
Diversified United	DUI	$465 m	Domestic — small cap
Carlton Investments	CIN	$438 m	Domestic — small cap
AMP Capital China Growth	AGF	$249 m	International
Platinum Capital	PMC	$229 m	International
Global Mining Investments	GMI	$227 m	International

Source: Bell Potter Securities Ltd.

Choosing an LIC that suits your needs means knowing what to look out for:

✔ **Performance:** As with managed funds, historical performance is no guarantee of future performance (refer to Chapter 9). With LICs, though, historical performance and dividend payments influence an LIC's share price.

✔ **Price:** The price of an LIC quoted on the ASX doesn't necessarily reflect the value of the underlying assets. An LIC can trade at either below or above its value, otherwise known as *trading at a discount* or *at a premium*. I cover valuing LICs later in this section.

LICs are likely to benchmark their performance against a market index such as the S&P/ASX 200. Doing this helps the manager and investors alike see how well the LIC's manager is doing compared with the market. LICs even have their own index, the ASX LIC Index, which is the average price of 45 LICs. For more information, visit the ASX website at www.asx.com.au.

Valuing an LIC

In theory, valuing an LIC should be pretty easy — add up the value of the investments and subtract any expenses owing. Then divide the result by the number of shares on issue. And this is pretty much how it works in practice but with some small points to watch out for.

The usual way to measure an LIC's value is its *NTA*, short for net tangible assets. Sounds impressive, but what does it mean? *Net* means after expenses and *tangible assets* means the investments can be sold. In other words, NTA is the value of the underlying investments minus any outstanding costs.

Working out an LIC's NTA is all very well, but investors may find that the ASX quoted price won't be the same as the NTA. An LIC might trade as follows:

✔ **Discount:** When an LIC's NTA is greater than its share price, it's said to be trading at a discount to NTA. For example, an LIC with an NTA of $1.10 per share and a share price of $1.00 is said to be trading at a 10 per cent discount to NTA. A poor history of returns makes investors wary of paying above the NTA.

✔ **Premium:** The opposite to discount! When the ASX quoted price is greater than the LIC's NTA. LICs may trade at a premium because they have a history of strong dividends, which investors are prepared to pay a price for over the value of the LIC.

The market has a habit of setting consistent discounts or premiums to NTA for each LIC. Knowing the average discount or premium of an LIC makes judging when to buy or sell if the price falls outside that average relatively easy. Stockbrokers provide research on LICs that gives the information needed to work out the average discount or premium, as does the ASX at www.asx.com.au.

Exchange-Traded Funds

Exchange-traded funds (ETFs) are a natural extension of listed investment companies. Born in the USA, ETFs have been in Australia for a while but have only recently started to catch on here. *ETFs* are listed index managed funds that give investors the opportunity to buy a diversified portfolio of securities in a single transaction. ETFs provide the benefit of trading ASX-listed entities, coupled with the low cost and diversification advantage of index managed funds (refer to Chapter 14 for more on index managed funds).

Investing in the next big thing

ETFs have become a central part of many investors' portfolios in the United States. ETFs now account for around one-third of the US stock market volume. Australia still has some way to go to match the US experience but ETFs are growing in popularity in Australia.

So what do ETFs do? ETFs aim to track the performance of a market index such as the S&P/ASX 200 in Australia or the S&P 500 in the United States. Some ETFs establish their own index rather than use the standard indices available. So you have to understand the basis for the index before deciding to invest. ETFs are very similar to their cousins, the index managed funds I talk about in Chapter 14. The difference is that ETFs are listed on a stock market and trade just like shares.

How do ETFs track an index? First, I need to explain what an index is. An *index* gives an average weighted price of a number of underlying shares at any particular point in time. For example, the S&P/ASX 200 is made up of, not surprisingly, 200 stocks. Those stocks are given a weighting in the index according to how big they are, or what their total market value is. The largest stock on the ASX by value is BHP Billiton, which makes up 12.3 per cent of the S&P/ASX 200. So BHP's price movement on the ASX has more of an impact on the index than any other stock. What ETFs do is buy all 200 stocks in the index according to each stock's weighting. In the case of BHP, it would make up 12.3 per cent of the ETF's portfolio.

The value of an ETF is never going to reflect exactly the value of the index it's tracking. ETFs pay out distributions to investors from dividends they receive from the portfolio of shares. Indices don't pay out distributions. The price of an ETF also has the annual management fee deducted from it.

Valuing ETFs

ETFs are valued in a similar way to managed funds and listed investment companies. The value is worked out by adding up the total value of all the underlying investments and deducting any expenses, to arrive at a net asset value (NAV) per unit. The NAV is calculated daily and the issuers of ETFs publish the NAV on their websites. Some issuers even calculate the NAV on their ETFs every 30 seconds.

Following the NAV of an ETF before you buy or sell can help you to determine if the price quoted on the ASX is fair. If the price is nowhere near the NAV, then ask your broker to speak to the market maker (read on) to get a better price.

Advantages of using exchange-traded funds

Reading about ETFs from the companies that provide these products, you may wonder why you'd bother with any other product. They love 'em! And ETF providers think you're mad not to love them the way they do. ETFs have a lot to like about them and I list the main reasons here:

- **Easy access:** Investing in ETFs is as simple as buying shares. ETFs are a great way to access a range of different markets that may usually be tricky for investors to get exposure to, especially overseas markets and commodities such as gold, silver and platinum.

- **Income:** ETFs distribute income quarterly, half-yearly or annually, depending on when they receive income from the underlying investments. Investors can also take advantage of *franking credits*, a tax deduction that investors can claim for the tax already paid by the companies before they pay a dividend. Refer to Chapter 5 for more on franking credits.

- **Liquidity:** A stockbroker can trade ETFs in one of two ways on behalf of investors. The first method is via the ASX, in the same way shares are traded during market open hours. The second way is through what is called a market maker. The *market maker*, usually a company, guarantees to buy or sell an amount of ETF shares at an agreed price for the investor. The agreed price is at or very close to the market value of the underlying investments. Using a market maker is a big plus for investors who want to get in or out of ETFs at the price they want, when they want.

- **Low cost:** The two main costs are an ongoing management cost and the cost of buying or selling ETFs through a stockbroker. The ongoing annual management fee is similar to that charged by managed funds (check out Chapter 5 for more on annual fees). Fees typically range from around 0.09 per cent per annum to 0.85 per cent per annum. The bigger the index, the cheaper the annual management fee tends to be. For example, investing in the iShares S&P 500 (United States) ETF costs 0.09 per cent, whereas the iShares MSCI Taiwan ETF costs 0.82 per cent per annum.

- **Taxation:** *Turnover*, or trading, of the underlying shares is low, so minimises the level of capital gains in the fund. For more on tax in managed funds, refer to Chapter 5.

- **Transparency:** You know exactly what investments are in an ETF.

- **Value:** ETFs are designed to trade very close to the value of the underlying investments. Any difference is usually because of annual management fees, which are deducted from the quoted price.

Disadvantages of using exchange traded funds

ETFs also have their downside, of course. The most obvious downside is that ETFs are a passive investment, meaning you're never going to outperform the selected index with these instruments. Here are the main risks of ETFs:

✔ **Currency risk:** Investing in ETFs that track overseas indices exposes investors to currency risk. ETFs do not hedge against that currency exposure. Movements in currency against the Australian dollar can enhance or detract from returns. So, for example, the S&P 500 Index ETF might increase 10 per cent over a period. At the same time, the Australian dollar may increase in value against the US dollar by 10 per cent, effectively wiping out the gains from the movement in the index. Of course, currency movements can favour investors as well.

✔ **Market risk:** Investors are never going to do better than the market index selected by the ETF provider, although this index may outperform the general market — for example, a resources index versus the S&P/ASX 200. The investment value of an ETF moves in tandem with the market.

From stocks to commodities and international shares

Investors have a large choice of indices to invest in across different markets and sectors within markets, such as resources. Three types of ETFs trade on the ASX:

✔ Australian domestic index ETFs following major indices

✔ International index ETFs following major global and regional indices

✔ Sector index ETFs following major domestic and global sector indices

ETFs cover a range of different indices. Table 15-3 lists some of the main ETFs available on the ASX.

To find out more on ETFs, visit the ASX website at www.asx.com.au/etf. Also take a look at PennyWise Investment at www.pennywiseinvestment.com.au, which provides research and strategies for investing in ETFs (for an annual cost of around $495). Another great site is ETFMate at www.etfmate.com.au, which has research on all the issuers of ETFs, as well as educational articles.

Table 15-3	Some of the Main ETFs in Australia		
Issuer	*ETF*	*ASX Code*	*Market*
Australian Index Investments (Aii) www.aii-etfs.com	S&P/ASX 200 Energy	ENY.axw	Australia
	S&P/ASX 200 Financials	FIN.axw	Australia
	S&P/ASX 200 Industrials	IDD.axw	Australia
	S&P/ASX 200 Resources	RSR.axw	Australia
iShares (Barclays Global) www.ishares.com.au	MSCI BRIC	IBK.axw	Brazil, Russia, India, China
	MSCI Emerging Markets	IEM.axw	Emerging
	S&P Europe 350	IEU.axw	Europe
	S&P Global 100 Basket	IOO.axw	World
	MSCI EAFE	IVE.axw	Europe, Australasia, Far East
	S&P 500	IVV.axw	United States
	FTSE/Xinhua China 25	IZZ.axw	China
Russell Investments www.russell.com/au	Russell High Dividend Australian Shares ETF	RDV.axw	Australia
SPDR (State Street Global Advisers) www.spdr.com.au	S&P/ASX 50	SFY.axw	Australia
	S&P/ASX 200	STW.axw	Australia
	S&P/ASX 200 Listed Property	SLF.axw	Australia
Vanguard www.vanguard.com.au	S&P/ASX 300	VAS.axw	Australia
	FTSE ALL-World ex US Index	VEU.axw	World
	MSCI US Broad Market Index	VTS.axw	United States

Typical investing strategies

One reason investors buy ETFs rather than managed funds is because many managed funds don't beat their benchmark index. So why take a chance on a fund manager when you can buy an ETF and be guaranteed to match the index? For many, ETFs are a no-brainer.

Taking a look at exchange-traded commodities

As well as exchange-traded funds, you can also invest in what are known as exchange-traded commodities (ETCs). These work in the same way as ETFs — instead of tracking an index, they track the price of underlying commodities such as gold, palladium, silver and platinum. Overseas stock exchanges, such as the London Stock Exchange, list many other types of ETCs, including livestock, oil, wheat and soy, to name but a few.

ETCs can either buy the physical commodity, such as gold, or they can track a commodity's price *synthetically*, meaning they use commodity futures. The Gold ETC listed on the ASX (ASX code GOLD) actually buys physical gold, which is kept in a vault on behalf of investors. ETCs offer a great way for smaller investors to access commodity markets, something usually reserved for sophisticated investors.

But why stop there? Investors can use ETFs to enhance a portfolio in other ways. ETFs are an efficient way to create a *core* equity portfolio giving you exposure to some or all of the market, depending on what type of ETF you buy. With this strategy, you won't have to buy several stocks to give you broad market exposure — you can achieve the same advantage through a single transaction in an ETF. For a low cost you can get immediate access to the performance of the market index. In fund-manager-speak this is known as the *beta* and means the return is equal to that of the market. Investors can then add specific stocks or sectors to sit beside the ETF and potentially add what is known as *alpha* returns. These are returns over and above what the market index makes.

For example, say you invest $50,000 in a broad S&P/ASX 200 index as you're positive about the market outlook. Too easy! You don't have to pick stocks; the ETF does it all for you. But you also fancy resource stocks; in particular, BHP Billiton and RIO Tinto. So you add $5,000 worth of each stock to your portfolio. Immediately, you can potentially earn some above-market returns, or alpha, by tilting your portfolio to resource stocks. This approach is also known as a *core and satellite* investing approach.

Ethical, or Values-Based, Investments

Investing with a conscience — now there's a thing! But values-based investing is just that, investing with a motive in addition to a desire to make money. In this section, I look at what values-based investing is all about and cover what are known as ethical investing, socially responsible investing (SRI) and sustainable investing.

This section also looks at how fund managers make *ethical investing* decisions, usually by avoiding or excluding certain companies. Avoiding the *sin-stocks* in gambling, alcohol, tobacco and weapons is one way funds can invest ethically. Others may exclude heavy environmental polluters such as those found in the resources sector.

Socially responsible investing (SRI) involves the strategy of selecting an investment to achieve environmental or social aims as well as financial returns. SRI investing may screen out investments that don't meet these objectives from a portfolio.

Sustainable investing, on the other hand, is more about looking for positive attributes in a business, such as how well a company is managed, as well as how well it meets its social responsibilities. Former US vice president Al Gore and his business partner David Blood (yes, Blood and Gore!) run one of the largest sustainable funds in the world, the Generation Global Share Fund. The fund is available through Colonial First State and 'recognises that economic, health, environmental, social and governance factors can impact a company's long-term performance'.

Investing ethically or responsibly is all very well. Surely, I hear you say, the price for investing with a clear conscience must be to sacrifice returns? Well, not necessarily. Performance need not be any worse than traditional funds just because they exclude the sin-stocks. In many cases, values-based funds perform as well, if not better, than traditional funds. Here I look at performance and give a brief run-through of the main ethical funds in the market.

Ethics and investing can go together

Ethical investing grew out of fund managers responding to the needs of their not-for-profit clients, such as charities and religious organisations. Managers developed a means of investing to suit their clients' ethical, environmental, religious and social values or beliefs. Imagine an Islamic fund investing in alcohol, a landmine clearance charity unwittingly investing in weapons manufacturers or a cancer foundation investing in tobacco companies? It doesn't make sense and the charities figured the same. With values-based funds, changing the world can now be part of your investment philosophy.

Some of the ways fund managers select values-based investments are:

- **Best of sector:** Looks for the best sustainable companies in each sector. The idea is that a company judged to be sustainable is likely to be better managed.

- **Negative screening:** Not a bad movie review but the way managers 'screen out' companies they don't want to invest in. Out go companies involved in tobacco, gambling, factory farming, logging of old-growth forests, armaments and uranium mining, and companies suspected of human rights violations.

✔ **Positive screening:** Having eliminated the bad guys, funds may decide then to 'screen in' investments that are considered good. These stocks may not change the world but can have a positive impact. Companies screened in may include clean energy (wind farms) or socially responsible companies such as those conducting *fair trade*, giving fair prices to their suppliers in third-world countries.

✔ **Sustainability:** This method looks at how likely it is a business will continue to operate into the future. The method is different from ethical or SRI investing, which apply negative screens to exclude stocks. Sustainable investing looks at positive aspects that will maintain a business well into the future and maximise returns for investors.

✔ **Themes:** These funds look to invest in companies that have a certain ethical or environmental theme, such as medical research, water, waste management or solar power.

Not all ethical funds are as ethical as the next. Some still include *negative stocks* in their portfolio but restrict the holdings to no more than, say, 10 per cent of the total value of the fund. These funds take the view that no-one is perfect and a little bit of sin is not such a bad thing. Woolworths stock is an example; the retailer sells tobacco products and is a significant pokies operator, but makes the bulk of its profits through its grocery operations. BHP Billiton is another example. Being one of the biggest miners in the world, its operations may often conflict with environmental considerations. But the stock is such a large part of the Australian market it is difficult for investors to ignore.

Fair trade for fair investments

Jumping on the ethical bandwagon makes good business sense for many companies, not just fund managers. Customers are forcing many companies to change and show they are socially responsible. Two sectors that are responding to growing consumer concerns about the way they do business are the fast-food industry and the automotive industry.

Fast-food chains, long criticised — rightly or not — about the source of their ingredients, have begun to answer their critics. Consumers have said, 'We want to know how the food is reared or grown.' Some fast-food chains now make a great play of having sourced 'fair trade' or 'green alliance' coffee, for example. Coffee where the growers get a fair price is not only seen as ethical but is great marketing for the fast-food chains and keeps customers coming through the door.

Equally, the automotive industry has woken up to the fact that oil is going to run out. Big-engine, petrol-guzzling cars may be great to drive but the reality is many consumers want to drive into a sustainable future.

The changes make good business sense for both the fast-food and car industries. Making the changes to more ethical and sustainable products keeps their customers happy and sees the money continue to roll in.

Make money from ethical investments, really!

So who are the main providers of values-based funds in the Australian managed funds market? For some providers, such as AMP, ethical funds are part of a stable of many different fund types. For other managers, such as Hunter Hall, values-based investing is all they do. Table 15-4 shows some of the main players in the market and the funds they offer. The Responsible Investment Association of Australasia (RIAA) has certified the fund managers listed in Table 15-4.

Table 15-4	Values-Based Fund Managers and Their Funds	
Fund Manager	**No. of Values-Based Funds**	**Retail Funds Offered**
AMP Capital Investors www.ampcapital.com.au	5	Balanced, Conservative, Growth, Australian, International
Australian Ethical Investments www.australianethical.com.au	6	Balanced, Smaller Companies Trust, Larger Companies Trust, Income, Property, International
BT Investments www.btim.com.au	2	Sustainable Balanced, Sustainable Conservative
CVC Sustainable Investments www.cvcsi.com.au	1	Sustainable Investments
Hunter Hall www.hunterhall.com.au	4	Value Growth, Australian Value, Global Ethical, Global Deep Green
Perennial Investment Partners www.perennial.net.au	1	Socially Responsive Shares
Perpetual Investments www.perpetual.com.au	1	Ethical SRI Fund
Vanguard Investments www.vanguard.com.au	2	Sustainability Leaders Australian, Sustainability Leaders International

Source: *Information compiled from Responsible Investment Association of Australasia website.*

To find out more about values-based or responsible investing you can visit the website of ASIC's consumer watchdog FIDO at www.fido.gov.au. You can also visit the Responsible Investment Association of Australasia (RIAA) at www.responsibleinvestment.org for more information.

So how do values-based funds stack up performance-wise? Figure 15-1 shows how responsible investment funds investing in Australian shares performed against traditional funds and the broader S&P/ASX 300 Accumulation Index. Figure 15-2 shows how responsible investment funds investing in overseas shares performed against traditional funds and the broader MSCI World ex-Australia Index. Both charts show values-based investing can beat the traditional funds!

Figure 15-1:
Relative perform-ance of Australian responsible-investing funds against traditional funds and the S&P ASX 300 Accumula-tion Index.

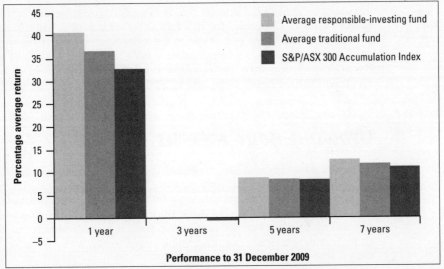

Source: Responsible Investing Association of Australasia, Morningstar and fund manager data.

Figure 15-2:
Relative perform-ance of overseas responsible-investing funds against traditional funds and the MSCI World ex-Australia Index.

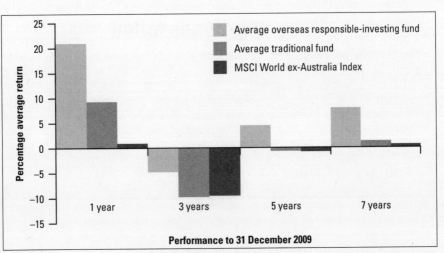

Source: Responsible Investing Association of Australasia, Morningstar and fund manager data.

Agricultural Investments

Sounds like a good idea. Get a patch of land, plant some long-maturing crops and package it up as an investment. Throw in generous government tax relief and you have the makings of a great product. But it's not that simple!

Agricultural investments, or *agrifunds*, take many forms. They invest in food or crop production directly. Those most easily accessed by everyday investors are packaged and sold as a managed investment scheme (MIS — refer to Chapter 2 for more details) via a product disclosure statement (PDS). Born out of generous federal government tax incentives, agrifunds were designed to stimulate local economies — I'm not touching the politics of that with a barge pole! But I do run through what agrifunds are, how they may suit some investors and the traps for the unwary.

Growing your returns, literally

So you're a townie who has never set foot on a farm but you quite like the idea of owning a stand of trees, growing some olives or perhaps a beef cow or two. These investments may be accessible using agrifunds. The best bit is that someone else does all the hard work of growing, harvesting and selling for you. For the manager, a fund is a quick way to raise enough money to start planting. Banks tend to shy away from lending to such long-term projects.

Agrifunds felled

The GFC claimed a number of agrifund operators, including Great Southern, Timbercorp and Forestry Enterprises Australia. All these operators — and Great Southern was one of the biggest — have gone bust. Some of these operators were set up such that, after the initial investment had been made, the investor had no more to pay. In theory, it was up to the operator to pay for ongoing expenses out of the initial investment funds. But it didn't work out like that. The funds relied on getting new investors through the door to pay for their existing operations! These funds appeared to be a classic version of a Ponzi scheme, where money from new investors is taken to pay back existing investors or, in this case, finance existing operations.

Agrifunds offer investments in forestry projects, usually for wood pulp; other plantation projects, including sandalwood; orchard fruits such as mangoes, almonds and avocados; and livestock, including cattle. With tree plantation projects, the investor effectively leases a piece of land from the grower and then employs the grower to cultivate the trees. At the end of the project term, which can be 15 to 20 years, the trees are harvested and sold. Any money left after expenses is returned to investors. No return or income is paid to investors until completion, usually after many years.

Understanding the difference between tax-advantaged and tax-driven

So what is the difference between tax-advantaged and tax-driven investments and why is it relevant to agrifunds?

- ✔ **Tax-advantaged:** Also known as tax-effective investments, these investments have tax breaks on the income and costs of the investment. For example, margin loans could be called tax-effective as the interest charged on the loan is potentially tax-deductible.

- ✔ **Tax-driven:** The best way to describe these investments is that you probably wouldn't invest in them if they didn't have the tax breaks. The investments just wouldn't make sense otherwise, let alone make money. Some agrifunds have fallen into this category in the past and many still do. These funds rely on tax rulings from the Australian Taxation Office (ATO) allowing tax deductions on the product. Without the tax rulings, the funds rarely stack up as a viable investment.

Determining the tax deductions

Investors may get 100 per cent tax deductions against other income — sometimes even more — on the initial investment and ongoing expenses. But agrifunds should be looked at exactly the same way as any other fund — potential for performance first and tax breaks second.

Each investor in the fund incurs costs from day one, as well as ongoing costs. Initial costs include the lease of the land or purchase of livestock. Annual ongoing costs include the planting and cultivating of crops and rearing the animals. The initial set-up costs are usually tax-deductible immediately against other income, as are ongoing costs.

Investors sitting on large capital gains from other investments may use the tax deduction on agrifunds to offset those gains. Always seek advice from a tax professional though.

Avoiding the traps for the unwary

Apart from all the usual risks from weather and disease that goes with growing anything, you need to watch out for how agrifunds are set up:

- ✔ **Fees:** Some of these funds can pay a whopping 10 per cent entry fee to financial advisers or brokers for recommending their products.

- ✔ **Income:** Proceeds from the sale of the crop upon harvest is income assessable for tax.

- ✔ **Land tenure:** With forestry projects, investors don't buy the land the trees are growing on; they just lease it for as long as the project lasts.

- ✔ **Length:** Check out how long you can expect to wait before the project starts harvesting and you start to see a return. Forestry projects can be 15 to 20 years long; livestock a lot shorter.

- ✔ **Tax rulings:** Investors should be very wary of products that don't have a tax ruling from the ATO. You won't get a tax deduction for your costs otherwise. A product ruling means the ATO is happy that the scheme has been set up to produce income and not as a tax dodge. The PDS should disclose this but always consult a tax adviser if in doubt.

Understanding private equity funds

Private equity has an air of mystique about it. Talked about in hushed tones by finance professionals, private equity is seen as something for serious investors. *Private* refers to the fact that funds are investing in private companies rather than those listed on a stock exchange. The people who run these funds have a reputation as being the smartest guys in the room. And they need to be, because investing in unlisted companies throws up all sorts of interesting challenges and risks.

Private equity funds don't usually buy a small part of a company like a traditional fund manager does. They may take a 30 per cent stake in a company, but usually a lot more. Usually offered to corporate investors or wealthy individuals, private equity has an exclusive tag. Managers want sophisticated investors in for the long haul, usually five years or more.

Private equity managers look to take an active involvement in the day-to-day management of their investments. They have seats on the board of directors and develop the strategy for the company. If the managers get it right, they can be paid a stack of money for their efforts.

Few private equity managers offer funds to retail investors in Australia. Four private equity companies are listed on the ASX, so investors can get an indirect exposure to their funds through the management companies. These four companies are Charter Pacific, CVC Limited, ING Private Equity and Souls Private Equity. Private equity funds tend to raise money over a relatively short period, such as eight to ten weeks, before closing to new investors. Investors' money is then locked up for between five and seven years.

Chapter 16

Lifting the Veil on Hedge Funds and Structured Products

In This Chapter

▶ Understanding what hedging means

▶ Discovering available hedge funds

▶ Checking out the fees attached to hedge funds

▶ Taking a tour around structured products

To many investors, hedge funds inhabit a parallel universe where the normal rules of investing have been thrown out the window. I doubt that any other type of investment has polarised the media and the investing public as much as hedge funds have done.

During the good times, hedge funds are the rock stars of the investing world, lifted almost to the status of miracle workers. During the bad times, all bets are off. Hedge funds are demonised and blamed for everything that's wrong with the market. The truth, as always, is probably somewhere in between.

More than 8,000 hedge fund managers and well over 25,000 funds exist globally, managing around A$1.7 trillion. Fortunately, available funds are a lot fewer in Australia. In this chapter, I shed some light on the different types of hedge funds and the strategies they use. I also show that hedge funds can be used in a portfolio as a way of spreading risk and look at funds available to investors in Australia.

I also cover what are called structured products. These funds usually aim to give investors a way to minimise or eliminate losses, called *downside protection*. This type of investing is a form of hedging. Sounds like a great idea but, as always with investing, anything fail-safe usually comes with conditions attached.

Understanding What's Meant by Hedging

Ever heard the phrase 'hedging your bets'? I'm sure most investors have and, in the world of investing, it means managing risk. Investors can't entirely remove risk from an investment. In short, *hedging* is about minimising losses and maximising returns. Here I explain what hedging is and what you should consider before using hedge funds.

Hedging: A simple explanation

Reading the papers, any mention of hedge funds is usually about how much money they've made or how much investors have lost. These funds generally represent a small minority of funds that have taken big one-sided bets on the market. Most hedge funds aim to make a decent return for their investors and some do better than others. And, for most funds, successful investing is about managing risk.

Going back to the beginning

A little-known fact is that the man credited with creating the first modern-day hedge fund, Alfred Winslow, was born in Australia — Melbourne, to be precise, in 1901 — and later moved to the United States with his parents.

In 1949, Winslow decided to try his hand at managing money and set up a fund aiming to minimise losses by *shorting* stocks (selling stocks he didn't own). Winslow also developed the idea of borrowing money to invest, generating potentially even higher returns. The fund was the first to tie in the manager's personal interest in being rewarded for the performance of the fund. The $100,000 he invested in 1949 grew to several million by the mid-1960s.

Perhaps an element of myth and legend has crept into the story of Alfred Winslow. But why ruin a good story with the facts! Although Winslow gets all the credit today, Karl Karsten, an American academic writing in the 1930s, was the first to write about hedging investments. Karsten defined in theory exactly what Winslow did in practice.

So why the history lesson? Winslow's fund was the first to be called a hedge fund because it 'hedged' so that market movements did not impact his investments (called *market-neutral* investing). The term *hedging* evolved into one that seems to cover every fund that isn't a traditional managed fund. Some of the 'hedge' funds available today are not hedged, don't protect their portfolios and have highly risky strategies. These funds have less to do with investing and more to do with gambling.

In the true sense of the word, hedging is all about managing risk. Hedging is what investors do to protect their investments and can be thought of as a form of insurance. So, if you think the price of gold will go up, you may decide to buy gold stocks. But you want to be sure you don't lose money if the price moves down. You 'hedge' your portfolio by using gold futures (a form of derivative — refer to Chapter 14) that increase in value if the gold price goes down. You may lose money on your gold shares but you make money on the gold futures, cancelling out the losses.

Finding a place in your portfolio for hedge funds

Hedge funds can add a different dimension to a portfolio. Many hedge funds are highly volatile and make the average rollercoaster ride at the local funfair look tame. Treat these investments in much the same way as you would any other investment. Here are two aspects to keep a close eye on:

- ✔ **Diversification:** Hedge funds can provide diversification to a portfolio both in terms of the assets they invest in and the way they manage risk. Investments may be international across a range of asset types, such as shares and bonds. Many funds adopt *market-neutral* strategies, where movements in the market are largely neutralised.

- ✔ **Risk:** Understand the risk of any hedge fund you're interested in. The research agencies such as Morningstar are a good starting point. Volatility (read risk) in hedge funds can be high, so you need to have a longer term investment horizon of at least five years. The level of risk in a fund can change the level of overall risk in a portfolio.

Comparing hedge funds can be tricky. Funds use different hedging strategies and the differences can be subtle. You need to look at each fund on its own merits and seek out funds with a good track record of performance. Also be prepared for potentially wild swings in performance. Hedge funds can exaggerate both positive and negative returns.

Examining Types of Hedge Funds

Hedge funds use many different ways to manage money. In fact, ways to manage money — strategies — are almost as varied as the number of hedge funds. Some strategies take investors deep into the realms of sophisticated mathematical models built by highly paid rocket scientists. Others are more straightforward and look a lot like traditional managed funds. In this section, I look at some of the more common strategies you may come across.

As many types as there are funds

Looking at the types of hedge funds and their strategies can leave investors feeling bamboozled. Identifying hedge funds is made simpler by the fact that they tend to be named according to the type of strategy they use. Here are the main types of these funds and strategies:

- **Absolute return:** Simply put, *absolute return* is the percentage return on any investment. In fund-management-speak, it means that the return ignores what a benchmark index has returned (refer to Chapter 14).

- **Arbitrage:** This strategy is employed when a fund manager looks to exploit differences in asset prices that can happen, for example, when a company is listed on two different stock markets. A classic example is BHP, which is listed on the Australian Securities Exchange (ASX) and on the London Stock Exchange. BHP's share price may not be exactly the same on both markets at the same time, for a number of reasons, such as currency movements. Fund managers try to use those differences to make money but making money this way is a tough game. Get it right and you can do well.

- **Distressed debt:** Investing in company debt considered to be *junk debt*, or not investment grade. These companies may be very sick, on the edge of bankruptcy or being turned around. Most traditional bond funds cannot own junk debt and that drives the prices of these investments down further, leaving many undervalued. Distressed debt funds believe companies will turn around and the price of the debt instrument will increase.

- **Event-driven or special situation:** Funds that look to exploit certain situations, such as merger and acquisition activity.

  For example, Company A may want to buy Company B, and offers shareholders $1 a share. The hedge fund takes a view that the shares are worth $1.20 a share and that Company A will have to make a higher offer to get Company B's shareholders to accept the takeover. Importantly, returns for these funds are not dependent on the movements in the underlying stock market.

- **Fixed income:** These funds invest in fixed-income securities — both long and short (read on for definitions of long and short) — using a range of different strategies, including borrowing to invest.

- **Long or short:** Investing *long* simply means buying investments in the way traditional managed funds invest in shares. Investing *short* means selling shares that you don't own, expecting the shares will go down.

  How does that work? An investor borrows stock and sells that borrowed stock at, say, $2.00. The share price then falls to $1.50, at which point the investor buys the stock back and returns it to whomever it was borrowed from. The investor has made 50 cents less any borrowing costs. Shorting stock is a well-accepted method of investing and stock can easily be borrowed with the help of a stockbroker. Long or short funds buy investments they think will go up, and borrow and sell investments they think will go down.

✔ **Macro:** These are the big-picture guys and the ones who make the headlines for taking huge bets on currencies or commodities. They look at what's happening to economies globally and try to pick the big trends in markets. The size of some of these funds can make life very difficult for governments when they see their currencies getting hammered by hedge funds.

✔ **Managed futures:** These funds invest in currency and commodity futures and options to generate returns in both rising and falling markets.

✔ **Multi-strategy:** These funds use a mix of the strategies listed here.

✔ **Relative value:** Funds that try to exploit price differences in similar assets.

For example, Bank A and Bank B are listed on the stock market, have similar relative values and their share price performances usually match. However, Bank A's share price starts to underperform Bank B's. A relative value fund will pounce on both banks' shares, shorting or selling the overperforming Bank B in the expectation its share price will fall and buying Bank A, expecting its price to rise.

Many strategies noted in the preceding list are market neutral. Investing in shares exposes an investor to broadly two types of risk — market risk that the market will go down and stock risk that the shares will go down. Under a market-neutral strategy, the fund manager is interested only in the stock risk and looks to get rid of the market risk. These funds look to benefit from both rising and falling prices, so it doesn't matter which way the market moves. These funds rely heavily on the skill of the manager to make money.

Understanding the level of risk involved with each type of strategy can be tricky. Many funds can leverage, or borrow for, their investments by more than a hundred times. So, for every $1 million dollars of money they have, they can get $100 million or more of exposure to a particular investment. These funds are at the extreme end of the hedge fund spectrum and cater to highly sophisticated investors.

Unravelling black-box investing

Black-box investing is a part of the hedge fund industry that is shrouded in mystery. Most people know the black box as the device that acts as a plane's memory, recording every bit of data while in flight. In investing, the *black box* is a general way of describing a model or structure that a fund manager uses to make investment decisions. The more sophisticated models can be a way for fund managers to analyse huge amounts of market data. Investment decisions are made on the back of that information.

The mystery around black-box investing is that, apart from the people operating these models, most investors on the outside have little idea of how they work. The fund manager can describe in general terms what the model does. But that is like explaining to someone who has never seen a car that it has an engine that makes it go. The first question they ask is 'What's an engine?' Black-box investing is sometimes called *quantitative* (or *quant*) investing. Quant investing looks at and analyses data such as market prices, performance, company balance sheets and reported earnings, and a heap of ratios that go with all of that. Some fund managers take the results of that analysis and add their own judgements to any investment decisions. Other funds are purely quant-driven. If the model says buy shares in Company A, then the manager buys Company A.

Finding out about hedge funds in Australia

Managed fund research house Morningstar Australia categorises hedge funds as either Australian (investing solely in Australian assets) or global funds. Some of the bigger hedge fund managers with funds available to everyday investors are listed in Table 16-1. In addition, Macquarie Fund Management has a number of hedge funds, all of which are closed to new investors. Platinum Asset Management (www.platinum.com.au) is sometimes called a hedge fund manager because it has funds that use the long or short investing strategy. However, Platinum does not regard itself as a hedge fund manager.

Table 16-1	Some Hedge Funds Available to Retail Investors		
Hedge Fund Manager	**Type of Funds**	**Number of Funds**	**Minimum Investment**
BlackRock Investment Management www.blackrock investments.com.au	Tactical asset allocation strategies globally across equity, cash, fixed-interest, property, commodity and currency markets	1	$5,000
Hedge Funds Australia (HFA) www.hfaam.com.au	Single-strategy fund and hedge fund-of-funds investing in a range of different global share-focused absolute-return funds	1 single-strategy fund; 2 fund-of-funds	$20,000
K2 Asset Management www.k2am.com.au	Equity long or short absolute-return funds	3	$20,000
PM Capital www.pmcapital.com.au	Equity long or short absolute-return funds	5	$20,000

Many other hedge funds are available in Australia. The problem is that most funds only want wholesale investors (refer to Chapter 3). These funds don't sell their products by a product disclosure statement (PDS) but by an information memorandum for wholesale clients. You need to prove you are a wholesale (sophisticated) investor. Some funds have a minimum investment of only $25,000; others set the bar high, at $1 million.

To find out more about hedge funds, visit the Alternative Investment Management Association in Australia (AIMA) at www.aima-australia. org. For research on hedge fund managers and the industry, head to EurekaHedge at www.eurekahedge.com. This site does have some free articles but the good stuff you'll have to pay for.

Fees to Make Your Eyes Water

Fees, fees and more fees! Well, when you've got a private jet and several homes around the world to look after, the standard managed fund fees just won't cut it. Okay, I'm exaggerating a bit. Yes, certainly some hedge fund managers make the headlines for their lavish lifestyles. Many do exceptionally well, others do okay out of it and equally many others crash and burn. Such is the high-risk nature of running a hedge fund. Of course, investors do pay for the skill that the hedge fund managers bring to the table — and it's all around performance fees.

Understanding the 2-and-20 rule

The *2-and-20 rule* is commonplace among most hedge funds — 2 per cent annual management fee and 20 per cent performance fee.

The 2 per cent annual management fee is a generalisation and can vary from around 1 per cent to more than 2 per cent. The annual management fees, along with contribution fees, transaction spreads and others work in exactly the same way as for managed funds (refer to Chapter 5).

Performance fees are a different thing altogether. The 20 per cent performance fee is, by and large, standard across the industry. These fees can work in slightly different ways, as either high-water marks or hurdle rates.

Floating above high-water marks

High-water marks are a way of giving an incentive to a hedge fund manager to keep producing good performance numbers. Think of high-tide marks left by the sea on a beach and you begin to understand what is meant by high-water marks. In short, managers can't get paid a performance fee unless they beat previous performance measures for the fund. Bear with me while I explain the high-water mark in a bit more depth.

The performance fee is only paid if the current value of a unit in the fund is more than the high-water mark. The high-water mark is the previous value of a unit when the last performance fee was paid.

If you invest in a fund for $1.00 a unit, for example, that price is regarded as the first high-water mark. Over 12 months the fund's value increases to $1.10 a unit. A performance fee of $0.02 per unit is paid to the manager (20 per cent of the $0.10 increase in value). Paying the fee reduces the value of each unit by $0.02, so the high-water mark is reset at $1.08 per unit. If, 12 months down the track, the fund is worth only $1.05, then no performance fee is paid. If, however, the fund increases to $1.15, then a performance fee is payable on the difference between the reset high-water mark of $1.08 and $1.15, or $0.07. And so it continues ...

High-water marks keep hedge funds honest, when it comes to charging fees anyway. Hedge funds have to perform better than they've done in the past to get paid. And that's fair enough. If a hedge fund can produce great returns for its investors on an ongoing basis then it's only fair they get paid for it.

Handling the hurdles

Some funds set a *hurdle rate* return they must beat before a performance fee can be paid. For example, a fund may set a hurdle rate of 8 per cent or more each year (a common rate). If the fund produces performance better than 8 per cent, it pays a performance fee to the manager. The fee is 20 per cent of the difference between the hurdle rate and performance.

So, if the fund returns 20 per cent, the performance fee is 20 per cent less 8 per cent. The resulting 12 per cent is then multiplied by the 20 per cent performance fee with a resultant 2.4 per cent of the fund being paid to the manager. If the fund has $100 million of investments, 2.4 per cent of that ($2.4 million) is a fair chunk to the manager. No wonder these guys can make a mint in the good times!

Structured Product Investments

Never invest in a business you cannot understand.

—*Warren Buffett, investment guru*

Warren Buffet's quote could equally apply to *structured products* — managed funds with a twist — a big twist. The ultimate managed fund investment is one that can only go up in value. And that's what many structured products set out to do. Wonderful! Or are they? This section sets out the main types of structured funds, a brief explanation of how they work and why you might invest in them. I also explain fees and other nasties to look out for.

These funds are effectively hedge funds with a different name. Using sometimes complex investment techniques involving derivatives, the fund manager sets up a structure to protect investors' money. So, many of these funds are also known as *capital-guaranteed* funds as they look to preserve your initial investment. These funds can be sold only to retail investors via a PDS or sometimes a *prospectus* — like a PDS but used when a product is offering shares for sale instead of units like a managed fund.

Watching out for the guarantees

As any professional investor will tell you, the only thing guaranteed in investing is that nothing is guaranteed. But the guys who put structured products together tell you that they can guarantee to give you at least your money back — with conditions. These products are called capital protected or capital guaranteed. Most funds offer a choice of guarantee between 100 per cent and 90 per cent of the initial investment. With a 100 per cent guarantee, if you invest $15,000 you will get at least $15,000 back at the end of the investment's term. The guarantees are typically provided by a large bank such as ANZ, so, even if the company providing the fund goes bust, you should eventually get your investment back in full.

Look out for how long the investment runs for. Most guaranteed funds give the full guarantee only at the end of the term. Take your money out early and you lose the protection. Guarantees also cost money and add to the fees investors pay for investing in the fund.

Types of structured products

Many different types of products are available. However, unlike a managed fund that can usually be bought at any time, structured products tend to be open for a short six- to eight-week period before closing. The most common products that appear at regular intervals during the year are the ones based on a theme. Managers of these products love a theme. Themes might be emerging markets, such as China, or a group of markets such as Brazil, Russia, India and China (BRIC). Others may offer exposure to particular global sectors such as infrastructure, commodities or utilities (electricity generation, water treatment and the like). Gold has been a popular theme in recent years.

How are products structured?

Guaranteed products have essentially two moving parts — the guarantee and the underlying investments. Investors may come across two types of guarantee. One guarantee gives you back your money at the end of the fund's life; and the other rises over the life of the product, so you get back a little more than your original investment. Underlying investments are what the fund invests in to make its returns (or possibly lose money), usually derivative products of some sort. Some funds even offer a chance to enhance any returns with what is known as a *participation rate*. These rates provide a potential extra kicker to a fund's returns.

Here is a little more detail on each of these aspects of structured products:

- ✓ **Guarantee:** The simple piece to the puzzle is the guarantee. Usually, the fund manager takes a portion of the investor's money, typically 70 per cent, and puts it in a relatively safe investment called a *zero coupon* or *deep-discounted bond*. The idea with these products is that the fund buys them at, say, $70 a bond and, because of the way the product works, it pays back $100 in, say, five years' time. Hey presto! The initial investment is guaranteed to be paid back in full. Big banks like Commonwealth Bank of Australia or ANZ usually provide the guarantees for these products.

- ✓ **Rising guarantee:** Some funds offer a rising guarantee over the life of the investment. So, over the course of a seven-year investment — say, after year three — the guarantee may be locked in at 105 per cent and at the end of the product life, the guarantee may be 110 per cent of your initial investment. Rising guarantees effectively take into account some of the effects of inflation — $100 today is going to be worth less than $100 in seven years' time.

- ✓ **Underlying investment:** If $70 of a $100 investment is going towards the guarantee, what about the other $30? This is where the fund manager gets to have some fun. The $30 may be invested in a range of derivatives, such as futures, and options that look to make a return over the life of the product. Using derivatives and options can multiply the returns on a particular investment — this is called *leveraging*, a form of borrowing. The $30 can become the same as investing the full $100 or even more. The $30 is used to produce the return on the fund, all of which — less fees — is the fund's performance and is returned to investors at the end of the product's life.

- ✓ **Returns (performance):** Apart from getting their money back, investors can potentially get a return on their investment over the life of the product. Returns can either be whatever the underlying investment returns, say 50 per cent over the period, or a multiple of that return — the participation rate.

So what is a participation rate? A participation rate is a way for investors to get an even better return on their investment. Say a fund is investing in something simple, the S&P/ASX 200 index. Performance of the index over seven years might be 50 per cent in total, so that $100 invested grows to $150. A structured product may set a participation rate of 150 per cent, meaning that it will give investors a return equivalent to 150 per cent of the return it actually makes. In this example, the 50 per cent return becomes 75 per cent (50 per cent return times 150 per cent participation rate). So, instead of $150, the investor receives $175. Not all funds offer this and it depends on how the manager structures the fund. Rates are set at the launch of the product and remain in place until the end of the product's life.

Derivatives and options are not 'real' investments in that they aren't backed by assets. They are just bits of paper, contracts with another party. Buying shares, on the other hand, gives an investor a stake in the underlying company, its assets and earnings. Derivatives and options are contracts between two investors to buy or sell a particular underlying share or commodity at some future date for a predetermined price. Derivatives and options reflect the price of the underlying investment, such as the S&P/ASX 200 share index or the price of gold.

Why invest in a structured product?

So, you like taking a risk but like being able to protect your investment even more. Perhaps you've a hankering to invest in China but want some safeguard when doing so. Structured products give investors a level of surety. Self-managed super fund investors looking to add a bit of zing to their investments but without the risk may be especially attracted to these products. Some other reasons why you may want to invest in a structured product are:

✔ **Access:** Structured products give investors the opportunity to invest in alternative asset classes, such as commodities, and access to different economies or markets, including emerging markets and commodities.

✔ **Diversification:** These products can help to spread your risk across a range of different assets.

The rise and fall of structured products

Structured products have long inhabited the realms of the sophisticated professional investor. Back-room bank boffins, with more degrees in astrophysics than you can shake a calculator at, dream up complex investment structures for their big corporate clients. Inevitably, these products, albeit very much watered-down versions, have made it to the general public.

During the bull markets of 2003 to 2008, many of these products came into their own. Catching a wave of optimism, providers churned out these products like there was no tomorrow, some becoming ever more complex than they already were.

When the fall inevitably hit markets in 2008, the products did what they were supposed to do, protected investors' capital. However, some products didn't. Some promised annual income of 12 per cent plus per annum, but the structure producing these returns was destroyed in the market fallout. Not even the product providers had expected such deep falls in the market. So, when the market did fall, their fancy models and assumptions fell apart. The guarantee was still in place, but investors were left with their money locked up and another seven years or so to get it back intact.

Lesson: Know what you're buying!

✔ **Investment strategy:** Some funds aim to generate a return regardless of whether markets are rising or falling. Funds may be *index unaware*, which means they don't set a target of beating any particular index, just to make as much money as possible.

✔ **Risk reduction:** So you like the idea of China but know how erratic the market can be. A capital guarantee lets you take a risk in the market, knowing you'll get your money back.

The main providers of these products available to the public include:

✔ **Commonwealth Bank of Australia:** CBA, through CommSec, issues its Capital Series products a couple of times a year. Check the website at www.commsec.com.au for more information, including the performance of existing funds.

✔ **Man Investments:** One of the largest hedge funds in the world, Man's OM-IP products have a long track record in capital-guaranteed products. It launches about three new products a year, investing mainly in managed futures or instruments that can make money in both up and down markets. Find out more at www.maninvestments.com.au or speak to your financial planner.

✔ **Macquarie Bank:** Different product types are issued occasionally. Some of Macquarie's products were devastated during the global financial crisis. Visit www.macquarie.com.au.

Four things to be wary of when investing in structured products:

✔ **Borrowing to invest:** Some companies offer 100 per cent loans to invest in their products. Most products give little or no annual income, so you need to pay back the interest on the loan from other income.

Many of these funds use leverage, or borrowing, to increase their exposure to certain markets. If you borrow to invest, you're effectively borrowing to invest in a fund that is already borrowing to invest. That increases the risk profile of the investment quite a bit.

✔ **Risk and complexity:** These products can be complex. Don't fall into the trap of not looking beyond the capital protection and not understanding what the underlying fund is doing. Risks can be involved, so take advice from a professional. If your adviser can't tell you what the product does, think very carefully about investing.

✔ **Return of investment:** When you invest, you pay by cheque or bank transfer. At the end of the investment term you may get your money back via cheque but you could also get the equivalent value of shares in a company like BHP. The product provider may do this for tax reasons. Check the details in the PDS.

✔ **Tax:** Some of these products are set up offshore. This could be a real headache from a tax point of view. An offshore entity selling investments in Australia is likely to be subject to the Foreign Investment Fund (FIF) rules. Even though investors are resident in Australia, their tax situation may also be impacted. Under these rules, affected investors have to work out the annual increase (or decrease) in the value of their investment and include it in their tax return. So you could potentially be stung for tax on gains you haven't realised!

Fees, more fees and the fees you're not told about

The product disclosure statement should disclose the fees payable, as with any managed fund. Some of the fees investors are likely to pay include:

✔ **Sales fee:** Like a managed fund contribution fee, sales fees are paid to financial planners and advisers for selling the product — typically 4 per cent.

✔ **Establishment costs:** Fees paid to the company for setting up the fund (printing, legal and mailing costs) — can be up to 1.5 per cent of the monies raised.

✔ **Management fee:** Ongoing management fee charged annually — typically 0.5 per cent.

✔ **Performance fee:** Paid on the increase in value of the investment after expenses — around 20 per cent of the gain.

✔ **Other fees:** Can include valuation fees, directors' fees, brokerage costs and a bank guarantee fee paid to the bank organising the capital protection, to name a few.

Saying the list of fees is long is like saying a tiger snake can bite. Yes it can, but the snake's bite can also cause some serious damage. Structured product fees can also do some serious damage to your investments. So funds may have to perform very well to be worthwhile investments.

Chapter 17

Looking at Administration Services and Managed Accounts

In This Chapter

▶ Discovering how to keep track of your managed fund investments

▶ Finding out what wrap accounts and master trusts do

▶ Working out if a managed account is what you need

▶ Cutting through fees and charges

Administration services and managed accounts are slightly different things but both have a lot to do with managed funds. Administration services were first designed for financial planners to help them administer their clients' money, most of which was in managed funds. Managed accounts also help track your investments but in a slightly different way. Big banks, as well as a few fund managers and specialist companies, offer many of the services.

In this chapter, I cover the two main types of administration service most investors are likely to come across — master trusts and wrap accounts. I refer to the providers of administration systems as *operators*. Investors may also come across the term *platform*. This is a general term for the more sophisticated administration services across investments, superannuation and pensions. The more basic services vary in sophistication depending on who uses them — wraps for financial planners and master trusts for both planners and the general public. Knowing about wraps is useful should you decide to use a financial planner.

Managed accounts are a different kettle of fish. Part managed fund, part share investment and part administration system, managed accounts are seen as an alternative to managed funds. Here I explain the differences between managed accounts and managed funds, and why you may want to use an account.

Understanding Administration Services

For some people, tax time involves little more than tipping out the shoe box of statements and receipts gathered during the year. Even those who are organised can find piecing together their investment transactions a challenge. Well, struggle no more! When it comes to keeping track of your portfolio, administration services can make life easier.

Uncovering how administration providers and financial planners work together

The big banks and fund managers — the latter usually owned by the big banks — need to sell as many managed funds and other services as possible. The biggest users of retail managed funds are financial planners. For the banks, having their own financial planners selling their managed funds makes sense. Bingo! Selling is so much easier when you've locked in your customer base.

If you use a financial planner, chances are that the planner either works for or is aligned to a major bank or fund manager. Chapter 11 talks more about financial planners but, to give an idea of how financial planners use administration systems, the three different types of planners are:

- Bank planners, who are employees of a bank and sell bank products
- Dealer group planners, who belong to an umbrella group of planners, many of which are owned by banks
- Independent planners, although *independent* is a controversial term in the industry because most planners become aligned to a product provider over time

The closer a financial planner is to the administration service provider, the more likely you'll end up being recommended that service. Not that there's anything wrong with a little cosiness, but you need to be aware of it. A good financial planner should be able to give the best advice regardless of the administration service they use.

What do administration services do?

To make life easier for financial planners, administration services help professionals keep track of their clients' investments. Some services are also available to the general public to monitor their investments.

Transacting

Administration services are like a supermarket for buyers and sellers of financial products. The more sophisticated services let investors — most often through a financial planner — buy and sell a range of investments. The operators offer a menu of up to 300 or more managed funds. Investors can also trade shares in the top ASX-listed 500 companies.

The administration service takes care of all the paperwork when you buy and sell. The service's agreements with the relevant fund managers allow it to deal directly with them on your behalf through a limited power of attorney. Arrangements with stockbrokers are in place for investors who want to buy and sell shares. Wrap accounts also offer a bank account to manage your cash when you put money in or take money out. After you've transacted, the service sends you or your financial planner the paperwork. Most also let you see your account details online.

Reporting

One of the main advantages of using an administration service is the reporting that it gives. Here are the main reports you get:

✓ **Holdings:** This report shows your investment holdings, the number of units in a managed fund or shares in a company.

✓ **Income and expenses:** Sets out the income received and any expenses during the year from each investment. This report also shows the gains and losses from the sale of investments during the year.

✓ **Portfolio valuation:** The value of your investments at a particular date.

✓ **Transactions:** Lists the investments you have bought and sold during the year, the date of the transactions and the price paid.

✓ **Tax returns:** Details relevant income, deductible expenses and capital gains.

Reporting is at least once a year at the tax year end and, in most cases, is available for investors to view online. Even if you have a financial planner, you still should be able to see your account information. You won't be able to transact online though.

Making sure you need the services

Do you really need an administration service? Your financial planner will say you do and he may be right, as it helps him to give you a better service. The answer, though, is that it depends. These services cost money and I go through the fees in the section 'Fees and Charges' later in this chapter. The more money you have to invest and the more investments you have, the more likely you need help with the administration. The information you receive from the operator should help you complete your tax return and may even help you save money at tax time.

Weigh up the pros and cons of using an administration service. It might save you money if you have a large number of holdings. If you have only a couple of managed funds, then you're unlikely to benefit. Many of the wrap accounts also set a minimum of $100,000 or more to be invested.

Most wrap services are available only through a financial planner. I have found it notoriously difficult getting my hands on wrap PDSs without going through a specially accredited planner.

Exploring Wraps and Master Trusts

Although wraps and master trusts both offer similar administration services, they are different beasts. Wraps are equivalent to the four-wheel-drives of the administration services world, able to navigate terrain off-limits to master trusts. Wraps can report on a range of different asset classes, from managed funds and cash to direct property and bonds. Master trusts, on the other hand, are the on-road, around-town runabouts — you get where you want to go as long as you stick to the roads and don't try anything fancy.

Table 17-1 lists the main providers of master trust and wrap services (most wraps are generally only available through a financial planner).

Mastering master trusts

Master trusts are relatively simple to understand. *Master trusts* offer a straightforward service for buying and selling, administering and reporting managed funds. I cover the reporting that master trusts offer in the section 'What do administration services do?' earlier in this chapter. The menu of funds on offer by master trusts usually covers most investors' needs. The operator chooses funds across all the different asset classes from cash and shares to fixed interest and property, both locally and overseas. The operator has agreements with various fund managers covering fees, transactions and marketing, and especially minimum entry levels, which can be significantly lower than for an investor entering a fund individually.

For most fund managers, having a fund listed on a master trust can be a significant boost to their business. Marketing, administration and dealing with investors are all done by the operator on behalf of the fund manager. And master trusts give fund managers access to a large audience of financial planners, as well as retail investors. Investors get choice and convenience. Having one set of forms and being able to invest with several fund managers has to be a good idea.

Table 17-1	Wrap and Master Trust Providers in Australia	
Operator	**Master Trust**	**Wrap**
AXA Australia www.axa.com.au	AXA Generations	AXA Summit
Asgard (St.George Bank) www.asgard.com.au	N/A	eWRAP and Elements
BT Financial Group www.btfinancial.com.au	BT Investment Funds	BT Wrap
Colonial First State (incl. wholesale) www.colonialfirststate.com.au	FirstChoice Investments	FirstWrap
OnePath* www.onepath.com.au	OneAnswer Investment Portfolio	N/A
MLC Ltd www.mlc.com.au and www.masterkeycustom.com.au	MasterKey Investment Service	MasterKey Custom
Macquarie Investment Managers www.macquarie.com.au	N/A	Macquarie Wrap
Perpetual www.perpetual.com.au	WealthFocus Investment Advantage	N/A

__Note:__ OnePath is the new name for the former investment division of ING

Wraps with a choice of filling

Wraps are a way of managing many investments. *Wrap accounts* do just as their name suggests — they wrap up a whole range of investment types and provide transaction, administration and reporting services. The investments are selected from a menu of investments listed by the wrap provider. Some wrap accounts also let clients include the details of direct property investments, letting them get a whole view of their portfolio. Some let investors include collectibles and the like. The wrap relies on third-party valuations for these types of investments. However, investors could get charged a fee based on the value of these assets.

Scouring a wrap's product disclosure statement (PDS), investors may notice that wraps are referred to as *investor directed portfolio services* (IDPSs). Apart from being a mouthful, it's also the legal name for wraps. Easy to see why the industry came up with the name wrap!

Wraps buy and sell investments on your behalf, acting on your instructions, and give you a consolidated report of your holdings. When you invest through a wrap, your investments are held for you by the operator as custodian, rather than by you directly. With a custodian holding the investments, you're not the legal owner of the underlying investments but you do have all the benefits of ownership, such as income.

Figure 17-1 shows how wraps work. A wrap account revolves around a cash account, which is used to pay for investments, receive income, pay expenses and receive monies from the sale of investments.

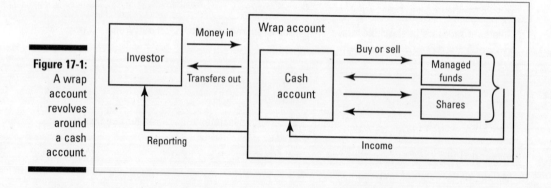

Figure 17-1:
A wrap account revolves around a cash account.

Wraps can be used for investments outside superannuation or built specifically for super accounts. No prizes for guessing that these superannuation services are generally called *super wraps*. These wraps are set up to handle investments in the superannuation environment and, most importantly, to comply with the superannuation law. Super wraps are obliged to have a trustee structure to look after the interests of its members — the investors. This is just like any super fund, whether a self-managed super fund or an employer super fund. These wraps can also be used to manage pension payments. For more on super, refer to Chapter 3.

Transferring holdings from one wrap account to another is usually possible without any tax consequences. Holdings can be transferred in or out of wrap accounts using an *in-specie transfer*, which is just a way of moving investments from one wrap to another without triggering any capital gains tax. Check with the provider though. Transferring super wraps is different. Transferring from one super wrap provider to another may see you end up with potential capital gains. The trustee of the super wrap owns the assets on behalf of the members. Changing a super wrap means changing trustee, and investors may have to sell their investments to make a transfer. Any gains could be liable for capital gains tax.

Most wraps are available only to financial planners acting on behalf of clients. In fact, you'll find it virtually impossible to get hold of a PDS for some of the wraps. These wraps are kept very much under wraps unless you plan to invest via a financial planner.

Financial planners brand their wraps

Many of the larger financial planning organisations have what are called *badged* wraps. For these planners, their wrap of choice has their name and brand across all the paperwork. However, the systems and administration will be run by one of the big wrap operators, such as Macquarie Bank.

In return for the badge arrangement, the planners must put a certain amount of their clients' money into the badged wrap. This amount can be as high as $100 million a year. The advantage to the end client is that the fees for using a badged wrap may be cheaper than using a financial planner who goes direct to the operator.

For the operators of wrap services, attracting and keeping financial planners means providing ever more bells and whistles. Operators spend millions of dollars every year updating their technology and providing ever more services. This spending and updating has become like an arms race between the operators and means they have to attract even more money through the door to justify their costs.

Using wraps and master trusts

Working for a bank a few years ago, I decided to take advantage of the staff discount to get some financial advice from a bank planner. I didn't have a lot of money to invest but the planner took me through all the possibilities, from buying some funds to using a wrap. The process was a real eye-opener. I had dealt with the people who built the bank's wrap service and reckoned I knew generally how it worked. But the planner showed me how to weigh up the pros and cons of wraps from a customer's point of view. This lesson made me think closely about how to value these services.

Considering a master trust

Master trust investment menus let investors choose from a selection of managed funds. If an investor isn't sure about what funds to pick, she can choose a risk profile, such as conservative or aggressive. Chapter 6 looks at risk profiling. The master trust then selects the underlying investments based on that profile. So, why would you use a master trust? I explain reporting and administration in the section 'What do administration services do?' earlier in this chapter. Other things to consider are:

- **Fund selection:** Master trusts offer a choice of managed funds from a range of different fund managers all in one place.

- **Wholesale funds:** By pooling money from many investors, master trusts can negotiate deals with fund managers to offer wholesale funds (refer to Chapter 3). These funds are normally only available to investors with large sums of money, sometimes $500,000 or more. Through a master trust, the minimum investment can start from $1,500.

Considering wraps

Using a wrap is only likely to be an option if you use a financial planner. Wraps make life easy for financial planners but do they do the same for you? Here are a few questions you need to ask before using a wrap:

- ✔ **Are the fees worth the service?** I cover off fees in the section 'Fees and Charges' later in this chapter, but you need to understand what you're paying for. Generally, the more money you have in a wrap, the better value it is.

- ✔ **Who's benefiting — you, the planner or both?** A good financial planner can show you at least a couple of options for managing and administering your managed fund investments. Get the right service and you may not mind paying for it.

- ✔ **What are you investing in?** If you're investing only in managed funds, you may be better off using a master trust. If you want to hold shares and cash as well, then you should consider wraps.

If you're self-employed or you use a financial planner for your advice or don't want to use your employer's default superannuation provider and/or want to manage your own super, then consider using a wrap. Using a wrap service for your superannuation may be a more cost-effective solution than setting up a self-managed super fund (SMSF), especially if you have less than $200,000 in your super account. Anything less than $200,000 in an SMSF is generally regarded as not cost-effective and, in fact, the Australian Taxation Office (ATO) recommends $200,000 as a minimum for an SMSF.

Understanding Managed Accounts

Although not strictly managed funds, I include this section on managed accounts because they so closely resemble managed funds. Managed accounts do the same thing as many managed funds — they invest in portfolios of shares and can provide comprehensive reporting. Often touted as the next big thing, managed accounts aim to offer the convenience of managed funds with the advantages of direct share investment. Here I explain why managed accounts are different from managed funds.

Different types of managed accounts

Managed accounts sit between managed funds and traditional direct share investing. Clients own stocks directly in managed accounts, unlike with managed funds, where a trust owns the investments. Managed accounts can be divided into two types — separately managed accounts (SMAs) and individually managed accounts (IMAs).

✔ **Separately managed accounts:** Like a managed fund but without the unit trust structure, investors can access portfolios of shares in their own name. This differs from managed funds, which hold investments on trust for investors. Portfolios in an SMA are developed by a panel of fund managers. SMAs are managed investment schemes (MISs — refer to Chapter 3) available through a PDS, as with managed funds.

✔ **Individually managed accounts:** The portfolio of shares in an IMA is put together by either a professional or an individual investor. IMAs are usually found in the full-service stockbroking houses and offered to investors with oodles of money. The stockbroker may provide a tailor-made portfolio of shares, along with a fancy reporting and administration service.

SMAs typically take smaller amounts of money and portfolios can't be changed much. IMAs take larger licks of money and portfolios are developed in conjunction with the investor. Table 17-2 outlines the key features of separately managed and individually managed accounts, alongside managed funds.

Table 17-2	Comparing Managed Accounts with Managed Funds		
Feature	*Managed Fund*	*SMA*	*IMA*
Investment types	Unit trust	Direct shares	Direct shares
Legal type	Managed investment scheme — PDS	Managed investment scheme — PDS	A service (not a product so no PDS)
Legal ownership of underlying investments	Fund has legal and beneficial ownership of the investments	Investor has beneficial but not legal ownership	Investor has full legal and beneficial ownership
Underlying investments	Fund managers	Fund managers	Equity specialists
Control over buying or selling of shares	No	Limited	Yes
Dividend entitlement	No; by law, income has to be distributed	Yes	Yes
Typical minimum investment	>$1,000	>$25,000	>$100,000
Tax advantages of beneficial or legal ownership	No	Yes	Yes

The level of control you have over your investments increases as you move from managed funds to SMAs and finally to IMAs, where you can have almost complete control.

IMAs are classed as a service, not as an investment product, meaning they're not sold through a PDS. So, any financial planner or broker offering an IMA must have accreditation to advise on equities. Financial planners selling an SMA via a PDS do not need to be equities accredited.

Using managed accounts

So, what are the advantages of using managed accounts? Listed here are some of the reasons why you may want to use a managed account:

- **Franking credits:** These are tax credits available on dividends paid to investors by companies. Franking credits can be used to offset against an investor's tax liabilities.

- **Holdings:** Investments are held directly by you, as the investor, in your name in the case of an IMA. With an SMA, you usually have beneficial but not legal ownership. Shares can be easily transferred to a stockbroking account from an IMA if you no longer wish to hold them through the managed account.

- **Portfolios:** You can select from a range of portfolios provided by a range of fund managers, much the same as for a master trust. Yor may also be able to build your own portfolio with the help of an adviser.

- **Reporting:** Managed accounts provide portfolio valuation and reports on transactions, income and expenses, and tax on holdings.

- **Tax:** Managed accounts have no embedded capital gains tax — a brand new portfolio is created for each new investor in a managed account and so the investor doesn't inherit an existing tax position on entry. Managed funds investors inherit any capital gains tax built up since the start of the financial year. Refer to Chapter 5 for more on tax.

- **Tax management:** Investors can decide which assets are sold and when, to help them minimise capital gains tax. Also known as *tax lot management*, where you can sell loss-making investments to offset any capital gains tax liabilities on other investments.

Managed accounts typically cover only one asset class — shares. If you want different types of asset class in your portfolio, such as bonds, unlisted property and the like, you may be better off using a managed fund.

Consider using a managed account, especially an SMA, for a self-managed super fund (SMSF). SMAs combine the flexibility of share ownership with the discipline of a professionally managed portfolio. SMSF trustees need to ensure that the holdings of the SMSF meet the requirements of its investment strategies. Using an SMA can be a way to fulfil that obligation.

Some of the main providers of managed accounts are listed in Table 17-3.

Table 17-3	Managed Account Providers	
Provider	*Managed Account*	*Minimum Investment*
AMP Capital Investors www.amp.com.au	AMP Personalised Portfolio	$100,000
Aviva Group www.avivagroup.com.au	Aviva SMA	$30,000
BlackRock www.blackrockinvestments.com.au	Customised Portfolio Service	No fixed minimum but some model portfolios have a minimum $25,000
BT Financial www.btfinancial.com.au	BT Elect Portfolio	$100,000
OneVue www.onevue.com.au	OneVue SMA	$25,000

Most of the larger stockbrokers have a managed account service of some sort. A stockbroker's managed account service can be an informal affair where the broker pulls together a portfolio of shares in consultation with the client. Others can be more formalised, call themselves IMAs and offer a set of portfolios that are managed in-house and offered to clients. Some stockbrokers, such as Macquarie, offer both SMAs and IMAs.

Even more managed accounts: The birth of UMAs

Great, another acronym — UMA (pronounced *ooma*)! Unified managed accounts are the new kids on the block. UMAs take separately managed accounts to the next level and offer reporting on a wide range of assets, not just shares. Reporting includes managed funds, fixed-interest securities and term deposits, warrants and stapled securities, property and mortgages, collectibles including art, wine and cars, and direct property investments. In many ways, UMAs offer similar services to a wrap account but the difference is that all the investments in an UMA are held in your own name. Keep an eye open for these. I predict many of the fund managers and platform operators will start launching these types of services in the not-too-distant future. Whether investors want them is a different matter!

Fees and Charges

Fees can quickly eat up a chunk of your money, especially if you're not sure what you should be charged. Fees can also make a big difference to your returns. I cover fees in a lot more detail in Chapter 5. This section looks at fees for master trusts, wrap accounts and managed accounts. The main fees charged by wraps, master trusts and managed accounts are shown in Table 17-4. The listing for managed accounts refers mainly to SMAs. The fees for IMAs can vary enormously, depending on who is providing the service. As a general rule, IMAs tend to be more expensive than SMAs because of the more hands-on approach.

The fees charged by a wrap account may be tax deductible. Check with your financial planner or accountant.

Table 17-4	Fees for Master Trusts, Wraps and Managed Accounts		
Fee Type	**Master Trusts**	**Wraps**	**Managed Accounts**
Administration fees	Usually nil	Yes, usually tiered, depending on value of portfolio. Fees from <$100,000 = 1.85% to >$1 million = 0.09%	Yes, usually tiered, depending on value of portfolio. Fees from <$100,000 = 0.6% to >$1 million = 0.33%
Adviser service fees	Yes, as agreed between investor and financial adviser	Yes, as agreed between investor and financial adviser	Yes, as agreed between investor and financial adviser
Contribution fees, each time you add money to your account	Yes, up to 4% plus one-off payment on value of contribution	Yes, up to 4% plus one-off payment on value of contribution	Nil
Establishment fees, for setting up your account	Usually nil but one or two funds may charge a fee	Usually nil	Nil
Management fees, charged by the fund manager	Yes, from 0.6% to 2.5% or more p.a.	Yes, from 0.9% to 2.5% or more p.a.	Yes, 0% to 0.9% p.a.
Transaction fees	Buy–sell spread on managed funds	Buy–sell spread on managed funds; brokerage on share trades from 0.1%	Brokerage on share trades

Part V
Following Some Sensible Ideas for Happier Returns

Glenn Lumsden

Although it sounded too good to be true, the hapless investors could not resist the call of the Venus funds-eater.

In this part ...

This part rounds out investing with managed funds by looking at techniques to hopefully enhance your returns. These include using margin loans to borrow to invest and dollar-cost averaging, which is a fancy way of saving money every month into a managed fund. Alarm bells may be ringing when I mention borrowing. Used sensibly, borrowing can be a way, if not of turbo-charging, then certainly of boosting your returns at least.

Although you certainly don't have to, if you've read this book from the beginning or at least read quite a bit of it, hopefully you've picked up enough tips to know where to look for the traps. Nothing is ever certain and some funds may hit some turbulence. So, if the fund does go pear-shaped and you lose money, what do you do? This part explains the non-violent ways you might be able to get your money back, who to shout at and how loudly. You also find out about knowing your rights and who is looking after them, as well as what to do if your money is frozen in a fund.

Chapter 18

Borrowing to Invest

. . . .

In This Chapter

▶ Getting to grips with gearing and margin loans

▶ Building your returns with someone else's money

▶ Stacking up the risks and rewards, and managing margin calls

▶ Taking the easier option with geared funds

. . . .

*B*orrowing to invest is a widely used method for potentially increasing investment returns in a portfolio. Also called gearing, borrowing to invest is usually done through a margin loan. Specialist lenders, mostly owned by one of the larger banks or stockbroking houses, are the more common providers of margin loans. In this chapter, I cut through the margin-lender-speak to show how margin lending works and how it can be used in a managed fund portfolio. I also look at the advantages of margin lending, ranging from potentially bigger returns to possible tax benefits.

The idea of borrowing to invest may send shivers down the spines of a few investors. The global financial crisis highlighted some of the risks of this strategy. Many investors received dreaded margin calls from their lenders and an unfortunate few even lost most of their money. Given the not inconsiderable potential risks involved, I show you what to watch out for, including how to avoid those pesky margin calls.

If you like the idea of borrowing to invest but aren't sure what to do, you can always leave it to the professionals. Some managed funds, known as geared managed funds, are allowed to borrow to invest. These funds give the advantages of borrowing without you having to take out a loan. In this chapter, I also look at how the funds work and explain the pros and cons of using them in your portfolio.

Gearing Up Your Portfolio

Using a *margin loan* is usually the way investors borrow (gear) to invest in shares and managed funds. *Gearing* is just a fancy word for borrowing. The idea is that an investor can use cash, shares and managed funds as security to take out a loan. The result is a larger amount of money to invest and all the benefits (and risks) that come with having a bigger portfolio.

This section explains margin lending (gearing) and lists some of the main providers in the market. But, where margin loans are used, you also have the risk that the lender will apply a margin call. If the investment value decreases beyond a certain level, the lender calls on you to put more funds (or investments) into your account to make up for the shortfall. (See the section 'Understanding margin calls' later in this chapter for more information.)

Understanding what gearing means

So why would investors borrow to invest? Think of a traditional investment portfolio as a bicycle with one gear — forward. You get to where you want to go but, if you add some more gears, you might get there faster. Here are some of the main reasons why investors borrow:

- ✔ **A larger portfolio:** Borrowing lets investors with limited funds increase the size of their portfolio. Like taking out a mortgage on a home and using the money to buy an investment property, margin loans let investors release some value in an existing portfolio of funds to buy more funds.

- ✔ **Capital gains:** With a bigger portfolio, investors can potentially increase the size of capital gains on investments (Table 18-1 shows how this works).

- ✔ **Diversification:** Investors with limited funds can diversify their portfolios across a broader base of asset classes and investment types. Importantly for managed funds, this diversification may mean spreading your investments across different fund managers.

- ✔ **Tax benefits:** Having a bigger portfolio means investors can potentially get their hands on more income and possibly *franking credits* (tax credits that let investors claim back the tax paid by companies on dividends). Interest on margin loans is also potentially tax deductible.

You should ask yourself a couple of questions before diving into a margin loan: Do you understand what gearing is? And do you understand what a margin call is? If you can't answer yes to these questions honestly, then you should think very carefully before taking out a margin loan. Seeking professional advice is always strongly recommended.

Table 18-1 shows the effects of using a margin loan on a simple portfolio of one managed fund, the Hunter Hall Value Growth Trust. The portfolio goes back to 30 June 2000, with the fund at $1.7367 a unit. After ten years, the fund's price had grown to $2.0285 a unit, or 15.7 per cent. You may think this growth doesn't sound a lot for ten years, and I agree. However, the fund also distributed income of $1.6843 per unit over the same ten-year period. Add that to the capital growth and the fund returned a healthier 114 per cent. Table 18-1 shows the effect on returns of using a portfolio with no loan, one with a 40 per cent loan and one with a 70 per cent loan. For more on how gearing levels or loan-to-value ratios (LVRs) work, see the next section, 'Multiplying Your Returns'.

Table 18-1	The Effect of Gearing on Returns		
Hunter Hall Value Growth Trust	*Ungeared Portfolio*	*Geared Portfolio (40%)*	*Geared Portfolio (70%)*
Initial investment	$15,000	$15,000	$15,000
Margin loan	Nil	$10,000	$35,000
Value at 1 July 2000	$15,000	$25,000	$50,000
Distributions (income)	$14,548	$24,247	$48,494
Value of units at 30 June 2010	$17,520	$29,200	$58,401
Total return at 30 June 2010	**$32,068**	**$53,447**	**$106,895**
Less total interest costs	Nil	–$8,000	–$20,000
Gain	$17,068	$20,447	$36,895
Return on $15,000 before tax	**114%**	**136%**	**246%**

Source: Unit pricing and distribution information from Hunter Hall. Assumes an interest rate on the margin loan of 8 per cent p.a. and assumes the interest is paid off each year and not capitalised. Excludes franking credits, foreign tax credits and contribution fees.

The example in Table 18-1 demonstrates the importance of income (distributions) from an investment when using a margin loan. Without the income, the return on the fund wouldn't have been enough to justify taking out a margin loan. The portfolio geared at 70 per cent produced the greatest return of 246 per cent for the simple reason that the investor was able to buy more units, receive more income and generate bigger capital returns (increase in value).

Finding a loan to suit you

Before you decide which loan to take out, you need to think about whether you're suited to margin lending or not. I look at the potential benefits earlier in this section and go through the risks in the next section. Investors should establish a few things about themselves before going ahead, possibly with the help of a financial planner:

✔ **Realistic financial goals:** Even margin lending has limitations on what it can achieve for investors. Be realistic in setting your goals and see margin lending as a tool to help you meet those goals, not as an end in itself.

✔ **Risk profile:** Margin lending adds another layer of risk to a portfolio. Investors need to work out their risk profile — I explain this in more detail in Chapter 6. If you're a conservative investor and want income with possibly some capital growth in your funds, then margin lending may not be for you. If, on the other hand, you want to potentially boost your investments and you have a high tolerance to risk, then margin lending may be worth a look.

Apart from the interest rate charged on a loan, other fees may include a transaction fee every time you buy or sell an investment, account-keeping fees and a set-up fee if investing through a trust or company. If using a financial planner, you may also pay an ongoing trail commission of around 0.25 per cent of the outstanding loan. Check with the margin lender for any other fees.

Table 18-2 lists the main margin lenders in Australia. All lenders offer loans for managed fund investing. Most of the lenders also provide calculators on their websites that let you play around with how much you may be able to borrow. Most also let you work out how much a loan is going to cost you.

Table 18-2		Margin Lender Comparison		
Lender	*Minimum Loan*	*No. of Approved Managed Funds*	*Managed Fund Loan-to-Value Ratio (LVR)*	*Managed Fund Buffer*
ANZ Margin Lending	$20,000	915+	40% to 80%	5%
BT Financial	$20,000	940+	40% to 95%	10%
CommSec (CBA)	$20,000	1,200+	40% to 90%	5%
Leveraged Equities (Bank of Queensland)	No minimum	1,200+	40% to 75%	10%
NAB Margin Lending	$20,000	1,100+	40% to 80%	10%
St.George Bank	$20,000	1,000+	40% to 95%	10%

For more of an explanation of the LVRs and the managed fund buffer mentioned in Table 18-2, see the next section, 'Multiplying Your Returns'. In short, the LVR is how much you can borrow against any particular fund and a buffer is how much leeway an investor has before a margin loan is called. Hit the buffer and you'll get a call from the lender asking you to keep an eye on the loan. Go above the buffer and you'll be in margin call territory.

The LVR varies according to how risky a fund is judged to be by the margin lender. For example, with a cash fund, seen as less risky, an investor may be able to borrow up to 95 per cent against the fund. A geared share fund is seen as the most risky and may have an LVR of only 40 per cent. See the section 'Finding Funds That Gear for You' later in this chapter for a better understanding of geared share funds and the risks involved.

Some lenders offer what is called *instalment lending* or *regular lending*. Investors can make regular contributions to their margin lending account, such as $250 a month, which is then invested in managed funds or shares. This allows the investor to build up a potentially sizable portfolio of shares over time.

The law gets stricter with lenders

Born out of the failure of some margin lenders during the global financial crisis, the federal government passed legislation in October 2009 giving consumers better protection when using margin loans.

By June 2011, all margin loan providers need to be licensed — why they wouldn't be already is a mystery — offer an external dispute resolution scheme and comply with new disclosure requirements. Advisers and financial planners wanting to offer advice involving margin lending will also have to be appropriately qualified. Margin loans are now regarded as a financial product and have to be sold via a

product disclosure statement (PDS) and all the disclosure that entails (refer to Chapter 12 for more on PDSs).

Margin lenders will also be required to make sure that you're suitable to take out a loan or, more correctly, that you aren't unsuitable for the loan. Previously, lenders didn't need to ask you questions about how you'd repay a loan. Now they need to know your financial history and work out if you could pay back the loan. Clearly, the new legislation is designed to bring margin lending kicking and screaming into the 21st century, in line with other lending practices!

Multiplying Your Returns

Margin loans have the effect of multiplying your potential gains, as well as your losses. By how much is determined by a lending ratio called a *loan-to-value ratio (LVR)*, which shows how much you can borrow against any particular fund or share. You can also potentially increase returns with the tax deductions that may be available to investors.

Working out how much you can borrow: LVRs and loan limits

Margin lenders lend against an existing portfolio of approved shares, managed funds and cash. The lender issues what's called an 'approved' list of shares and managed funds that it will lend against. Next to each share or fund is the loan-to-value ratio, or LVR — how much the lender will loan against that security. Each borrower has a loan limit, worked out as the total value of his investments multiplied by the LVR on each investment. Lenders should reduce that limit if they judge that the investor is taking on too much debt given his financial circumstances.

So, for example, if you take out a margin loan with BT Financial, the Hunter Hall Value Growth Trust may have a 75 per cent LVR. This means that you can borrow up to 75 per cent of your funds to invest in the Hunter Hall fund. A $100,000 investment can be split — $75,000 as margin loan from BT Financial and $25,000 as cash or shares, for example. The total loan limit is then $75,000.

Consider where the dividends from shares and distributions from managed funds are paid. Having income paid into your margin lending account helps to reduce the balance on your loan. Some lenders insist that income is paid into the margin account. Others give you a choice. Also consider whether or not you will capitalise the interest on your loan. *Capitalising interest* means adding the interest to the total loan. If you don't pay off the interest or have investment income paid into your account, then the value of your loan increases over time. The amount is paid off when you finally settle the loan by selling your investments.

Don't rely on income or distributions from your investment to meet the interest payments on a loan. In bad years, managed funds may not pay a distribution.

Increasing your returns with tax deductions

Tax should never be the main reason why you invest. But margin loans do have some distinct tax advantages that can make investing more attractive. Margin lending is sometimes seen as *good debt*, where the interest is tax deductible, such as with margin loans and investment property loans. *Bad debt* is where the interest is not tax deductible, such as residential home loans and credit card interest. Investors may be able to take advantage of two types of tax benefits with margin loans:

- **Franking and deferred tax credits:** As with any investment in shares and managed funds, investors may be eligible to receive tax franking credits on dividends received by the managed fund and paid as part of the distribution to investors (unit holders). Deferred tax credits are usually available to investors in property managed funds. Arising out of a revaluation of a property asset or from various other tax allowances, the tax on the distribution is deferred and is usually only taxable on sale of the asset. Flick back to Chapter 5 for more on tax and franking credits.

- **Interest payment deductions:** The interest paid on a margin loan is generally tax deductible by an individual.

Taking out a margin loan means you can buy more units in a fund. With those additional units you may receive distributions as well as the associated tax credits.

Arrange to pre-pay the interest on your margin loan for the next financial year just before the end of the current financial year. Paying the interest ahead of time means investors can potentially claim the interest paid as a tax deduction in that year's tax return, rather than having to wait another year. If you expect a large credit at the end of the tax year, you may be able to reduce the amount of tax deducted from your earnings during the year. This is called a *witholding variation*. Talk to a tax adviser to find out more.

Managing Your Risk

Margin loans add a whole new dimension to potential investment returns. Unfortunately, adding potentially higher returns to a portfolio can also increase the risk. You need to give careful consideration to the level of risk you're happy with. Regardless of how much you borrow, understanding the worst-case scenario can help you manage your loan and manage your risk.

Looking out for the downside

Many things can go wrong with margin loans, regardless of whether you're investing in shares or managed funds. Following some sensible strategies means most of the downside risks can be managed to a greater or lesser degree. Here are some of the risks (you get the strategies in the next bullet list):

- **Capital losses:** Borrowing to invest increases the risk of losing your money. Not only do you have to take account of the money lost on your initial investment but also on the part that you've borrowed.

  Say, for example, on a $100 investment you borrow $50 and use the total $150 to buy a managed fund. The fund loses 10 per cent in one year. Your initial investment of $100 goes down $10 and the borrowed amount goes down $5 for a total loss of $15. You still have to pay back the $50, so your holdings are now worth only $85 ($150 minus the $15 loss and minus the $50 loan).

- **Gearing ratios:** The lender may change the ratio that money is lent against a particular managed fund. The lender may decide that it should lend only 40 per cent of the value of the fund rather than 50 per cent. Investors may need to stump up more cash or investments to meet the new ratio.

- ✔ **Interest rates:** The interest rates charged by the lender may increase at any time.

- ✔ **Legal liability:** Investors should remember that they are legally liable for the debt.

- ✔ **Margin calls:** This is when the value of your investments falls below a point where you need to give the lender more security — I explain margin calls in the next section.

- ✔ **Power of attorney:** When you sign up for a loan, you also give the margin lender a power of attorney over your investments in the account, enabling the lender to sell investments without needing your approval.

Managing these risks can start with how you construct a portfolio of managed funds (or shares). Here are some strategies to cushion your investments:

- ✔ **Diversification:** Putting all your money into one managed fund concentrates your risk of losing money should the fund perform badly. You may want to consider diversifying into a few funds, possibly covering different sectors and managed by different fund managers. Any diversification of your investments, though, should fit in with your overall investment strategy.

- ✔ **Gearing levels:** The most sensible strategy you can adopt is to not borrow too much. Being able to finance 70 per cent of a portfolio on borrowed money may sound great but, in reality, can leave you exposed to sharp falls in the market.

- ✔ **Interest rate:** You can usually fix your interest rate for 12 months before the start of the tax year.

- ✔ **Liquidity:** How easy is it to get your money out if you need it? Not usually a problem with most managed funds that arrange daily redemption of units. You need to be careful, though. Some funds have limited redemption dates and others make it very difficult to sell until the fund is wound up (closed-end funds).

- ✔ **Other resources or income:** If you don't have access to other resources (such as investments or cash) to meet a margin call, then the lender will sell your managed funds to raise cash.

Understanding margin calls

A _margin call_ happens when the total value of your fund falls below the LVR set for that fund. The lender will ask you to put some more cash or assets (or investments) into your account to make up the shortfall.

For example, Ella starts off with an investment in XYZ Managed Fund of $50,000, split $25,000 of her own money and a $25,000 margin loan. The fund has an LVR of 75 per cent, with a buffer of 5 per cent. The value of the fund takes a beating from poor markets, falling to $30,000, but the value of the loan remains unchanged at $25,000. Ella's security against the loan effectively falls by $20,000 and the LVR increases to 83 per cent ($25,000 divided by the fund's value of $30,000).

With a new total value for the fund at $30,000 and a maximum allowable LVR of 75 per cent plus the buffer of 5 per cent, the maximum loan against that investment can be only $24,000 ($30,000 multiplied by the LVR of 75 per cent plus 5 per cent buffer). Given the original loan was $25,000, Ella's margin call would be a minimum of $1,000 to bring down the LVR to the maximum 80 per cent. Ella has three choices:

✔ Sell some or all of her fund and use the proceeds to pay back some of or the entire loan

✔ Offer more security for the loan in the form of managed funds or shares

✔ Put extra cash into the account

Figure 18-1 shows the price of Ella's fund falling and the LVR increasing over time. The two lines look a bit like the jaws of death!

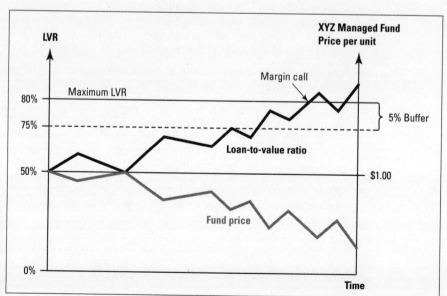

Figure 18-1: How LVRs and margin calls work.

Figure 18-1 also shows a line called the *buffer*. Most margin lenders provide a buffer of between 5 and 10 per cent, which means, in reality, you get a bit of extra leeway before your investments attract a margin call. For example, an LVR of 75 per cent with a buffer of 5 per cent means the investments will face a margin call only when the loan is equivalent to 80 per cent of the value of the investment.

Margin calls can be managed with some careful preparation. Investors may want to consider some of the following pointers when taking out a loan:

✔ Target a gearing level you're comfortable with and below the maximum LVRs available. For example, you may only want to borrow up to 50 per cent of the value of the fund, giving yourself more room to manoeuvre before facing a margin call.

✔ Pay off debt over time using income from your investments. To do this you need to make sure your income from investments is more than the interest payments due.

✔ Have a margin call strategy in place. Facing a margin call means either putting up more security (cash, shares, managed funds) or selling all or part of your investment to cover the loan. Decide whether you'll meet a margin call by selling your funds or adding more cash.

✔ Always consider getting professional advice when taking out a margin loan.

For further information on the risk involved in using margin loans, visit the Australian Securities and Investments Commission's corporate watchdog website FIDO at www.fido.gov.au (click on the About Financial Products tab and then choose the Borrowing and Credit link).

Even if you sell your investments to meet a margin call and pay back your loan, if the proceeds don't cover the amount you owe, you're still liable for the shortfall. This is one way you could lose all of your money and more.

Learning the hard way

The global financial crisis and the resulting sell-off in shares in early 2008 threw up some nasty surprises for investors and regulators alike. As share values dived, investors with margin loans were caught on the hop and many were unable or unwilling to meet their margin calls. Shares were sold and many investors lost everything. Some investors who were able to tip more money in to keep the loans alive still lost everything.

So what happened? It was all in the way the margin loans were set up or, more precisely, the way some providers were set up. Investors borrowed money from their stockbrokers to buy shares using margin loans. The brokers then borrowed money from another provider to finance the loans. That provider, in turn, then went to the big banks to again finance those loans.

In hindsight, this multilayered borrowing was a disaster waiting to happen. Added to that was the fact that the investments of the original investors taking out the margin loans were pooled into the one investing pot and used as security for the bank loans. The shares went down in value, one or more of the providers couldn't meet their debts and the banks called in their loans.

The fallout affected all of the margin loan clients, not just those who were in the margin call. The shares in the investment pool were sold off, regardless of whether or not the clients had breached the terms of their loans. These loans were called non-standard margin loans. I'd be very surprised if any lender offers these types of margin loans any more, but be very careful if you find one that does!

Finding Funds That Gear for You

Most traditional managed funds cannot borrow money to invest. However, some funds have been set up so they can borrow. Funds do so in a similar way to individual investors using a margin loan. These funds tend to be known as geared share funds or internally geared share funds. Gearing can add a rocket under a fund's returns but equally amplify any losses.

In this section, I set out what makes a geared fund tick and what to watch out for. Non-traditional funds such as hedge funds or structured products also use gearing — mainly through the use of exotic products like derivatives — as a standard investment strategy. I talk about these funds in Chapter 16.

Examining geared funds

In a nutshell, *internally geared share funds* borrow on behalf of investors to increase the fund investments in Australian or overseas shares. *Gearing* is a general term for using existing assets, such as cash or equities, as security to borrow money. Internal gearing is just when a fund borrows money rather than the investor borrowing. Gearing does add more risk and funds may typically borrow up to 50 per cent of the value of the investments it holds. For example, a fund with $100 million in investments might borrow $50 million, giving a total amount of $150 million to invest in the market.

So, how are returns magnified with a geared fund? Compare two funds with exactly the same investments: Fund A has no borrowings and Fund B borrows 50 per cent of its money at an interest rate of 6 per cent per annum. Figure 18-2 shows the results for both Fund A and Fund B. Janice invests $10,000 in both funds and both return 10 per cent per annum. Fund A, without the borrowings, has grown after ten years to $25,937. Fund B, with the borrowings, has increased to $29,125, a difference of $3,188, or around 12.4 per cent extra. The example excludes any management fees and other costs charged by the managed fund or margin lender.

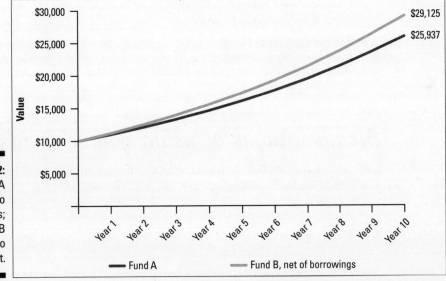

Figure 18-2:
Fund A has no borrowings; Fund B borrows to invest.

Note: Borrowing cost is 6 per cent p.a. and returns on both funds are 10 per cent p.a.

Advantages of using geared share funds

Geared funds offer investors a quick and easy way to borrow money to invest without having to go through the rigmarole of taking out a loan. The fund managers offering these types of products tend to be able to borrow money more cheaply than individual investors. Here are the main reasons for using a geared fund:

✔ **Accelerated returns:** Gearing can magnify the gains that a fund makes.

✔ **Access to limited recourse loans:** The borrowing by the fund is known as limited recourse, meaning that only your initial investment in the managed fund is at risk if the manager doesn't pay back the loans. Contrast this with a mortgage on a residential house that is full recourse, where the lender can recover the loan by selling off any assets you have.

✔ **Availability to self-managed superannuation funds (SMSFs):** SMSFs can invest in geared share funds but are restricted from most other forms of borrowing to invest.

✔ **Convenience:** Investors can access all the advantages that borrowing can give, without having to take out a loan.

✔ **Lower rates:** Geared funds can usually borrow money at much cheaper rates than the average investor.

✔ **Positive gearing:** Funds are set up so that most of the dividend income from the shareholdings goes to pay the interest on the loan. Any tax losses that arise (income less than interest payments) can't be passed on to investors.

Disadvantages of using geared funds

Inevitably, using geared share funds has some potential downsides, as much as it has advantages. Here are some of the disadvantages:

✔ **Accelerated returns:** Gearing can magnify the losses that a fund makes.

✔ **Increased risk:** Geared share funds have a much higher level of risk than the same share funds without the borrowings.

✔ **Limited income:** Don't expect much income from a geared fund. Most of the income is used to pay interest on the borrowings.

✔ **Rising loan to value ratio:** As with a margin loan, the borrowing in a geared share fund also has an LVR (refer to the section 'Understanding margin calls' earlier in this chapter for an explanation). If the value of the fund's assets falls below the LVR, it is forced to sell investments, possibly at much lower values than the fundamental value of the investments.

✔ **Volatility:** Yes, these funds exaggerate the moves in the market. Say a fund borrows 50 per cent of the value of its holdings. The shares go up 10 per cent but the return on the fund is twice that, at 20 per cent, and vice versa if the shares go down 10 per cent. So, even the smallest moves in the market can be greatly magnified in the fund.

Figure 18-3 demonstrates how much the fund moves up and down over a particular period — the volatility noted in the last bullet point. The chart shows the value over ten years of $100 invested in the S&P/ASX 300 Index versus $100 invested in the Colonial First State Managed Investments Geared Share Fund at the end of June 2000. I use the CFS MI Geared Share Fund for no other reason than it was one of the first geared share funds in Australia. The fund's performance is typical of other Australian geared share funds over the period.

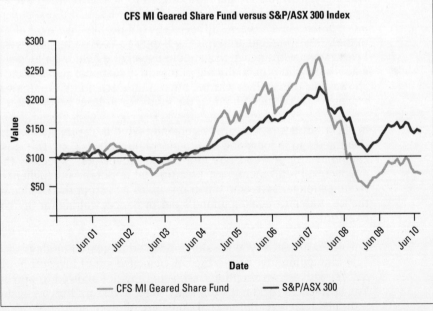

Figure 18-3: Comparing performance of a geared share fund against a market index shows the fund's volatility.

Source: Compiled using data from Colonial First State and from IRESS. Does not take account of fees.

As shown in Figure 18-3, the CFS MI Geared Share Fund from the start of 2004 to mid-2007 significantly outperformed the S&P/ASX 300 Index. After mid-2007, the fund's performance fell off a cliff. The effects of the gearing in the fund magnified the losses in the market.

Be careful not to double-gear. Using a margin loan to invest in a geared managed fund is doubling up your gearing — you're borrowing to invest in a fund that borrows. You need to watch out for two things with this strategy:

- ✔ Geared funds don't usually pay much income, so you shouldn't rely on distributions to finance your margin loan.

- ✔ With the increased risk of geared funds, if the market falls substantially, not only will your fund manager potentially face a margin call but so will you.

Working out when to use a geared share fund

Geared share funds are generally suited to investors who have a growth or aggressive growth investor profile. (Chapter 6 sets out investor profiles in more detail.) Investors with these types of profiles like a bit of excitement in their investing and are typically happy to take on higher levels of risk. Investments with higher risk should usually be held for a longer term to smooth out the potentially big swings in investment performance (Chapter 4 shows how this works). Geared share funds are no different. Most fund managers recommend holding the funds for at least seven years.

In short, investors who are largely interested in capital gains, who don't need an income and are comfortable with risk, are the most likely candidates for geared share funds. Other investors, especially those a long way off retirement, may be attracted to potentially higher returns. Having a longer investing timeframe gives investors the chance to ride out the inevitable troughs in a fund's performance, waiting for the good times to return.

The other investor type possibly attracted to geared funds is the superannuation investor — the self-managed super investor in particular. SMSFs, with a few exceptions, are generally not allowed to borrow to invest. The lawmakers reckon it's too risky to let investors borrow against their retirement savings. But geared funds are allowed and let SMSFs get the potential benefits from borrowing — without actually borrowing.

Chapter 19

Investigating Other Investment Strategies

In This Chapter

▶ Taking a look at regular savings plans

▶ Adding up the benefits of dollar-cost averaging

▶ Revealing the wonder of compound growth

*I*nvesting is all about growing your money, whether it's like a slow-developing fig tree that delivers in the end or a plot of fast-growing petunias. Just as with gardening, you can apply some simple techniques and strategies to help your investments along. And the beauty about these strategies is how simple it is to set them up — and then they take care of themselves (unlike most potplants).

Committing to a regular savings plan means investors don't have to commit a big dollop of cash to a managed fund in one go. You can drip-feed money into your investment over time, gradually building up your pot of managed funds. In this chapter, I take a look at what you need to consider and how simple it is to set up a regular savings plan.

Dollar-cost averaging, as well as being a strategy in its own right, is a likely spin-off benefit from having a regular savings plan. Dollar-cost averaging is the antidote for those trying to time the market (refer to Chapter 7 for more on market timing). A regular contribution to a managed fund at frequent intervals over a period of time may help reduce the risk of market timing — that is, buying at a high price and then losing money. I explain how it works, as well as the potential benefits, and explore some of the trade-offs.

I finish off this chapter with a look at the power of compound growth — how you can use the returns from your investments to generate even more returns.

Benefits of a Regular Savings Plan

The hardest part about setting up a regular savings plan is sticking to it — I know it is for me anyway! Set up the plan right and you may be able to put temptation far enough out of reach for it to work. At the risk of stating the obvious — one I'm happy to take — savings plans are a convenient way to build up a decent-sized investment over time. Time is an important element in this strategy, along with the discipline to see it through. Adding a little each month to a managed fund not only helps you build up a bigger nest egg, but also lets you benefit from the strategy of dollar-cost averaging. I deal with this strategy in the next section, 'Examining the Difference between Savings Plans and Dollar-Cost Averaging'.

Most managed funds offer regular savings plans — I list some of the major fund managers and plans in Chapter 2. Regular savings plans typically let you set up an investment with a lower amount than the fund manager's usual minimum investment. For example, Colonial First State has a minimum $5,000 initial investment. Take out a regular savings plan and the minimum falls to $1,000, as long as you add a minimum $100 a month to the plan.

Setting up a regular savings plan

For most people, money is a scarce resource and, like any scarce resource, it needs managing. The first thing you need to do before setting up a savings plan is to have worked out a budget. From that you can then figure out what money you want to put towards your savings plan. Inevitably you have to redirect some of your scarce resource to your investments. Whether it's deciding not to put petrol in the motor yacht this week or giving up one coffee every day (one sacrifice too far, I'd say), you may have to make sacrifices. Flick back to Chapter 7 for more on goal setting.

Okay, so after running your slide rule (yes, I'm showing my age) over the budget, you've laid off the domestic staff and are now doing your own ironing. Now what do you do with all the extra cash you have in your pocket? This is as simple as setting up a direct debit arrangement from your bank account to the fund manager. The fund manager's product disclosure statement (PDS) will have the relevant form for you to complete. It's exactly like the form for any regular direct debit. If you resist the temptation of withdrawing money, you're on the way to building a bigger pot of money.

Benefiting through dollar-cost averaging

Dollar-cost averaging is one benefit of a savings plan, but it's also a separate strategy to help smooth out or reduce the impact of movements in the market on your investments. In an ideal world, investors buy managed funds at a low price and sell at a high price. Back in the real world, few things in investing are more depressing than buying a managed fund only to see its value fall during the following months.

Dollar-cost averaging reduces the risk of buying at the top of the market by spreading out your buys over time. Put simply, *dollar-cost averaging* is a method of investing regular amounts in an investment over a long period. This spreads out the price you pay for your managed fund. Dollar-cost averaging is usually used for investing in funds that invest in volatile assets like shares, where values can move up and down a lot. You probably wouldn't use dollar-cost averaging for bond or cash funds as values tend not to move as much.

Examining the Difference between Savings Plans and Dollar-Cost Averaging

So what's the difference between dollar-cost averaging and a regular savings plan? Not a great deal on the face of it. The difference is in the way you think about your investments and implement your strategy. Dollar-cost averaging is about trying to reduce risk and a savings plan is about building capital. Both can have similar results for your investments though.

An example of a regular savings plan

The best way to show how a regular savings plan and dollar-cost averaging can work hand in hand is to look at an example. The most important point about dollar-cost averaging and savings plans is that time is of the essence. By that I mean keeping the plan in place for a long time to get the full benefits of the strategy.

Table 19-1 shows how a regular savings plan works over a 12-month period, investing $250 every month after a $2,000 initial investment. By the end of the year, the total $5,000 investment has grown to $5,513 (based on the pricing outlined in the table). Not only does a regular savings plan mean not having to commit a big lump sum (of $5,000 to begin with), but the investor also ends up with a few more dollars ($13 to be precise). Extend this result over a few years and already you can begin to see the benefits of regular savings (and dollar-cost averaging).

Table 19-1		How a Savings Plan Produces Dollar-Cost Averaging				
Month	Amount Invested	Price per Unit	Number of Units Bought	Total Number of Units	Value	Average Purchase Price
Initial investment	$2,000	$1.00	2,000.00	2,000.00	$2,000	$1.0000
January	$250	$1.01	247.52	2,247.52	$2,270	$1.0011
February	$250	$1.02	245.10	2,492.62	$2,542	$1.0030
March	$250	$1.03	242.72	2,735.34	$2,817	$1.0054
April	$250	$0.98	255.10	2,990.44	$2,931	$1.0032
May	$250	$0.96	260.42	3,250.86	$3,121	$0.9997
June	$250	$0.91	274.73	3,525.59	$3,208	$0.9927
July	$250	$0.95	263.16	3,788.74	$3,599	$0.9898
August	$250	$0.98	255.10	4,043.85	$3,963	$0.9892
September	$250	$0.99	252.52	4,296.37	$4,253	$0.9892
October	$250	$1.01	247.52	4,543.90	$4,589	$0.9903
November	$250	$1.04	240.38	4,784.28	$4,976	$0.9928
December	$250	$1.10	227.27	5,011.55	$5,513	$0.9977
Total	$5,000					

Table 19-1 shows an initial investment of $2,000 made in January and $250 each month after that. By December, a total of $5,000 is invested at an average unit price of $0.9977, though the price of the fund had swung between $0.91 and $1.10 over the period. If you had invested the same $5,000 at the start with no further contributions, the return would have been 10 per cent (the $1 you paid less the $1.10 value at the end of the year), or $500. However, because you're investing throughout the year at different prices, your return is slightly trickier to work out. Having done the sums, the return using dollar-cost averaging is 15 per cent (you work out the individual returns on each contribution and then add them up).

Looking at Table 19-1 in terms of dollar-cost averaging also shows that when markets are low you end up buying more units and when markets are high you buy less. The effect of dollar-cost averaging is to smooth out the fluctuations in purchase price over time. The idea is that you can reduce the risk that you pay too high a price for your managed fund.

Any strategy that aims to minimise risk also has its trade-offs. Dollar-cost averaging can mean you avoid putting all your money into a fund at a high price. You also miss the benefit of buying a fund at its cheapest.

Making the most of dollar-cost averaging

Dollar-cost averaging is particularly suited to investing in managed funds. Why? Well, the fact you can buy parts of a unit of a managed fund makes it easy to contribute regular dollar amounts, knowing it will be fully invested. Contrast this with shares, which have minimum order or lot sizes on the stock exchange. On the Australian Securities Exchange (ASX), the minimum lot size is $500 and investors can buy only whole shares. Inevitably, buying shares means bigger ongoing contributions and some loose change after you've invested.

The other positive for managed funds is the cost. You pay a spread (refer to Chapter 13) —

the difference between the buy and sell price a fund manager quotes daily, of usually about 0.4 per cent. But you may avoid paying any transaction costs, such as the contribution fee, if you negotiate with the fund manager or go through a managed fund broker.

Invest in an index fund and your ongoing costs (management expenses charged by the fund manager) can typically be a low 0.9 per cent per annum. Buying shares inevitably means paying brokerage fees every time you invest but you don't have to pay ongoing management fees when holding shares in your own name.

Planning your strategy

Before investing, bear in mind three things to help you make the most of a savings plan and dollar-cost averaging strategy:

- ✔ **How much to invest:** Work out how much you can afford to invest every month and over what period of time. The strategy depends on a consistent amount of money being invested over a long period. Only this way is the risk of loss reduced. It doesn't mean you always avoid a loss — it just reduces the potential size of a loss.

- ✔ **Investing intervals:** Decide if you will invest monthly, quarterly or some other interval. You probably don't want to stretch it out beyond quarterly or you run the risk of lessening the averaging effect.

- ✔ **Investment type:** Select your managed fund carefully. Okay, that sounds a bit dumb because you wouldn't select a fund recklessly! What I mean is you don't want to get hammered by underperformance. If you select a poor-performing fund that continues to underperform, you're unlikely to see the full benefit of dollar-cost averaging.

Dollar-cost averaging can work well in bear markets, or markets that are falling. A successful dollar-cost averaging strategy is one that keeps on investing through the good times but especially through the bad times. Poor markets mean cheaper fund prices, which in turn give you a better average purchase price ready for when the markets improve.

To show how dollar-cost averaging can reduce a loss, take a look at Figure 19-1, which uses the unit pricing figures of the Perpetual Australian Share Fund. The chart shows an investor buying $5,000 worth of units on 1 January 2008 and the value of that fund up to 1 July 2010 — about $4,133. The chart also shows an investor buying $2,000 worth of units on 1 January 2008 and buying another $100 worth of units at the beginning of each month until 1 July 2010. The value then is about $4,764. The important point is that both investors have ended up investing $5,000.

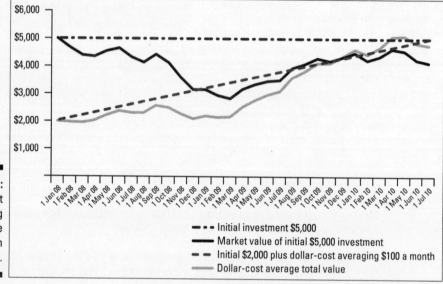

Figure 19-1:
Dollar-cost averaging can reduce a loss in tough times.

Source: Unit pricing data for Perpetual's Australian Share Fund from 1 January 2008 to 1 July 2010. Assumes distributions are reinvested and excludes contribution fees.

The period I use in Figure 19-1, January 2008 to July 2010, was a tricky time for investors. The chart shows that the investor who put in $2,000 to begin with and $100 every month after that just about preserved her wealth. The investor who put in $5,000 in January 2008 — near the top of the market before the sell-off during the global financial crisis — is a lot worse off than the dollar-cost averaging investor, losing $867 versus the dollar-cost average investor losing $236, a difference of $631.

Every time you add to a managed fund, you may be charged a contribution or entry fee of 4 per cent of the value of your contribution. You can have this fee rebated as additional units if you invest through a managed fund broker, negotiate a deal with your financial planner or speak to the fund manager direct.

Compounding Your Investment Growth

The power of compounding is one of those fundamentals of investing that work so well for investors. Compound growth is popularly understood in the context of bank accounts and interest. Compounding is simply leaving income you earn from an investment (such as interest) as part of the sum invested — earning interest on your interest.

Reinvesting your distributions

Shares listed on the stock exchange have dividend reinvestment plans whereby shareholders can put dividends back into the company's shares, usually at a small discount to the quoted share price. Fund managers are the one set of investors who won't reinvest the dividends they receive on investments in shares. Fund managers instead give the dividends back to investors in the fund in the form of distributions. Investors have the option of reinvesting those distributions back into units in the fund.

Managed funds have financial years the same as the tax year, from July to June. Fund managers are obliged to distribute income at least once a year to their unit holders. Distributions are usually made after 30 June each year in time for tax return season. Some funds have more regular distributions, such as half-yearly or even quarterly. The frequency of distributions is all down to what type of fund it is. Funds set up to produce regular income, such as cash, bonds and fixed-interest funds, may distribute quarterly; growth funds may only distribute annually. Table 19-2 shows how reinvestment of a distribution can work.

Table 19-2	Reinvestment of Managed Fund Distribution		
EFG Managed Fund	**Price per Unit**	**Units**	**Value of Units**
Unit buy price at 30 June	$2.5500	1,000	$2,550.00
Distribution per unit	$0.1500	1,000	$150.00
Unit buy price at 1 July	$2.4000	1,000	$2,400.00
If Distribution Is Reinvested			
Reinvestment price	$2.4096	62.25	$150.00
New holdings value	$2.4000	1,062.25	$2,549.40

In Table 19-2, the distribution has the effect of reducing the value of each unit in the managed fund by the equivalent amount of the distribution, so $0.15. The fund manager also quotes a price at which the reinvestment of the distribution is made. This price is lower than the quoted price on the day because it takes into account the typical spread of 0.4 per cent charged by most fund managers. This difference is shown in the value at 30 June of $2,550.00 and the new holdings value of $2,549.40. The *reinvestment price* is what you pay for your new units.

The reinvestment price is important. It becomes the base cost for those units you bought with the distribution when you eventually come to work out any capital gains tax liability on the sale of the investment.

Figuring out the effect of compounding

If you don't need to use the income from an investment, then reinvesting it may be a way of boosting your returns over time. Compounding is best explained using an example. Table 19-3 shows the effect of compounding, by reinvesting distributions, on the performance of a fund. In this case, I take the example of a $5,000 investment in 2000 and show its value in 2010, with 7 per cent annual growth and 3 per cent distribution each year, excluding costs, inflation and tax. The second column shows the effect of the investor taking out the distributions and deciding the income would be more enjoyably spent supporting his local publican. The third column shows the result when distributions are fully reinvested. Over a ten-year period, reinvesting the distributions has seen the investment beat its non-reinvested cousin by 15 per cent.

Table 19-3	Effects on Performance of Reinvesting Distributions	
	Value at 1 July 2010, No Reinvestment	**Value at 1 July 2010, Fully Reinvested**
Initial $5,000 investment 1 Jan 2000	$9,836	$12,786
Distribution retained	$2,218	Nil (reinvested)
Total value of investment	$12,054	$12,786
Percentage total return (before tax)	241%	256%

Chapter 20

Understanding What Can Go Wrong and What to Do If It Does

An unfortunate fact of investing in managed funds — like any investment — is that investors can and do lose money. Falling market values, incompetent fund managers and downright fraud can all take a chunk out of your investments. In this chapter, I take a tour through the land of the regulators, the watchdogs in the world of financial services, and describe what they do — or should be doing — to protect investors.

Fraud is an unpleasant reality when large sums of money are involved. Here, I show you some of the warning signs that shout *Scam!* and set out the usual way for making a complaint to fund managers if you think they've done something wrong. I also explain what to do — apart from shouting louder — if you're not happy with the outcome and where to go next.

Markets go up and down and that's a hazard of investing. If markets go down and you lose money, you're unlikely to find a sympathetic ear with the regulators. But, if values fall far enough, funds can be forced to freeze their funds or stop investors getting their hands on their investments. In this chapter, I also take a look at why this can happen and what options are available to recover your money.

Policing the Fund Managers

In an industry that relies on trust, reputation is as important as performance to most fund managers if they want to attract and keep customers. The slightest hint of wrongdoing can send customers scurrying for the exits, switching the lights off as they leave. Reputation is all very well but the law — enforced by the regulators — sets the minimum standards by which fund managers must operate. If managers fail to stick to the rules, the regulators quickly bring the shutters down, regardless of reputation. Here I set out the main regulators and what they do.

Industry watchdogs and organisations

If you're investing in managed funds, you're likely to come across at least four financial services regulators keeping an eye on companies and product issuers. The regulators have varying degrees of responsibility, listed here from highest down, in relation to managed funds:

- **Australian Securities and Investments Commission (ASIC):** Australia's corporate, markets and financial services regulator, ASIC is the key regulator responsible for supervising fund managers.

- **Australian Prudential Regulation Authority (APRA):** APRA supervises regulated superannuation funds, other than self-managed super funds (these are supervised by the Australian Taxation Office) and approved deposit funds (bank accounts and the like).

- **Australian Securities Exchange (ASX):** Monitors compliance with the ASX's operating rules, although much of the supervisory responsibilities of the market sit with ASIC. Supervises all listed companies, including listed investment companies, listed managed funds and exchange-traded funds.

- **Australian Taxation Office (ATO):** Apart from collecting tax, the ATO is also responsible for regulating self-managed superannuation funds.

Although not a regulator, the Financial Services Council (FSC) is the peak industry body in Australia for the managed funds industry. According to its website, the FSC is committed to 'upholding the highest standards of integrity and ensuring that client and investor interests are paramount in all decisions and transactions'.

Virtually all the major fund management companies are members of the FSC. The FSC issues guidelines to its members covering a range of topics, from a code of ethics, to how to calculate after-tax returns for managed funds, through to management fee calculations. Standards are compulsory for all members and the FSC has its own disciplinary committee to deal with non-compliance. The FSC sees its role as being part of the regulatory process, even though it doesn't have a formal responsibility under law.

Australian Securities and Investments Commission

ASIC is Australia's key regulator for managed funds. ASIC is an independent government body with the main purpose of enforcing the relevant law under the Corporations Act. Among other things, ASIC is responsible for regulating Australian companies, financial markets (like the ASX) and financial services companies. ASIC also supervises all professionals who advise and deal in financial services products such as superannuation and managed funds. ASIC has three main responsibilities, which are, in order of importance:

- **Corporate regulator:** To make sure company directors act honestly and in the best interests of their companies

- **Markets regulator:** Making sure financial markets such as the stock market work fairly and transparently

- **Financial services regulator:** Responsible for licensing and monitoring a range of financial services companies, including managed funds, shares, insurance and superannuation

So what does this mean for fund managers and investors? Companies managing investors' money must be licensed, as does anybody selling or advising in managed funds, such as financial planners. Getting a licence means fund managers must meet certain requirements, such as:

- **Complaints procedure:** Having in place a documented complaints procedure available for clients to view

- **Compliance:** Having a plan in place to make sure the business and its employees comply with financial services law

- **Insurance:** Having adequate professional indemnity insurance to meet any claims by investors

- **Regular reporting:** Giving regular reports to ASIC on the company's financial situation, as well as reporting any breaches of ASIC's regulations

- **Security bond:** Lodging a bond of $20,000 with ASIC

- ✔ **Sufficient resources:** Having financial as well as technological and human resources; fund managers need to have — with some exceptions — at least $5 million in net tangible assets (all assets of the fund management company after deducting outstanding debt)

- ✔ **Training:** Providing adequate training for representatives and employees

Regulators can do only so much to protect investors. If a person is determined to defraud investors, the regulators may not pick up on the fraud until well after the event. The regulators provide a check and balance, keeping the majority of operators honest. But there will always be some so-called advisers who intentionally set out to deceive.

Identifying the Crooks and Conmen

Hardly a month goes by in Australia without ASIC banning a financial adviser for dodgy practices or prosecuting someone for running off with investors' money. In this section, I run through a few likely warning signs that investors should keep in mind before committing their money.

Making sure you don't get conned

Some basic checks before you invest may help you avoid a lot of pain later on. In Chapter 2, I explain that a managed fund is legally known as a managed investment scheme (MIS). Properly set up by the issuer (read fund manager) with a product disclosure statement (PDS), the scheme provides protection to investors under law. MISs cover a whole range of opportunities, from cash trusts, managed funds and agricultural investments to property trusts. More unusual schemes are also covered, such as betting, time-share and lottery schemes.

Illegal schemes catch out many investors every year and seem to target particular groups within the community, such as retirees and church groups. Illegal schemes may be started by well-meaning individuals who have no idea what they're doing. These schemes rope in friends or community groups and, because the operators have no idea, investors can lose money with devastating consequences for those involved. Such schemes may be as simple as pooling a group of investors' money together and investing in complex derivative products, for example, or even just unwittingly recommending a scheme that may be illegal. Other schemes may be set up by outright fraudsters who know what they're doing and operate outside the law to defraud investors. I set out the more common fraud in the next section, 'Too good to be true: No such thing as a guaranteed return'.

MISs must be registered with ASIC. If a scheme is not registered with ASIC — with some exceptions — then it is an illegal scheme and offering that scheme to investors is also illegal. If a scheme is offered only to wholesale investors (see Chapter 3 for a definition of wholesale investors) or has fewer than 20 investors (members), then it doesn't need to be registered with ASIC. These exceptions needn't complicate matters but require a few more checks before you invest.

Using ASIC's website at www.asic.gov.au, on the Noticeboard box in the middle of the page click on Company, ABN and Other Searches to search the register of PDSs. If the product you're looking for isn't listed with ASIC, take this as a hint to do more research. Heaps of other searches can be carried out, including on banned and disqualified persons.

ASIC sets out three safety checks for investors to apply before they invest. Table 20-1 summarises those checks.

Table 20-1	ASIC Safety Check
Managed Investment Scheme Information	*Investor Check*
MISs need to set up a public company (Ltd not Pty Ltd after its name) that is registered with ASIC	Search ASIC database (National Names Index)
Scheme operator must have an Australian Financial Services Licence (AFSL)	Search ASIC register of Australian financial services licensees
Scheme must be lodged with ASIC as a registered MIS	Search both the product disclosure statement and the offer list databases. If not registered, it may be an illegal scheme and you won't be protected under the law (with some exceptions)

Too good to be true: No such thing as a guaranteed return

In investing, especially with managed funds, guaranteed returns don't exist. Or perhaps I should qualify that by saying guarantees don't usually exist, except those heavily dependent on meeting certain conditions and backed up by a raft of legal disclaimers. Schemes offering guaranteed returns should always be viewed with a healthy dose of suspicion — definitely guilty before proven innocent.

The biggest scam of them all

After Bernie Madoff rampaged through the global investment community with his investment scam, it's any wonder Ponzi schemes aren't renamed after him. Billed as the biggest modern-day Ponzi scheme, Madoff is said to have lost more than $50 billion (by his own estimates) of investor money through his hedge fund manager, Ascot Partners.

Madoff claimed to be investing in blue-chip investments using hedging techniques to enhance returns. Statements he sent to clients showed consistent returns of 10 to 15 per cent per annum. These returns are good returns but not outrageous, which is perhaps why Madoff was able to keep the scam running for several decades without being found out. Madoff was so trusted by the market he was even made Chairman of the NASDAQ stock exchange in New York! Only when the markets turned, in early 2008, and investors headed for the exit did the smoke and mirrors stop working and the scheme come unstuck.

But investors don't need to go overseas to get a taste of what Ponzi schemes can do. You only have to check the local Australian media to see the latest scam to be prosecuted. Do an internet search on *Australian Ponzi schemes* and see what you come up with — you may be surprised to see people still losing their money to these schemes.

The most common fraud scheme offering guaranteed returns is what is known as a *Ponzi scheme*. Taking their name from Charles Ponzi, who operated in 1920s America, these schemes promise exceptionally high returns. Ponzi's own scheme promised returns of 50 per cent in 45 days or 100 per cent in 90 days. These schemes are best summed up in the saying 'robbing Peter to pay Paul', because that's what happens. Rather than earning money through investments, these schemes rely on new money coming into the scheme to pay early investors ostentatious returns. Seeing such great returns, early investors unwittingly become the scheme's unpaid promoters, telling their mates and family and drawing more money into the scheme.

As long as new money coming into a Ponzi scheme exceeds money going out, the scheme will survive. Eventually, though, Ponzi-like schemes see new investments slow and the money to pay existing investors runs out. Schemes inevitably collapse at this stage, leaving investors with massive headaches, not to mention a large hole in their wallets.

With managed funds, watch out for the asterisks in advertising and be careful of guaranteed returns. Any fund manager offering guaranteed returns on an investment is either being economical with the truth or delusional, or is heavily qualifying the offer with various conditions.

Visit ASIC's consumer watchdog website, FIDO, at www.fido.gov.au to find out more about the type of scams you may come across. Use the Scams and Warnings tab to find out the latest and to contact ASIC if you think you've come across a scam.

Finding Out Where to Complain

Complaints against a fund manager can cover anything from poor service, mispricing of units and mishandling of money through to not investing your money correctly. This sections looks at your rights under the law, how to complain and who to complain to.

Knowing your rights

Fund managers must clearly set out the complaints procedure in place for aggrieved investors. The process must be included in the fund manager's financial services guide (FSG). I explain FSGs in Chapter 12. The FSG sets out the following information on how to make a complaint:

- **Compensation claims:** The fund manager states that, should compensation be payable, money will come from its normal cash flows or from its insurer. The manager generally also says that its compensation arrangements comply with the Corporations Act.

- **Contact details:** The FSG sets out who to contact in the event of a complaint (usually a complaints resolution officer) and the contact details, such as phone, email and postal addresses.

- **Further action:** If you're not happy with the outcome of a complaint, you have the right to take it to an external mediator, in this case the Financial Ombudsman Service (FOS).

- **Response time:** Fund managers need to commit to a time to get back to you, usually within 14 days of receipt of your complaint.

An FSG must be given to you before you invest so that you understand your rights, the fees that may be charged, what the fund manager does and how to complain. Many fund managers build the FSG into the product disclosure statement to make sure investors do receive it before investing.

Figuring out compensation and claims

Unless you can show that a fund manager was somehow at fault when managing your money, you're unlikely to get compensation just because the market goes down, for example. If the manager was investing according to the way it was supposed to invest (as stated in the PDS), the chance of a complaint succeeding is low to zero. If the manager invested in international equities and the PDS said the fund invested in cash products, proving the fund manager has been negligent with your money may be easier.

Complaining can be a two-step process. Whatever the complaint, you need to go first to the fund manager. If you're not happy with the outcome, your next port of call is to go to the Financial Ombudsman Service (FOS). Also let the fund manager know you're going to FOS.

The process with FOS is as follows:

1. **Lodge a complaint.**

   You can lodge online or by post.

2. **Complaint registered.**

   FOS will register a complaint but take no immediate action if your complaint to the fund manager is less than 45 days old or you haven't yet received a direct response from the fund manager.

3. **Check the progress of your complaint.**

   If you've not received a response from the fund manager within 45 days or you're not happy with the fund manager's response, you can ask FOS to progress your complaint.

4. **Complaint reviewed.**

   FOS is intended for retail Mum and Dad investors to resolve disputes. If you fit that definition, FOS looks at the complaint. FOS also only looks at certain types of complaints, such as those about money mishandling that sees you out of pocket, but FOS won't consider complaints about levels of fees, unless you weren't correctly told about them.

5. **Complaint resolved.**

   FOS aims to act impartially as a mediator between fund manager and investor. It sorts out complaints through discussion and negotiation and, failing that, makes a decision based on the facts.

Setting out a complaint to a fund manager can be an art in itself, especially when it comes to a claim for potential loss. Including evidence of your loss in your complaint letter is helpful, both for you and the fund manager. Emotions can understandably be running high when lost money is involved!

Frozen Funds

Frozen funds are the unfortunate side effect of something major happening to the fund, which throws it completely out of whack. Such is the impact that the fund manager is forced to stop investors getting access to their money in the fund. The term *frozen funds* refers specifically to managed funds that normally let you take money out — otherwise known as *open ended* — but no longer allow you to do so. This section explains why funds may be frozen and what you can do to recover some or all of your money.

Finding out why funds may be frozen

Why funds may be frozen is best explained by looking at what happened during the global financial crisis. Many investors saw the value of their investments in some managed funds hit hard. Looking to at least prevent further losses, investors decided to head for the hills, selling their managed funds. Most managed funds were able to give investors their money back. However, some funds, especially in the property sector and those investing in mortgages, went into meltdown and struggled to meet investors' sell orders.

Fund managers couldn't raise enough cash by selling the underlying investments to pay back investors. Not only were fund managers forced to sell investments to meet payments to investors, some of those investments couldn't be sold — no-one wanted them. At this point, the law says that if a fund ceases to be *liquid* — liquid funds have less than 80 per cent of investments that can't be readily sold at market price — a fund has to freeze redemptions. Devastating for investors, yes, but a lifeline for struggling fund managers.

Getting out of a frozen fund

Many funds investing in mortgages, real property schemes, enhanced cash schemes and retail hedge funds were frozen during the global financial crisis and remain so at the time of writing. Some of the biggest funds affected include:

- ✔ Centro Direct Property fund, with $1.3 billion in assets
- ✔ AXA Wholesale Australian Property fund, with $883 million in assets
- ✔ APN Property for Income fund, with around $587 million in assets

Freezing of funds doesn't mean investors won't get their money back or that distributions dry up. Investments should be returned but it may take two to five years, sometimes longer, depending on the scheme. Fund managers — or, more correctly, the responsible entities — are obliged to try to help investors who want their money back as much as possible. Currently, investors have three avenues to try to get their money back:

- ✔ **A withdrawal offer:** An offer made by the fund manager to all investors, inviting them to make a withdrawal when the fund is judged to be liquid again. If not enough money is available to meet all requests, then withdrawals are apportioned across all investors.

- ✔ **A hardship application:** Normally, no exceptions are made to the rule that no redemptions are allowed unless the offer is to all investors. However, ASIC modified the law so investors could apply for release of funds in exceptional circumstances, or hardship relief. Circumstances include not being able to meet day-to-day living expenses, threatened foreclosure on your residence and not being able to meet medical bills. The amount is currently capped at $100,000 per annum with up to four transactions a year. If the fund is in the process of being wound up, then it must apply to ASIC before granting the relief.

- ✔ **A 'rolling' withdrawal offer:** An offer is made to all investors, open for a calendar year. The fund manager sets out which dates it will pay the withdrawal offer and investors can put in a request to withdraw money on any future withdrawal dates during the year.

For most investors, frozen funds mean waiting until the markets improve, which is cold comfort for those affected. Most investors would have invested in property funds and, in particular, mortgage funds for the income those funds deliver. Most of the funds are still paying an income, although not as much as they were before the funds were hit. Equally, the performance of the funds has not been pretty since the crisis.

For more information on frozen funds, you can visit the ASIC website at www.asic.gov.au (click on the Publications tab and choose Media Centre from the dropdown menu). Here you can search for press releases relating to frozen funds.

Part VI
The Part of Tens

Glenn Lumsden

'Wow, you have grown over the last ten years ... I'm going to have to build us a bigger nest!'

In this part ...

This part of the book is where you'll fold over the corner of the page for easy reference — the part of the book with the well-thumbed pages and the coffee stains. This is the part that becomes your easy guide to managed funds; the part that you tell your friends is the reason you bought the book. Like an old pair of slippers, you'll turn to this part for comfort when you head down the DIY road and everyone else has deserted you for a financial planner.

Okay, perhaps I'm getting ahead of myself, but the Part of Tens *is* useful. It serves up some practical advice on ten things to watch out for with managed funds, as well as ten tips for choosing and investing in them.

I encourage you to make this part your own — make notes and write questions as you go along. So get out the ballpoint and start marking the margins, scribbling in the borders and doodling in the paragraphs. Armed with a set of notes and an easy reference guide, you can begin your journey down the road to successful managed fund investing.

Chapter 21

Ten Tips for Managed Fund Investing

*D*ealing with managed funds is not necessarily a straightforward process. Sometimes you need help, whether that's through doing some research or seeking advice from a financial adviser, or, more likely, both. Managed funds aren't always set-and-forget investments either. Giving your portfolio a regular health check to make sure your investment plans stay on track is sound investing practice.

This chapter highlights my top ten tips for managed fund investing. Some of these tips are relevant to all forms of investing; others are specifically for managed funds. Some may sound familiar and you've probably seen some before. I cover off points from how your superannuation is probably your most important investment to what to consider when choosing a fund manager. I also look at how 20:20 hindsight or past performance is never recommended solely as a basis for making an investment decision.

Saving for Retirement

The one long-term plan investors should have is to make more money and have enough in their superannuation account to retire comfortably. For many people, though, reading or listening to the experts and trying to understand superannuation hardly gets the pulse racing. Understanding that superannuation is usually the most tax-effective way to save for retirement, you're halfway to developing a retirement savings plan.

The great thing about most people's superannuation is that managed funds are likely to make up some or all of their superannuation investments. Get to grips with the basics of managed funds and make a head start on getting your super to work for you. Chapter 3 gives loads of information on super.

Superannuation is complex. If you don't know what you're doing, pay for advice when it comes to super because it pays for itself in the end. The worst thing anyone can do is ignore super.

Lessons from History

The past does not repeat itself, but it rhymes.

—*Mark Twain*

Don't chase last year's best performing managed fund or asset class (shares, fixed interest, property or cash). Chances are that last year's standouts could be back-of-the-pack next year. If anything, look at those funds that performed badly in the year just gone and ask why the funds didn't do well. Was it a one-off bad year for the underlying investments because of poor market sentiment, or more of a long-term problem, say, with the fund manager? If it's longer term issues with the fund manager, then best to avoid. Equally, a blip in a managed fund's performance history may signal an opportunity to invest in a fund that could recover over the coming years. Refer to Chapter 9 for more on performance.

Historical performance on its own may not be a good predictor of future performance. You need to take into account other factors — overall market conditions and your investment goals, for example.

Being Patient Is a Virtue

The market does not beat them. They beat themselves, because though they have brains they cannot sit tight.

—Jesse Livermore, investor and author of
Reminiscences of a Stock Operator

Patience is a virtue when it comes to riding out not just storms in the market but everyday ups and downs. Plan your investments, buy the managed funds and then, unless something drastic changes with you or the fund, stick with it. Times of market panic see the price of managed funds (and the underlying investments) fluctuate more than is warranted by the value of the investments.

Keeping your nerve when markets are choppy can be like flying in turbulence. A piece of advice I once read in a fear-of-flying book can be applied equally to managed fund investing. In summary, a passenger's (investor's) tolerance for turbulence is a lot less than the pilot's (fund manager's) and the pilot's tolerance is a whole lot less than the plane's (managed fund's) tolerance for turbulence.

Never be eager to get into the market for fear of missing out, because you risk buying when prices are expensive. After you've invested, try to stay in the market but be flexible enough to change your plans if circumstances change. Chapter 7 has more on setting goals and plans.

Mixing It Up with Asset Allocation

The most important investment strategy is to get the mix right. The mix (your asset allocation) is what amount you put into shares, fixed-interest securities, property or cash, or any combination of the four. The mix determines the level of risk (the chance of losing money) in your portfolio and drives the likely returns you get. With one single investment, a managed fund can give investors exposure to some or all of the asset classes. This suits some investors but a diverse exposure potentially reduces returns. Others prefer to target their investments in managed funds to specific asset classes, such as property funds, fixed-income funds or high-yield funds.

Be aware of how mixing asset classes can affect how much risk you're taking on, or otherwise, and the impact on potential returns. Check out Chapter 4 for information on asset classes.

Doing Your Research

Three important things to remember when investing in managed funds — research, research and more research. Whether using a financial planner to help you invest or doing it yourself, research is vital. A heap of information is available if you know where to look, from the fund managers' websites to managed fund research houses such as Morningstar.

Key information on a fund is set out in the product disclosure statement (PDS — refer to Chapter 12), outlining what a fund invests in and how much it costs, among other things. In addition, research houses provide easy-to-follow five-star ratings on most managed funds available to the investing public. Managed fund brokers also provide online comparison tools, which help investors select and compare a range of different criteria, such as performance and star ratings. Chapter 8 gives you the lowdown on the ratings agencies.

Don't just rely on one source of information. If your financial planner says something about a fund, it's always worth backing it up with your own research.

Looking for Income? Distribution History Is Key

Most retirees need their investments to provide an income as well as to preserve their money. If you're an investor looking for income (yield), then it is important to look at a managed fund's long-term distribution history. Try not to be swayed by short-term distributions, either large or small. A good income fund manager should be able to produce a regular and reliable level of income for investors. However, the global financial crisis in 2008 took a chunk out of many managed fund distributions. This blip in distributions was exactly that for many funds, a short-term correction. Although distributions aren't back to where they were pre-crisis, they are on the way back up. Take a look at Chapter 14 for information on different types of funds.

Beware the yield trap. These investments (funds or shares) pay a good income but the value of the fund declines over time.

Choosing Fund Managers That Perform

At the risk of stating the obvious, finding a fund manager that performs — and I don't mean like a seal at the zoo — one that can produce decent returns, is important. But this may be no easy task. Then again, if you do find a fund manager that can catch fish in midair and produces decent returns at the same time, you may be onto a winner.

Follow the performers but be wary of the stars who have a habit of shining bright and burning out. Get to know the guys who have been around the traps and in the business for a while. With a little research, you can discover the fund managers who consistently produce good returns over, say, five years. Performance alone is never recommended as the basis for making an investment but some fund managers just keep coming up trumps year after year. These are the ones I want managing my money. Chapter 10 identifies the different types of fund managers.

Never overrate past performance, especially recent past performance. One year's good performance — relative to the market — doesn't necessarily mean the following year is going to be a repeat.

Managing Risk, Not Avoiding It

Never be afraid to try something new. Remember, amateurs built the ark; professionals built the Titanic.

—Anon.

Investors can't totally avoid risk. Like going outside and trying to avoid the weather, risk is always there. Even putting money in the bank carries some risk. Understanding your tolerance to risk — how much you're prepared to lose — is the first step to managing risk. The second step is using risk to build a portfolio of managed funds to help achieve your goals. Refer to Chapter 6 for information on risk assessment.

Managed properly, you can use risk to your advantage. Generally, the more risk you take on, the bigger the potential returns — but only up to a point. A dusting of risk across a portfolio can add more potential for a better return than simply trying to eliminate risk altogether. Too much risk and you may as well buy a lottery ticket.

Adding Fuel to the Fire: Dollar-Cost Averaging

Most managed funds offer investors the opportunity to set up a regular savings plan. This is good business for fund managers — they see a steady inflow of money to invest and charge fees on — but it makes a lot of sense for investors as well. The discipline of regular savings is not just good for the soul, financial experts say, but also good for growing your money.

One of the positive side effects of regular savings is what is known as dollar-cost averaging. Regular amounts invested over a long period of time help to smooth out the average price you pay. Sometimes you pay a higher price for your units (fewer units bought) and other times you pay a lower price (more units bought), depending on how the fund is performing. Investing this way reduces the risk of putting all your money into a fund at a high price. Check out Chapter 19 for more on this strategy.

Work out how much you can regularly invest, say, monthly. When you set up the plan, try to stick to it to get the full benefit of dollar-cost averaging.

Managing Your Funds

Every so often, perhaps once a year, you need to tend to your managed funds. As many plants need pruning, so your managed funds may also need a trim. Called rebalancing (refer to Chapter 13), this helps to keep your investment strategy on track. Setting and forgetting your funds sees them grow towards a particular sector or fund that has done well in the past.

Is this a bad thing? Well, it could be, because it means your investments are exposed to a part of the market that has done well. The risk profile of the investments changes and could be different from the risk you're prepared to take. The likelihood of the fund underperforming also increases over time. Better to trim some of the good performance and let your other funds have their day in the sun. Chances are that the funds that have not done so well may do better in different market conditions.

Chapter 22

Ten Traps and Pitfalls: What the Managers Don't Tell You

In This Chapter

▶ Understanding what you're buying and the costs involved

▶ Being sceptical of guaranteed returns

▶ Looking out for tax, economists and the marketing hype

▶ Discovering where fund managers invest

Read a managed fund's product disclosure statement and you'd be forgiven for thinking that much about managed funds smells of roses. From being seduced by the marketing hype to the comfort of investing with a big name, investors should take a step back before making the leap into managed funds.

In this chapter, I look at ten of the traps and pitfalls that investors may come across; things that are better to know before investing rather than afterwards. Knowing what you're buying sounds obvious. Looking at recent history and failed investments makes clear that many investors may not fully appreciate some of the risks in certain investment types. Costs and tax are other things investors need to keep an eye on, as well as some of the more exotic and sophisticated funds that are at the margins of most investors' investing radar.

Not Knowing What You're Buying

Never invest in any idea you can't illustrate with a crayon.

—Peter Lynch, fund manager

Suggesting that you may not know what you're investing in may be like saying, 'Don't eat what's on your fork before you know what it is'. Advice like this may seem obvious. However, the combination of a fancy product disclosure statement (PDS) and the advice of a professional can give investors false comfort.

Taking time to understand exactly how the investment works and the risks involved can avoid heartache and a hole in your wallet down the track. Chapter 3 helps you understand managed fund structures.

The need to understand the investment is especially important for the more exotic funds, such as capital-guaranteed (structured) products and hedge funds, which may rely on borrowing and complex derivatives. Agricultural investments may be primarily tax-driven. Without government tax concessions, these funds may not stand up as investments in their own right. Investors need solid, unbiased advice and a good feel for the risks involved before taking the plunge with these funds. (Chapters 15 and 16 go into more detail.)

A healthy dose of scepticism can help avoid a nasty cold down the track. Always question and don't always accept the first answer you're given.

Not Figuring Out the Costs

Like buying a car that needs registration and insurance every year to keep it on the road, so too managed funds come with running costs. If you don't know what those costs are, you could be in for a shock. Costs are deducted from the value of your investment, usually monthly. You don't receive a bill in the post and, because of this, costs can easily be ignored or missed. All the costs should be outlined in the PDS. Working out exactly which ones apply to you before you invest can be almost as hard as working out how a mobile phone contract works.

The level of costs ultimately affect the returns on your investment, usually taking off between 1.5 and 2 per cent per annum. Throw in the performance fees some funds charge and annual costs can be significantly higher. Check out Chapter 5 for more on fees and costs.

Some fund managers negotiate on costs, such as the contribution fee (usually 4 per cent), and may reduce some fees to zero. Managed fund brokers can also reduce contribution fees to zero and lower the ongoing management costs.

Not Appreciating Inflation

> *If inflation continues to soar, you're going to have to work like a dog just to live like one.*
>
> —George Gobel, comedian

More often than not, the fancy performance charts the fund managers roll out to illustrate a fund's performance don't take account of inflation. So, when you see a chart showing, for example, what $10,000 invested ten years ago might look like today if invested in a managed fund, check to see if inflation has been included. A decent return at first glance may, in fact, barely have kept pace with inflation or, worse, return less than putting your money in the bank. For more on performance, refer to Chapter 9.

 If inflation isn't included in performance comparisons, then you may have to make an adjustment of 2 to 3 per cent per annum. What starts off looking like a reasonable investment could end up looking mediocre.

Believing in Guaranteed Returns

In investing, the only sure thing is that there is no sure thing. Managed funds spruiking guaranteed returns should be handled with as much care as a rattlesnake. Believe them at your peril! Invariably, the fund manager may be economical with the truth or have a list of disclaimers longer than your arm. If you want guaranteed returns, then putting your money in the bank is probably as close as you can get. Even products that offer capital guarantees — where you get your money back, eventually — require investors to keep their money in the investment for the life of the product. Guaranteed returns are covered in Chapter 16.

 Watch out for the small print, because this is where you find out how strong any guarantee may be. If the documentation has no small print, be very sceptical!

Not Watching Out for Tax

Tax is often the forgotten cost of investing, not just in managed funds but in any investment. Tax may not usually be seen as a cost of investing but it should be viewed as such, as it can take a big chunk out of your investment's performance, more so than any fees charged by the fund manager. The problem is, because each person's tax situation is different, fund managers can't accurately tell investors what the impact of tax will be. Investors may not get a clear picture of the tax effects until it comes to filling in a tax return.

After-tax returns should be what matter most to an investor. After all, this is what you end up with in your pocket. Managed fund performance is virtually always shown before tax. Imagine buying a car, only to find when it's delivered it has no wheels. Tax has the same effect on an investment's returns — what you see is not always what you get. A fund's performance is usually split between income (from its investments) and growth (the increase in value of investments and gains made on the sale of investments). These figures are taxed slightly differently. Capital gains may be taxable even if the fund manager hasn't realised those gains by selling the investment. Check out Chapters 2 and 5 for more on tax.

Factor tax into your expected returns and watch out for the performance split between income and capital gains. The more a fund manager trades (buys and sells) the more likely investors will face capital gains tax liabilities.

Listening to Economists

The economy depends about as much on economists as the weather does on weather forecasters.

—Jean-Paul Kauffmann, journalist

Hanging on every word from economists can be a big mistake. I don't mean you should ignore economists at social functions or the like — that would be mean! Most economists are good at setting out where an economy is and how it got there. What is less certain is their ability to explain how investments (and economies) are going to do in the future. Economists can be forgiven for this because forecasting is a notoriously difficult process. Economists who do get forecasts right are idolised, shown by the very few — you can count them on one hand — who forecast the global financial crisis, against the many, many more economists who got it wrong. Chapter 11 gives you information on advisers.

Be wary about using economic forecasts to predict company values. Countries with relatively low economic growth can have the best performing stock markets (like Australia) compared with countries with high economic growth.

Believing the Marketing Hype

Big fund managers spend a lot of money telling you how good they are. But think about it, what are they really telling you — the only funds being advertised are the ones that have performed well recently. The fund managers aren't going to push an underperforming fund. Bear in mind, though, historical performance is not necessarily a good judge of future performance.

Fund managers may also use star ratings from research houses to push funds when advertising. Some star ratings, such as those provided by Morningstar, are a record of how the fund has performed in the past. Other star ratings are a combination of past performance and subjective views on how a fund manager is managing money. Ratings are a great starting point but should not be used as a predictor of future performance. Refer to Chapter 8 for more on the ratings agencies.

Managed fund marketers push funds that have done well in the past. Better to look at tax efficiency, costs and funds that meet your needs before looking at performance.

Not Following the Money

When you 'follow the money' you find out where the fund managers invest their money. Ignoring this aspect when investing could keep you from some valuable tips. Any fund manager worth her salt invests money with the fund she is managing. Do the same with any professional you may be relying on for advice — stockbrokers, financial planners and accountants.

When I started stockbroking, one of the first questions I was asked by most fund managers was what I was investing in. Fund managers and advisers can't be expected to have credibility with their clients if they don't believe in what they're recommending. Fund managers need to show that they have 'skin in the game'. Chapter 11 gives some tips on dealing with the professionals.

Funds Growing Too Big, Too Fast

Watch out for this trend when researching which funds to invest in, and don't get too excited. Funds that grow too big, too fast can suffer from growing pains. Looking after a large chunk of money, especially if that chunk of money has grown very rapidly in size, is different from looking after a small amount of money.

The first problem is that the fund manager ends up moving far greater amounts of money in and out of the market. This alone can make it difficult for a manager to invest without adversely affecting prices. The second problem is that more people and better systems are needed just to look after the money and investors. Bigger fund managers are more adept at managing large amounts of money and generally have better systems in place. The third problem is that a once-nimble fund manager, able to take quick advantage of opportunities in the market, may be left trying to turn an oil tanker, potentially affecting performance. Some fund managers put limiters on growth by keeping funds under management at a certain level. Check out Chapter 10 for information about fund managers.

A large fund is anything with more than $1 billion in funds under management. Before investing, see how long a particular fund has been around. If it's only a couple of years or so, consider the fund manager's abilities to manage such growth.

Following the Crowd

Following the crowd can lead you up the garden path if you're not careful. And by crowd I mean the financial commentators and the media. Usually, by the time a fund is mentioned in the media, it's too late to invest. The same goes for stocks that are recommended by market pundits. The media is good at picking the hot funds — those that have stormed to the top of the performance charts over the last 12 months. And that's the point — the fund has performed well over the last year. Leading performers can burn out as quickly as they arrive and end up bottom of the class the following year. All too often, individual investors get in on these hot funds just as they're starting to cool down. By the time you hear about the fund, the performance bandwagon has departed and your fund's left trying to get a lift to catch up. Chapter 9 tells you how to assess performance.

Doing your research may not lead you to the next top performer. However, stick to your plan and don't change funds midway just because another fund has done better than yours.

Glossary

absolute performance: A method of measuring the performance of a fund based on actual returns over a specified period, regardless of index performance; funds that adopt this as a strategy are known as absolute-return or index-unaware funds. See also *relative performance*.

account-based pension: See *market-linked pension account*.

administration platform: A reporting and administration system for managed funds, as well as *shares* and *cash* assets.

All Ordinaries (All Ords) Index: A market-capitalisation weighted index of the largest 500 Australian companies; widely recognised as the best measure of the overall performance of the Australian sharemarket.

alpha: A managed fund's return generated over and above the market performance, which is known as *beta*.

annuity: An annual income paid by a life insurance company from either a superannuation account or another fund; either market-linked or fixed-income based. See also *fixed-income pension account, market-linked pension account*.

Asia–Pacific Investment Register (APIR): The register that gives a unique industry code to identify each managed fund.

asset allocation: The practice of dividing assets into different *asset classes*.

asset class: A group of assets with similar underlying investments; typical asset classes are *cash, shares, fixed-interest securities* (*bonds*) and *property*.

Australian real estate investment trust (A-REIT): See *listed property trust*.

Australian Securities Exchange (ASX): The Australian national stock exchange, located in Sydney.

benchmark index: A financial index, such as the *S&P/ASX 200*, used to assess a managed fund's performance. See also *tracking error*.

beneficial ownership: The status of the party that has the right to receive benefits from *share* ownership; in relation to managed funds, the trust that is set up to have *legal ownership* of the shares.

beta: A managed fund's return that equates to the performance of the overall market. See also *alpha*.

bias: A fund manager's style, such as active or passive, *growth, value* or *style-neutral, hedged* or unhedged.

bond: A form of government or corporate debt that pays an income through interest.

bond fund: A managed fund that invests in *bonds*, typically with the aim of providing stable income with low risk to capital.

bond trust: A fund that invests in *bonds*, a *fixed-interest* product.

buy–sell spread: The difference between the price a fund will sell units for and the price it will pay for them.

capital gains: The profit realised from the sale of investments.

capital guarantee: The guarantee to return at least all of your initial investment after the term of the investment; offered by some *managed investment scheme* products also known as *structured products*.

cash: An *asset class* that includes cash in the bank and investments in *cash managed funds* and *cash management trusts*.

cash managed fund: A fund that invests in different low-risk *cash* assets, such as government and semi-government securities, bills of exchange, negotiable certificates of deposit, promissory notes and call deposits; technically can be classed as a *fixed-interest security*, but generally treated as a cash asset.

cash management account: Special account in which you leave funds you may wish to use as cash — and withdraw within 24 hours — that pays a higher rate than ordinary cash accounts offered by banks.

cash management trust (CMT): A trust that invests in *fixed-interest* products, such as company *bonds*, that pay a regular income; technically can be classed as a fixed-interest security, but generally treated as a *cash* asset.

CHESS: Acronym for Clearing House Electronic Subregister System, an electronic transfer and settlement system used by the *Australian Securities Exchange* that automatically issues updated holdings statements to the investor and details of all shareholdings on its register to the stock issuer.

closed-end fund: A managed fund that has a set date to be wound up, generally with all units issued at the outset. See also *open-ended fund*.

collateral: Assets such as property or securities provided by a borrower or guarantor as security for a loan.

commission: In the context of managed funds, monies paid to third-party intermediaries such as financial planners for recommending the product to clients; paid out of a fund's *indirect cost ratio (ICR)* and typically around 0.25 per cent per annum of the value of the investment.

concentrated fund: A managed fund that contains a small number of stocks, which magnifies risk and return; also known as a high-conviction fund. See also *diversified fund*, *index fund*.

concessionally taxed income: Also known as tax-deferred income, between 50 and 100 per cent of income received from investment in a *property managed fund* that is taxed at a lower rate, recognising that fixtures and fittings reduce in value over time, which can be claimed against the investment.

contribution fees: Also known as upfront fees, or entry fees, because they're paid as soon as the investment is made. Typically contribution fees are up to 4 per cent of the value of the investment; paid every time money is contributed to an investment, such as a regular savings plan.

core fund: A fund that invests in *shares* that produce consistent returns over time, reflecting characteristics of both *growth* and *value funds*; also known as style-neutral. See also *GARP fund*.

coupon: The income paid by a *bond*.

cyclical stocks: Shares in companies where the earnings and performance of the company are tied to the overall performance of the economy.

debenture: Debt backed only by the integrity of the borrower, not by *collateral*, and documented by an agreement called an *indenture*. Managed funds invest in debentures for the income that is generated by the notes in the form of interest.

debenture note: A type of listed or unlisted *fixed-interest security*.

derivative: A security that derives its value from the expected future price of an underlying asset such as *shares*, commodities or an *index*; a contract between two parties that may or may not trade on a recognised exchange.

distributions: Income and *capital gains* from managed fund investments distributed to unit holders in any particular year.

diversified fund: A managed fund that contains a diversity of stocks so as to increase the potential risk and rewards beyond that of an *index fund*, but not as great as a *concentrated fund*.

dividend: Payment made by a company to its shareholders, usually out of after-tax profits made during the year, known as a *franked dividend*.

dividend imputation credit: See *franking credit*.

dollar-cost averaging: A technique where an investor buys a small number of investment units and waits for the price to drop before buying more, thereby reducing the average cost of the units.

entry fees: See *contribution fees*.

establishment fee: A one-off fee that may be charged by the fund when setting up a managed fund investment. Charged as a percentage of the assets invested.

exchange-traded commodity (ETC): A fund that tracks movement in a commodity market such as gold or wheat.

exchange-traded fund (ETF): A fund that tracks an *index*, but can be traded like a stock; enables investors to buy a diversified portfolio of securities in a single transaction.

family bonds: An investment available for children under the age of 16 years; similar to managed funds in that they allow investors to choose from a range of different *asset* types.

financial services guide (FSG): A document that legally must be sent to all prospective retail investors and that describes the service that accompanies a financial product. See also *product disclosure statement*.

fixed-income pension account: An investment fund bought from *superannuation fund* providers to generate a regular income in retirement. See also *annuity, market-linked pension account*.

fixed-interest security: An *asset class* that pays a set interest rate, such as *bond trusts, debenture notes* and *mortgage trusts*.

franked dividend: A *dividend* paid by a company out of profits on which the company has already paid tax. See also *franking credit*.

franking credit: A tax credit received from the distribution of *franked dividends*, on which tax has already been paid at the company rate.

frozen funds: Money in a managed fund that has stopped or limited the ability of investors to withdraw it from the fund. Funds may be frozen due to poor market conditions making it difficult for the fund manager to sell the underlying investments and repay investors.

fund manager: The individual or organisation responsible for making investment decisions — selecting, buying, managing and reporting on the investments — on behalf of a managed fund.

GARP (growth at a reasonable price) fund: A fund that invests in *shares* that generate good earnings but also represent good value, in that the stocks may be undervalued but the underlying business is strong, reflecting characteristics of both *growth* and *value funds*, similar to a *core fund*.

geared funds: Managed funds that borrow money to invest in shares to potentially enhance returns; also carry greater risk of losing money.

growth fund: A fund that invests in *shares* that are expected to grow at a higher rate than the market or *index*. See also *core fund, GARP fund, value fund, yield fund*.

hedge fund: A fund that takes high risks in betting on the direction of currencies and commodities, for example, typically by *shorting* stock. See also *traditional fund manager*.

hedging: A method of locking in the price of foreign currency when converting back to the local currency, using *derivatives* such as currency futures.

hybrid securities: An investment mix of debt and equity, starting off like a *bond* with a fixed income but converting to a *share* in the issuing company.

imputation credit: See *franking credit*.

indenture: A written agreement between the issuer of a *bond* and the bondholders, usually specifying interest rate, maturity date and so on.

index: A stock market-issued list of the average weighted price of a number of underlying shares at any particular point in time.

index fund: A managed fund that mirrors the returns of a market *index*. See also *concentrated fund*.

index-unaware fund: See *absolute performance*.

indirect cost ratio (ICR): The standard method of showing annual expenses attributable to managing a fund, including management fees but excluding separately disclosed fees, expressed as a percentage of the total value of a fund's assets; replaced the management expense ratio (MER) in 2004. See also *management expenses*.

investment bonds: A tax-advantaged investment available for children aged between 10 and 16 years in their own name; have a minimum term of 10 years but can be as long as 40 years.

junk bond: A non-investment grade *bond* identified by a rating less than BBB by *Standard & Poor's*.

legal ownership: The status of the party whose name is on a *share* certificate; in relation to managed funds, the trust that is set up to have legal ownership. See also *beneficial ownership*.

leveraged investing: See *margin loans* and *geared funds*.

liquidity: The ability to sell an investment quickly.

listed investment company (LIC): A company that manages funds whose shares can be bought and sold on the stock market.

listed property trust: Also known as Australian real estate investment trusts (A-REITs), a fund that is listed on the *Australian Securities Exchange*, and invests directly in *property* and is responsible for all aspects of its management. See also *property securities trust*.

loan-to-value ratio (LVR): The percentage value of a *margin loan* as measured against the value of the underlying investment, either shares or managed funds; margin lenders lend up to a maximum LVR against a list of approved stocks or managed funds.

long-only manager: See *traditional fund manager*.

managed investment scheme (MIS): A managed fund, as defined by the Corporations Act 2001, which devotes pooled funds provided by thousands of individual investors to particular investments.

management expense ratio (MER): See *indirect cost ratio (ICR)*.

management expenses: The operational costs to run a fund, including audit, legal, administration and brokerage fees; make up the bulk of the ongoing fees in a managed fund. Also known as the *indirect cost ratio (ICR)*.

margin call: When the lender of a *margin loan* asks the investor to add more *collateral* or sell the holding, if the *loan-to-value ratio* on a margin loan exceeds a pre-set limit, to reduce the loan amount outstanding.

margin loan: A loan offered by specialist lenders specifically for investors to use to buy *shares* or managed funds.

marginal tax rate: The highest rate of tax an individual's income is taxed at.

marketable parcel: A parcel of securities not less than $500 in value based on the closing price if securities are listed.

market capitalisation: The total value of a company's *shares*.

market-linked pension account: Previously known as an allocated pension, an investment fund bought from a *superannuation fund* provider to generate retirement income based on investment returns. See also *annuity, fixed-income pension account*.

market maker: A professional investor who guarantees to buy or sell an amount of *shares* of an *exchange-traded fund* at an agreed price for the investor, at or very close to the market value of the underlying investments.

master trust: A single investment account that gives investors access to a menu of different funds, including funds from other fund managers.

Morningstar: An independent provider of investment portfolio information offering star ratings and commentary on managed funds.

mortgage trust: A trust that invests in residential and commercial mortgages to pay a *fixed-interest* income over the life of the loan.

net asset value (NAV): The total value of all the underlying investments of an *exchange-traded fund* after deducting expenses.

net tangible assets (NTA): The value of the underlying investments of a fund minus any outstanding costs.

ongoing or trailing commissions: Commission payments made by fund managers to financial planners, typically at around 0.25 per cent of the value of the fund paid annually to the financial planner; included in the *management expenses* charged by the fund.

open-ended fund: A managed fund that does not have an end date and can issue and redeem units in the trust at any time. See also *closed-end fund.*

performance fees: Fees charged by a fund should the fund meet or better predetermined performance hurdles for the fund, typically set at 20 per cent of returns the fund manager makes over and above the set performance hurdle.

platform: See *administration platform.*

Ponzi scheme: A fraudulent scheme that pays investors returns from their own money or money from other investors rather than from any underlying business. Named after Charles Ponzi, a career criminal operating such schemes in the 1920s.

product disclosure statement (PDS): A document that legally must be sent to all prospective investors and that describes the financial product they wish to invest in. See also *financial services guide.*

property: An *asset class.* See also *property managed fund.*

property managed fund: A fund that invests in different areas of the property market through *listed* or *unlisted trusts*, or *property securities trusts.*

property securities trust: A *property managed fund* that invests in the *shares* of property companies; can be unlisted or listed on the *Australian Securities Exchange*, but does not invest directly in property, unlike a *listed* or an *unlisted property trust.*

public offer super fund: An industry-based *superannuation fund* that is not-for-profit.

relative performance: A method of measuring the performance of a fund based on comparative returns of similar funds or a market *index.* See also *absolute performance.*

responsible entity: A public company that is appropriately qualified to look after the operation of a managed fund.

retail fund: A fund that can be bought into by retail investors, generally either inexperienced investors or investors with smaller (less than $50,000) amounts of money to invest, or both. See also *wholesale fund.*

reversionary beneficiary: A person who takes over the benefits of a *fixed-income pension* or *annuity* on the death of the beneficiary, usually the partner or spouse.

rising guarantee: Offered on some *structured products* and *capital-guarantee* funds whereby an investor's initial investment is not only guaranteed, but increases at a set rate over the life of the product.

risk-adjusted return: A ratings tool that deducts the risk measure from the total performance numbers.

risk profile: A description of an investor type, such as conservative or aggressive, depending on the amount of risk that investor is willing to be exposed to.

S&P/ASX Small Ordinaries Index: Comprises stocks that are included in the S&P/ASX 300 Index but not in the S&P/ASX 100.

S&P/ASX 200: The stock market *index* of the top 200 companies listed on the *Australian Securities Exchange (ASX)*, published by *Standard & Poor's (S&P)*.

sector fund: A fund that invests in stocks from different sectors, such as property, resources or financials.

self-managed superannuation fund (SMSF): A *superannuation fund* established by an individual taxpayer to administer superannuation contributions and investments.

shares: An *asset class* that includes investment in shares in both Australian and international companies.

shorting: The high-risk technique of borrowing stock, selling it and then buying it back at a lower price to return to the original owner of the stock, typically practised by *hedge funds*.

small cap: The market terminology for the *shares* of companies that have a *market capitalisation* of typically less than $2 billion, as defined by companies included in the *S&P/ASX Small Ordinaries Index*.

Standard & Poor's (S&P): An independent provider of investment portfolio information offering star ratings and commentary on managed funds.

structured product: A *managed investment scheme* that looks and feels like a managed fund but usually has a facility that guarantees to return some or all of your initial investment using *derivative* instruments. The guarantee is only available at the end of the life of the product. See also *capital guarantee*.

style-neutral fund: See *core fund*.

superannuation: A long-term savings vehicle for investment *assets* that operates primarily to provide income for retirement.

superannuation fund: A fund established primarily to provide benefits for members on their retirement, or alternatively, on their resignation, death, disablement or other specified events; usually a trust fund governed by a trust deed and administered by trustees.

superannuation guarantee: Employer contributions to a *superannuation fund*.

switching fees: Fees charged by a fund manager if an investor moves money from one fund to another within the same fund manager; rarely charged.

tax-deferred income: See *concessionally taxed income*.

tracking error: The measure of how a managed fund performs against a financial _index_, such as the _S&P/ASX 200_. See also _benchmark index_.

traditional fund manager: A fund manager that invests in shares purely to make money, without accepting the potentially higher risk of a _hedge fund_; also known as a _long-only manager_, in contrast to the practice of _shorting_ stock.

trailing commissions: See _ongoing commissions_.

transaction costs: Applied when units in a fund are bought or sold and expressed as the _buy–sell spread_.

turnover: The percentage value of an investment portfolio that is bought and sold each year.

underlying investments: The investments that a managed fund holds.

unlisted property trust: A _property managed fund_ that invests in _property_ but is not listed on the _Australian Securities Exchange_, so investors can invest directly with the _fund manager_; the trust can invest directly in property and be responsible for all aspects of its management, as for a _listed property trust_. See also _property securities trust_.

upfront fees: See _contribution fees_.

value fund: A fund that invests in _shares_ at a price less than the intrinsic value of the stock, on the basis that the stock is currently undervalued. See also _core fund_, _GARP fund_, _growth fund_, _yield fund_.

wholesale fund: A fund that can be bought into by a wholesale investor, generally an experienced investor, or through an _administration platform_. See also _retail fund_.

withdrawal fees: Fees applicable when some or all monies are withdrawn from a fund. Most fund managers don't charge this fee.

wrap account: An _administration platform_ that allows investors to manage a range of different investment types, including _cash_, directly held _shares_ and managed funds, in one place; allows transactions across a menu of investment options and provides extensive reporting and administration. Wraps are generally available to financial planners.

yield: The profit or income that an investment returns; usually expressed as an annual percentage of the initial investment.

yield fund: A fund that invests in stocks that provide good income in the form of _dividends_, known as _distributions_.

Index

● *N* ●

● *O* ●

● *P* ●

Business & Investment

978-1-74216-971-2
$39.95

978-1-74216-853-1
$39.95

978-1-74216-852-4
$39.95

978-1-74216-939-2
$34.95

978-1-74246-874-7
$19.95

978-1-74216-962-0
$19.95

978-0-73140-828-3
$19.95

978-0-73140-827-6
$19.95

978-1-74246-848-8
$34.95

978-1-74031-146-5
$39.95

978-0-73140-940-2
$39.95

978-1-74216-941-5
$36.95